A POISON STRONGER THAN LOVE

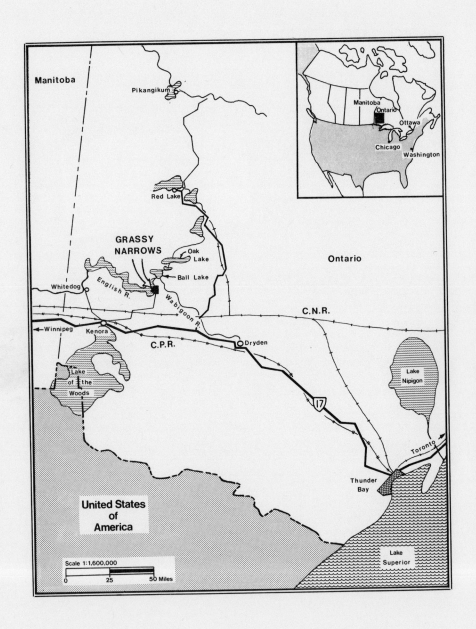

# A POISON STRONGER THAN LOVE

## THE DESTRUCTION OF AN OJIBWA COMMUNITY

**Anastasia M. Shkilnyk**
Foreword by Kai Erikson
Photographs by Hiro Miyamatsu

YALE UNIVERSITY PRESS · NEW HAVEN AND LONDON

Designed by Nancy Ovedovitz and set in Baskerville type by The
Composing Room of Michigan, Inc. Printed in the United States
of America by Murray Printing Company, Westford,
Massachusetts.

Library of Congress Cataloging in Publication Data

Shkilnyk, Anastasia M., 1945–
A poison stronger than love.
Includes index.
1. Grassy Narrows Indian Reservation (Ont.)  2.  Chippewa
Indians—Social conditions.  2.  Indians of North America—
Ontario—Social conditions.  4.  Water—Pollution—
Ontario.  I.  Title.
E99.C6S53  1984        305.8'97'071        84-40202
ISBN 0-300-02997-7 (alk. paper)
ISBN 0-300-03325-7 (pbk.: alk. paper)

The paper in this book meets the guidelines for permanence and
durability of the Committee on Production Guidelines for Book
Longevity of the Council on Library Resources.

10

TO MY MOTHER AND
THE MEMORY OF MY FATHER

I can't explain it to you, because I can't explain it to myself. The only thing I know about alcohol is that alcohol is a stronger power than the love of children. It's a poison, and we are a broken people. We suffer enough inside, and therefore we understand each other.

—Resident of Grassy Narrows

# CONTENTS

# TABLES

# FOREWORD

**Kai Erikson**

I normally don't see much point in asking anyone to write a foreword to a book as strong and compelling as this one. It stands firmly under its own considerable power. What can a colleague add?

It happens, though, that I have a special interest in the subjects dealt with in this account. I visited Grassy Narrows in January of 1979 for a long week in which the temperature never ventured above forty degrees below zero, and I came face to face—if only fleetingly—with all the human misery that Anastasia Shkilnyk describes so movingly here. Together with Christopher Vecsey, I interviewed a fair number of people, conferred with a fair number of others, and generally tried to develop some sense of what life was like on the reserve. I left with the conviction—one that I tried to communicate in a report Vecsey and I wrote to the band council—that Grassy Narrows was more deeply damaged than any community I had ever seen. Or heard about. Or even imagined.

In that sense, anyway, I feel like a partner in this undertaking, even if my role in the collaboration was a minor one, and that is the spirit in which I write what follows.

## I

The story of Grassy Narrows is told here in a single clear voice, but the reader should listen in two ways at once. In the first place, of course, the book should be read as the portrait of a community in desperate trouble. I had been asked to visit Grassy Narrows originally because thousands of pounds of methyl mercury had been dumped into the network of lakes and rivers surrounding the reserve, polluting the whole area. There were good reasons to suppose that the mercury had already found its way into living human tissues, which meant that the people of Grassy Narrows were already suffering from the effects of the poison or were doomed to wait for months, years—even generations—to learn whether harm would yet be done to them or their offspring. And if that did not seem peril enough, the contamination of the waterways had created wrenching problems of an economic and a spiritual sort as well. The Ojibwa of Northwest Ontario have always seen the waterways as a source of life itself, and this had become doubly the case in recent years among the people of Grassy Narrows because virtually all the men of the band had been employed in one or another aspect of commercial fishing. The closing of the waters simply spelled the end of meaningful employment at the reserve, and by the time I visited Grassy Narrows, that proud band of hunters and trappers and fishermen had begun a slide into dependency and humiliation that is the main subject of this book.

It turns out, however, that the susceptibility of the people of Grassy Narrows to the effects of mercury poisoning was all the greater because of an event that had occurred some years earlier, one that seemed quite routine at the time but looks now, with the sharper vision that time sometimes confers, as even more traumatic. This was the relocation of the Grassy Narrows band from its old reserve along the edges of the English and Wabigoon river system to the narrow strip of land it now occupies.

In the sixty or so years that had preceded the relocation, the people of Grassy Narrows had experienced several shocks that served to weaken the fiber of Ojibwa society. Each of these shocks can be traced directly or indirectly to white contact, and each of them can be justly described as a disaster from the point of view of the people exposed to it. There was an awful influenza epidemic in 1919, for example, that not only killed off more than half the population but placed an enormous strain on the Ojibwa belief system because traditional ways of controlling the rages of nature proved powerless. At the same time, Indian children were being taken to residential schools many miles from the reserve and, as a matter of deliberate policy, were being stripped of their language, their native skills, and their very identity as Indians. And, meanwhile, a combined force of missionaries and Royal Canadian Mounted Police—not such good guys as the movies of my youth taught me—did everything it could to discourage the practice of Ojibwa religion, raiding sacred ceremonies and harassing other religious activities until the old faith had been driven underground. In the end, then, native religion became a private preoccupation of the aging rather than an integrative force for the young, and the people of Grassy Narrows, like their Indian neighbors elsewhere, lost much of the spiritual insulation that had been their ancestors' major protection against the effects of disaster and disruption.

This roster of troubles could go on at greater length, of course, but the relocation that took place in 1963 belongs at its head. The reasons for the move, Shkilnyk points out, seemed wholly sensible at the time, not only to white authority but to Indian leadership. But the costs turned out to be enormous. For one thing, dwellings in the new reserve were tightly bunched together in the manner of an agricultural village, violating the sense of space that is natural to hunting and gathering people everywhere. Moreover, an Ojibwa band is, first, a gathering of clans, and the way land is parcelled and arranged in the new reserve mixes up clan alignments to the point that frictions increase and factions multiply. Most important of all, perhaps, the new reserve is laid out in such a way as to disturb the ancient relationship between the Ojibwa and the rest of nature, for people now feel separated from the land and the water and the creatures of the forest, with which they have always felt a special kinship. They are, in a very real sense, removed from their natural habitat.

As a result of all this, Shkilnyk shows movingly, the Ojibwa of Grassy Narrows are a truly broken people. They neglect themselves out of an inability to believe that they matter, and, though it may be difficult for those of us who live in secure comfort to understand, they not only neglect but abuse their own children. They live a life of sullen pain, blurred for days at a time by joyless bouts of drinking. And they die suddenly. Among these deaths are some that any coroner would feel compelled to call suicide, but there are others, impossible to document accurately, that come as the result of people destroying themselves out of a simple failure to care. Grassy Narrows is a place of rape and murder and incest and thoughtless vandalism. It is a place of tremendous rage and frustration. It is, as one of the older men said to us, "a diseased place to live."

## II

The second theme one should listen for in the pages that follow, although it is stated more implicitly than explicitly, concerns the lessons we might learn about life in general from the example Grassy Narrows provides us. What happened to the band over a period of years is unique, a singular tragedy, and it seems almost unfair to a group of people who have suffered so much to make of their story a moral tale, a parable, or a "case study." And yet the sustained disaster that took place at Grassy Narrows, for all the horrors that make it special, can nonetheless serve as a sample of something that humankind seems to encounter more and more frequently, and that is another reason why the story related here should be attended with particular care.

Let me try to make the point by drawing a distinction.

Any disaster, whether it takes the form of a sharp and furious eruption that splinters the silence for one terrible moment and then goes away, or whether it takes the form of a more chronic run of troubles, as in Grassy Narrows, has the capacity to inflict at least two kinds of damage. In the first place, obviously, it can injure the persons who are exposed to it in a number of direct and indirect ways, and the responsibility of those who undertake the job of rescue at the time or the job of repair afterward is to take care of those injuries as quickly as possible. Yet there is another kind of damage found in the wake of disasters that is not so obvious and deserves a great deal more attention than it normally receives. This form of damage does real injury to the persons who are exposed to it, but it does not leave visible marks on the body, and it cannot be measured by count-ing casualties. I am referring to the fact, so well illustrated by the catastro-phe of Grassy Narrows, that disasters sometimes have the potential for destroying the sense of communality that holds people together, for kill-ing the spirit of neighborliness and kinship that is so important a part of their world. One should speak of such things cautiously, but in a very real sense the cultural bonds that connect people to one another and to the places in which they live are a kind of tissue that can be damaged and even destroyed by too sharp and too sustained an assault.

I once tried to distinguish between these two kinds of injury by calling the first of them "individual trauma" and the second "collective trauma."

By "individual trauma" I mean to include those injuries that are im-posed on people as the result of an initial assault, both physical wounds and mental ones. In disaster situations it is normal for people to suffer deep shock as a consequence of the devastation they have been exposed to, and as a result they are apt, for the time being at least, to withdraw into themselves, feeling numbed, fearful, vulnerable, and very alone. We see dramas of that sort played out again and again in the everyday news—a tornado in Mississippi, a hurricane in Florida, an earthquake in Alaska, a dam break in Idaho, or any of the other terrible visitations that seem to interrupt the flow of human life so often.

By "collective trauma," on the other hand, I mean to include those kinds of injury that are inflicted not on individuals directly but on the tissues of community life themselves—injuries that act to damage the bonds attaching people to one another, to impair the prevailing sense of group cohesion. Collective trauma works its way slowly into the awareness of those who come to suffer from it, so it may not be visible in the days or even months following discrete moments of disaster. But it is a form of shock all the same, a gradual realization on the part of an already numbed people that their community no longer exists as an effective source of support and that an important part of their world has disappeared with-out so much as a sound. As people begin to emerge hesitantly from the protective shells into which they had reflexively shrunk at the time of the assault, they learn that they are isolated and alone, living in a kind of social wasteland with no one to turn to. They have lost the solace that comes from being in fellowship with one's kind. They have lost both the physical and the spiritual health that comes from being in communion with kinsmen and neighbors who can be counted on to care.

The terms I have elected to use in my own work to distinguish between the two species of trauma do not matter here, of course, but the larger point I am trying to make may be important in thinking about Grassy Narrows or any other scene of such reaching devastation. This is because the job of repair after a severe crisis, a project in which Shkilnyk has been deeply involved, is immensely complicated if one has to deal with both sorts of injury. When survivors suffer from loss of community as well as from individual shock, it is not just a question of getting them back on their feet but of seeing to it that there is some kind of communal ground, as it were, for them to stand on once they are upright. We can dress their physical wounds, provide food and shelter and clothing, console them for their losses, ease their grief, find ways to calm their anxieties. But until we restore the communal surround that was so vital to their sense of health and security, they will remain like refugees in their own land, damaged in spirit long after they have been put together again in body, and feeling a long way from home.

We in the United States and in Canada are a good deal more aware of individual trauma than we are of collective trauma, and we are better equipped to repair the kinds of damage inflicted on *persons* than the kinds of damage inflicted on *communities*. We know how to shelter people and feed them; we know how to tend physical wounds, and we are learning how to tend mental ones. But we do not know very much about how to restore a sense of community to people who have lost it, and this is true, at least in part, because we do not generally think of that loss as an injury requiring treatment.

It *is* an injury, though, and one of its symptoms, especially relevant to the case of Grassy Narrows, is a loss of the connective ties that held people together. When people who have been tightly enmeshed in the fabric of their community are ripped away from it by the force of some crisis, they find themselves exposed and alone, suddenly dependent on their own resources. And the cruel fact of the matter often is that they prove to have but meager resources once left on their own. This is not because they lack the heart or the competence, surely, but because they had always placed their abilities at the service of the larger community—the neighborhood, the clan, the parish, the band—and do not really know how to recall them for their own individual purposes. They do not think well in individual terms. They do not know how to be alone. They find that they are not very good at making decisions by themselves, and, worse, they find that they are not very good at getting along with others in the absence of familiar community supports.

Human relations in a true community take their shape, at least in part, from expectations pressing in on them from all sides like a firm but invisible mold. They are governed by the ways of the tribe, the habits of the neighborhood, the customs of the community. When the mold is stripped away, so to speak, something happens to those relationships. It is as if they existed in a kind of gravitational field. The human particles that make up the field are held in place by interpersonal charges passing between them, but they are also held in place by all the other magnetic forces—cultural, societal, communal—that constitute the larger field. And when those outer currents lose their force, as can happen when the assault is serious enough, the particles begin to separate because the interpersonal charge, by itself, turns out to be less than sufficient. So marriages break up, friendships dissolve, the bonds of kinship weaken, and, at the outer edges of human despair, parents lose the ability to care for their own children. Whole networks of ties begin to snap noiselessly as the particles, drifting now in a dead gravitational field, move farther and farther apart. And the pity of it is that people do not know why this is happening. They never realized the extent to which the old community validated those bonds and gave them strength, and, partly for that reason, they do not know how to breathe new life and meaning into them by deliberate expressions of affection or by deliberate offers of support. The battery on which they depended for emotional recharging, the community, is just no longer there.

And that, as you shall read, is an important part of the story of Grassy Narrows.

# ACKNOWLEDGMENTS

My debt to the people of Grassy Narrows is immeasurable. I am deeply grateful to the elders—John Beaver, Maryann Keewatin, Maggie Land, John Kokopenace, and Andy Keewatin—who shared with me their precious knowledge of the band's history and way of life. When we worked together on projects, the advice and kindness of Steve Fobister, Bill Fobister, and Pat Loon meant a great deal to me, and I thank them warmly. And Ivy Keewatin should know that each time she took me fishing, she left me with a keen sense of pleasure and a luminous memory of the old reserve.

Many non-Indian persons associated with the community also contributed to this volume. Father Lacelle, a retired Oblate missionary, provided invaluable historical information. Norman and Dorothy Schantz and Melva and Marvin Zook, Mennonite missionaries resident at Grassy Narrows since 1958, shared their knowledge of the community over many evenings of fine home cooking; their unflinching optimism and courage uplifted my own flagging spirits on more than one occasion. I was very fortunate to have been able to share the experience of everyday life at Grassy Narrows with Bill Morison, the band's forestry advisor; Karen Sheremeta and Peggy Halcrow, supervisors of the day-care center; Leslie Fraser and Marguerite and Alan Raslack, teachers at the federal school. And when I visited the Kenora office of DIAND, Dennis Wallace, Stu Martin, Brian Bennett, and Harry Veldstra always offered a sympathetic ear and a helping hand in my work.

I wish to convey my appreciation to those within DIAND in Ottawa who made it easier to devote two years to this study. I am grateful to Cam Mackie for arranging a six-month contract to begin research on the Grassy Narrows relocation. And I am indebted to Andy Mikita, Ian Cowie, and Keith Johnson for their moral and logistical support during the initial phase of my writing.

Many friends read portions of the manuscript, listened to ideas in gestation, or simply extended loving kindness when the business of writing got too lonely or when the wells of the creative imagination had run dry. I cannot return to them as much as I have received, yet they should know that they occupy a special place in my heart. A few deserve particular mention either because they have left an indelible mark on my life or because of their vital role in shaping my ideas and extending the boundaries of my understanding, insight, and compassion. They are Simon Fobister, Hiro Miyamatsu, Jack Beaver, Kai Erikson, and Jim Kingham. Others made the preparation of this book not only possible but an un-mitigated pleasure. Francine Whissell magically transformed sheaves of scrawled notes into fine typescript; and Gladys Topkis, my editor, "dreamed the poet's dream" and shepherded the manuscript through its life's stages. I am deeply grateful to all these extraordinary people for their wise counsel, their faith, and their abiding love.

My debt to my family, especially to my mother, goes beyond measure or description or metaphor. It is signalled by the dedication.

# INTRODUCTION

In the early morning of November 7, 1976, I climbed into a pickup truck in front of the Holiday Inn in Kenora, Ontario, and set out on a journey that would profoundly affect my life. My destination was a small Indian reserve called Grassy Narrows, about 1,200 miles northwest of Toronto, my hometown, and 120 miles east of Winnipeg. I did not know at the time, and could never have foreseen, that it would be my destiny to live in this village for two and a half years in order to bear witness to an awesome human tragedy.

I travelled sixty miles north and east from Kenora down a bumpy and winding logging road. On that jarring trip, I found myself more enchanted by the region's natural beauty than concerned about my immediate assignment. Winter had already come to this part of northwestern Ontario. Fresh snow hung loosely from the branches of pine, spruce, and birch trees, reflecting the sun with crystalline magic. There were countless lakes along the way, imposing outcroppings of rock, and high promontories that offered spectacular views of the landscape. This was God's country, the terrain of the Canadian Shield: rugged, sparsely populated, rich in fish and game, and quiet as the grave.

A sign on the road ultimately intruded on my thoughts: Grassy Narrows Indian Reserve—Population 520. I felt a moment of panic as I approached the village. I had been sent here by the Canadian Department of Indian Affairs to advise the federal government on programs to alleviate the economic disruption caused by mercury pollution of the English-Wabigoon River. I had read about this event in the newspapers and knew that Grassy Narrows and the nearby Indian community of Whitedog, both located on the river system, had been severely affected by the loss of their commercial fishing operations. But I knew very little about Canadian Indians and even less about the Ojibwa, the tribe that inhabited these villages.

Soon I came upon a little collection of frame houses in the middle of nowhere, all uniform in design, crowded together, and regimented into tight linear formations. One sensed disorder, even squalor, in the physical surroundings. Certainly the man-made environment presented a sharp contrast to the pastoral beauty of the natural setting. Later, I would come to understand an even sharper contradiction. For unlike the natural order of things, this community was headed not toward growth and renewal but toward self-mutilation and death.

1

It hadn't always been like this. I learned that at the beginning of the 1960s, the Grassy Narrows people were still living on the site of the "old reserve" of islands and peninsulas on the English-Wabigoon River. On these ancestral lands, allocated to them by the North-West Angle Treaty of 1873, the people had preserved an ethos that encompassed, among other things, a deep attachment to the land and the rhythms of nature, respect for the dignity of the person, and the independence and self-sufficiency of clan-based family groups. They lived, as they had for generations, by hunting, trapping, fishing, and gathering, now supplemented by occasional wage labor. The ebb and flow of life was reflected in their seasonal migrations between the winter trapping grounds and the summer encampment on the old reserve. Because of their relative isolation and limited contact with white society, the people managed to maintain considerable stability and continuity with the ancient patterns of Ojibwa life.

But in the summer of 1963, the Department of Indian Affairs began to relocate the people of Grassy Narrows to a "new reserve" about five miles south of the old settlement. The move was justified on the grounds that the new site, accessible by road from the town of Kenora, would make it easier to provide the Indians with some of the amenities of modern life—a school on the reserve, electricity, improved housing, and social services. The uprooting, however, proved devastating to the Ojibwa way of life. And before the people had had time to adjust, to establish new roots, they were hit in 1970 by another blow: the discovery that the river that had sustained them was poisoned by methyl mercury. In little more than a decade, the society that had held together and prospered on the old reserve was in shambles. And the people, finding themselves trapped in a no-man's-land, an abyss between two cultures, had begun to self-destruct.

This book is about the origins of suffering in the life of these Indian people. In sociological terms, it is a case study in the causes and symptoms of social disintegration; in the idiom of psychologists, it is a study in social pathology, an attempt to trace the sources for the symptoms of collective trauma. It crosses into the discipline of anthropology when it describes the intrusions on the way of life of an indigenous people and their response to the experience of forced acculturation. And it falls into the field of social planning when it documents the contribution of government planners to the history of an environmental and human disaster. But this book is also a chronicle of a personal voyage of learning and discovery. The Grassy Narrows people taught me a great deal about their history and culture, and in the process, they taught me much about myself.

Precisely because knowledge and insight arise out of a complex interaction between self and others, the issues of objectivity and moral judgment haunt the social scientist who is both a participant in and an observer of a way of life fundamentally different from her own. As intimately as I was involved in the life of the community, I could not help but look at the situation as an outsider. Even though I was committed intellectually to seeing things from the inside, I still had to rely on my developed senses of perception, ways of knowing, and value system to guide both my observation of present conditions and my analysis of past experience. I tried, however, to see the "pathology" from the perspective of what community life at Grassy Narrows was like before the troubles began. And I listened carefully, over a long period of time, to what the people themselves had to say about the significant events in their history. In this connection, I was particularly struck by the circumstances of their relocation and the effects of mercury contamination. Certainly these two events seemed to have a direct relationship to the symptoms of individual trauma and social collapse that began to appear in the early 1970s. Having said this, however, I feel that I should let the reader know something more about my own background, experience, role, and relationship to the community, for these surely influenced the book that eventually emerged.

In the summer of 1976, I took a leave of absence from my doctoral studies in urban and regional planning at the Massachusetts Institute of Technology and returned to Canada. When I was approached to work with Indian people, I saw a unique opportunity to bring my knowledge and experience in the Third World to the problem of underdevelopment in my own country. I thought I was adequately equipped to provide technical assistance to Grassy Narrows in the creation of alternative forms of economic enterprise.

But it did not take long for me to recognize that the situation in the community was far more complex and much less amenable to a technical solution than I had envisaged. All the indications of material poverty were there—substandard housing, the absence of running water and sewage connections, poor health, mass unemployment, low income, and welfare dependency—but something more fundamental seemed amiss. Its manifest symptom was widespread alcohol abuse, in the form of prolonged and frequent periods of spree drinking. In the day-care center where I lived, I could not help but be exposed to the difficulties this caused, because battered women and abandoned children came there to seek warmth, refuge, and food. My first experience with the aftermath of a weekend of heavy drinking left such a strong impression that I obtained a grant to support a resident community alcohol counselor and persuaded an alcohol treatment clinic in Thunder Bay to give priority to the Grassy Narrows people. As I tried to find my bearings in the community, I worked with band members to obtain government funding for short-term employment programs, organized files in the band office, and started feasibility studies on a number of development projects. Mostly I extended assistance in whatever form the people required, including filling out applications for old age pensions. By "doing things," I sought to gain acceptance by the people and to dispel their doubts—and sometimes my own—that I had anything of value to offer. I even organized a cooking and nutrition course as a last-ditch attempt to find a way to the heart of the community. But all my efforts seemed to have no impact in lifting the dark curtain of demoralization that enveloped the village.

I could never escape the feeling that I had been parachuted into a void—a drab and lifeless place in which the vital spark of life had gone out. It wasn't just the poverty of the place, the isolation, or even the lack of a decent bed that depressed me. I had seen worse material deprivation when I was working in squatter settlements around Santiago, Chile. And I had been in worse physical surroundings while working in war-devastated Ismailia on the project for the reconstruction of the Suez Canal. What struck me about Grassy Narrows was the numbness in the human spirit. There was an indifference, a listlessness, a total passivity that I could neither understand nor seem to do anything about. I had never seen such hopelessness anywhere in the Third World.

When my contract ran out in April 1977, I returned to Toronto and buried myself in other work. But that was not to be the end of my involvement with Grassy Narrows. One day I received a call from the young chief of the band, Simon Fobister, who asked me to return to the reserve to work directly for the chief and band council as a community planner. I accepted. And from September 1977 to June 1979, Grassy Narrows became my home.

The years passed quickly. I became deeply involved in a variety of research and developmental activities. My first large project, in 1977–78, was a comprehensive household survey to generate the basic demographic, physical, and social data needed for a community plan. I worked with Hiro Miyamatsu, a Japanese photojournalist who had been living at Grassy Narrows since 1975; together we administered questionnaires, analyzed data, and prepared a community profile for the band council. In a parallel research project, I sought information from government agencies about their programs and expenditures on the reserve. A third project involved Melva Zook, one of the resident Mennonite missionaries, in a genealogical mapping of Grassy Narrows clans since the treaty of 1873; this study of family trees was distributed to the major family groups. Research gave way to action when I joined a team of people in developing a community-based wild-rice industry. Together we were able to build a dam to control water levels for wild rice and to install appropriate technology for the local processing of the product. In this and other development projects, I was primarily responsible for raising funds and dealing with the federal and provincial governments. My role as ombudsman for

Grassy Narrows evolved out of countless meetings with, and submissions to, government officials on issues of program delivery, land use, and access to natural resources, in which I tried to persuade the authorities to be more responsive to community needs as defined by the Indian people themselves.

By late 1978, however, despite noticeable improvements in the levels of community income and employment generated by the new programs, it was clear that sharp and public suffering was continuing. Recognizing that the troubles at Grassy Narrows went far beyond those common to other Indian reserves in the region, Chief Simon Fobister and the band council decided to press for an out-of-court settlement for the extraordinary damages to community life inflicted by mercury pollution and the relocation. In December, the chief signed a formal mediation agreement with the federal and provincial governments. From that point on, as the band's fact finder, I began to document the damages to community life, the events and processes that had led to them, and the forms of compensation appropriate to the losses the people had endured. With the assistance of Pat Loon as translator, I recorded lengthy interviews with the heads of all the family groups; some interviews were also captured on film to buttress the written evidence. The work in preparation for the mediation process was intense, urgent, and personally rewarding in terms of community participation and support.

By June 1979, however, I was suffering from a classic case of burnout. I decided to interrupt my work at Grassy Narrows to take up two short-term assignments in Ottawa. The first was to write a policy paper for the National Indian Socio-Economic Development Committee; the second was to write a report for the Department of Indian Affairs and Northern Development (DIAND) on the circumstances of the Grassy Narrows relocation. But by mid-1980, things had changed in the community. The mediation process had failed to meet the expectations generated for it; the band did not reelect Simon Fobister as chief; and the people slid into an even deeper and darker depression. The change in leadership made it particularly difficult to return to the reserve, so I decided to resume my academic work. As I had been encouraged to write a doctoral thesis, I committed the next year to a search for more information on how the assault on the Indian people had been delivered. On the basis of data gleaned from public records and archives, additional interviews, and my own extensive collection of field notes, diaries, and transcripts, I wrote a dissertation on the origins of breakdown in community life. This book emerged from that document. It was inspired by the desire to make the story known to a wider public because, to date, the Grassy Narrows people have not been fully compensated for the personal and communal losses they have suffered.

Since much of the narrative contained in these pages unfolds in the words of the Grassy Narrows people or others who know them well, the reader should know how these voices came to be recorded. There are basically four sources for the quotations in the text. Most of the Indian voices are drawn from either the twenty-two mediation-related interviews or eighteen of my own interviews. The latter took place over the years, as people stopped by my house for tea or to ask or return a favor; with their permission, I recorded their stories of times past and times present. A much smaller number of quotations are drawn from filmed interviews or from conversations noted in my diary. As for the non-Indian voices, they were recorded in connection with either the mediation or the research for my thesis. Both Indian and non-Indian speakers remain anonymous at their request, and pseudonyms are used throughout.

# PART I
# GRASSY NARROWS: COMMUNITY IN RUINS

A ragged urchin, aimless and alone,
   Loitered about that vacancy; a bird
Flew up to safety from his well-aimed stone;
   That girls are raped, that two boys knife a third;
   Were axioms to him, who'd never heard
Of any world where promises were kept,
Or one could weep because another wept.
   —W. H. Auden, "The Shield of Achilles"

At the end of Sheba's Hill, named after the old woman whose house crests the steep climb, past the log icehouse, and at the intersection of the road going to The Point lies the cemetery of Grassy Narrows. Casual visitors to the reserve in winter would hardly notice its existence or pay heed to a miniature shelter that rises incongrously out of the deep snow to mark the grave of a child. Even as the snow melts and the grave sites become exposed, one can see that there are no monuments to the dead, just some simple markings, some crosses, and the remnants of plastic flowers strewn about the unkempt ground. But only those who do not know what happened at Grassy Narrows can pass by this burial ground without thought or memory. For those who belong to this community, memory is inescapable. There is no one on the reserve today who, in the past fifteen years, has not buried here a parent, child, husband, wife, brother, sister, or cousin. Death and violence have become the hallmarks of a community in crisis.

People who have never lived under such conditions may find it difficult to comprehend that there could be a human settlement in which the odds of dying a natural death from sickness, old age, or misadventure hover around 25 percent. Yet, at Grassy Narrows, if the trend continues, three out of every four persons will die from an act of violence. This extraordinary probability of violent death spares no one, regardless of age. For people under nineteen, the odds of dying violently are even greater, and their deaths still more disturbing, because they will probably die by their own hand.

Grassy Narrows cemetery.

There are other indications that Grassy Narrows is a deeply disturbed community. Cases of acute child neglect, for example, are in general extremely rare among Indian peoples, who are known for their indulgent devotion to their young. At Grassy Narrows, however, in just one year, the Children's Aid Society had to take away over a third of all children between the ages of five and fourteen because they had been physically abused, severely neglected, or simply abandoned. When this evidence of a discontinuity in the ability of a people to care for and protect their offspring is viewed alongside data on the extent of alcoholism and alcohol-related illness among adults, the inescapable conclusion emerges that aberrant and self-destructive behavior has become the collective norm for this community. Social pathology, usually confined to a minority of the population, becomes represented by the majority. The data speak for themselves. The social conditions at Grassy Narrows are very serious, far worse than those found among other Indian bands in the region, and comparable to those documented for indigenous populations that have been through a major upheaval or disaster.

However painful this portrait may be to a people seemingly disfigured and broken in spirit by historical circumstance, it is the price they have to pay to make us understand their case for social justice.

# 1 • A COMMUNITY
   DESTROYED

## Violent Death and Suicide

In the early hours of November 7, 1976, on the day of my arrival at Grassy Narrows, an eighteen-year-old youth was killed by a gunshot wound in the stomach. David Fobister, one of the most gifted young men of his generation, had been shot in the heat of a political argument during a drinking party. As the wave of shock and remorse subsided in the community and gave way to preparations for burial, I learned that this was the eleventh death from violence in less than a year in this small village of about five hundred persons (table 1.1).

There is no easy way to communicate the cumulative effect of a succession of violent deaths in a small community, only half of whose residents are over the age of fifteen. Grassy Narrows is a place where everybody is related by blood or marriage. Death therefore affects not only one's immediate kin but a much wider circle of relations. A not uncommon reaction in those who have been touched by violent death is to repress grief, guilt, or anger until these powerful emotions can be released by the disinhibiting effects of alcohol. The feelings of aggression and rage normally suppressed in face-to-face encounters find expression during drinking parties which are the context for beatings, rape, or other acts of violence that may lead to death. The drinking parties become part of a vicious circle in which the mourners often become those who are mourned.

People forgive each other for acts of violence committed under the influence of alcohol because, they say, "the pain has to come out sometime." As an overall commentary on the contemporary community, however, the record of death presents grim evidence of the progressive deterioration in the security and well-being of the people. One cannot help being awed by the dramatic change in the way people die at Grassy Narrows (figure 1.1).

The pattern of deaths over the past twenty years leaves no doubt that violent death is a recent phenomenon at Grassy Narrows, associated with the move to the new reserve in the mid-1960s. Prior to the relocation, in the period 1959–63, 91 percent of all deaths in the community were due to natural causes. By the mid-1970s, only 23 percent of all deaths could be

**Table 1.1  Record of Death at Grassy Narrows, 1975–1978**

| Year | Month | Name | Age | Cause of Death |
|------|-------|------|-----|----------------|
| 1975 | January | Sammy Assin | 21 | *Stabbing |
|  |  | Parker Keewatin | 14 | *Stabbing |
|  | March | Robert Pahpasay | 6 mo | *Child neglect |
|  | June | George Petiquan | 50 | *Assault |
|  | September | Camilla Loon | 60 | Illness |
|  |  | Theresa Fontaine | 40 | *Gunshot wounds |
|  | November | Alex Pahpasay | 63 | *Alcohol poisoning |
|  |  | Mary Necanapenace | 44 | *Alcohol poisoning |
|  |  | George Quoquat | 41 | *Alcohol poisoning |
| 1976 | April | Mary Loon | 56 | *Exposure |
|  |  | Joe Swain | 92 | Old age |
|  |  | Lawrence Fisher | 25 | *Alcohol poisoning |
|  | May | John Turtle | 19 | *Drowning/homicide |
|  | July | Mary Morison | 36 | *Suicide |
|  | August | Mary Pahpasay | 52 | Unknown |
|  | September | Gladys Pelly | 54 | *Exposure |
|  | November | David Fobister | 18 | *Shotgun wound |
|  |  | Baby Tanguay | 1 mo | *Infant death |
|  |  | Agnes Necanapenace | 80 | Exposure |
|  |  | Ann Marie Kabestra | 1 mo | Infant death |
| 1977 | March | Elizabeth Kokopenace | 40 | *Death by fire |
|  |  | Curtis Kokopenace | 4 | *Death by fire |
|  | July | Elizabeth Stone | 29 | *Hit by train |
|  | September | Alan Pelly | 25 | *Drowning |
|  |  | Twins/Strong | 1 mo | Infant death |
|  |  | Rosie Necanapenace | 70 | Old age |
|  | October | Mary Land | 72 | *Heart attack/alcohol |
|  |  | Mary Keewatin | 54 | *Heart attack/alcohol |
|  | December | Audrey Loon | 12 | †Suicide |
| 1978 | January | Sharon Keesick | 14 | †Suicide |
|  |  | Alice Fobister | 54 | *Gunshot wound |
|  | March | Alphonse Necanapenace | 17 | *Suicide |
|  | May | James Swain, Sr. | 59 | *Drowning/homicide |
|  | July | Paul Pelly | 44 | *Assault |
|  |  | Jane Meeseewapatung | 31 | †Suicide |

*Source:* Compiled from the records of Mennonite missionaries Norman and Dorothy Schantz, who have lived in Grassy Narrows since 1958.

*Death related to alcohol.
†Death caused by an overdose of drugs.

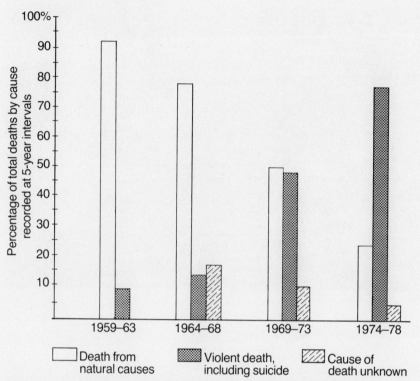

Figure 1.1. Incidence of Violent Death at Grassy Narrows, 1959–1978

traced to old age, illness, or accident. During 1974–78, 75 percent of all deaths were due to alcohol or drug-induced violence directed against others or against the self.

The incidence of death by violence is also considerably higher at Grassy Narrows than in the Kenora district and the province of Ontario generally. The Kenora–Rainy River District Health Council keeps regional statistics on causes of death. Its category "other accidents" corresponds to almost all alcohol-related violent deaths, such as those from drowning, fire, assault, or railway impact. In 1977, such deaths in the Kenora district represented 16 percent of total deaths; the comparable figure for Ontario was only 4 percent. In stark contrast, the average annual figure for Grassy Narrows in the period 1969–76 was 52.4 percent.

The higher incidence of violent death in the Kenora district relative to Ontario as a whole is related to the presence of twelve Indian reserves in this region. Social problems associated with alcohol abuse are common to many Indian communities. Yet Grassy Narrows is known as "the place

where sudden death from violence is most likely."[1] In this community, people have turned their anger inward, lashing out against those closest to them or against themselves. Their self-destructive response to intolerable conditions is clearly evident in the statistics on suicide.

At Grassy Narrows in 1977–78, twenty-six persons between ages eleven and nineteen tried to take their own lives (table 1.2). This number represents almost one-fifth (17 percent) of the entire population in this age-group. Three of these suicide attempts succeeded: two girls, twelve and fourteen, died from drug overdoses, and one seventeen-year-old boy shot

**Table 1.2   Attempted Suicide at Grassy Narrows, 1977–1978**

| Date | Time | Age | Gender |
|------|------|-----|--------|
| June 7, 1977 | 4:48 p.m. | 15 | female |
| June 21, 1977 | 4:10 a.m. | 14 | female |
| Sept. 2, 1977 | 5:35 a.m. | 14 | female |
| Sept. 2, 1977 | 5:35 a.m. | 16 | female |
| Sept. 21, 1977 | 5:35 p.m. | 12 | male |
| Oct. 5, 1977 | 10:34 a.m. | 17 | female |
| Oct. 6, 1977 | 9:45 p.m. | 14 | female |
| Oct. 15, 1977 | 5:45 a.m. | 17 | female |
| Oct. 18, 1977 | 5:15 p.m. | 49 | female |
| Oct. 24, 1977 | 8:28 a.m. | 11 | male |
| Oct. 31, 1977 | 7:45 p.m. | 11 | female |
| Nov. 17, 1977 | 7:00 p.m. | 14 | female |
| Nov. 17, 1977 | 7:00 p.m. | 11 | male |
| Nov. 26, 1977 | 4:50 a.m. | 49 | female |
| Jan. 4, 1978 | 2:50 p.m. | 20 | male |
| Jan. 13, 1978 | 1:30 p.m. | 32 | female |
| Jan. 26, 1978 | 11:55 p.m. | 14 | female |
| Feb. 1, 1978 | 10:45 p.m. | 13 | female |
| Feb. 1, 1978 | 10:45 p.m. | 14 | female |
| Feb. 5, 1978 | 3:30 p.m. | 13 | female |
| Feb. 5, 1978 | 3:20 p.m. | 17 | female |
| Feb. 7, 1978 | 10:30 p.m. | 18 | female |
| Feb. 12, 1978 | 7:00 p.m. | 19 | female |
| Mar. 10, 1978 | 11:00 a.m. | 22 | female |
| Mar. 13, 1978 | 7:30 p.m. | 16 | female |
| Mar. 24, 1978 | 7:20 a.m. | 12 | male |
| Apr. 1, 1978 | 12:05 p.m. | 16 | female |
| May 7, 1978 | 11:00 p.m. | 16 | female |

*Source:* Data are from the records of the Grassy Narrows detachment of the Ontario Provincial Police for the period June 1977 to May 1978.

himself in the head. But even this appalling record is incomplete, since it includes only those suicides and suicide attempts that came to the attention of the Grassy Narrows detachment of the Ontario Provincial Police. Other incidents are not reported. In the summer of 1978, for example, I became involved with two teenage girls who tried to kill themselves after having been raped by a close relative; their fear and embarrassment prevented them from talking to the police. The sense of violation, shame, and powerlessness following incestuous or gang rape very often triggers an attempt at suicide. But more often than not, these cases are not reported.

Certainly in the context of the Indian way of life, as in our own culture, suicide of the young is considered a tragedy. Attempted suicide indicates depression, hopelessness, a loss of moorings, an erosion of the symbols and points of reference essential to life's continuity. The high incidence of suicide and attempted suicide among the young at Grassy Narrows is therefore an unambiguous signal that community morale is very poor. When one asks young people why they want to kill themselves, they say they "have nothing to lose." Almost all come from families in which there is heavy drinking; almost all are physically neglected or abused children. Deprived also of emotional nourishment, they choose suicide as a means of protest against life without love. The story of Amanda Lynn, composed from notes in my diary dated December 1977, illustrates the lament of childhood at Grassy Narrows. This girl was only twelve years old when she took her own life.

> Amanda Lynn used to come to the day-care center to make chocolate chip cookies. Her little band of friends would come to visit, because they had nowhere else to go when their families were drinking. If they couldn't take refuge in the day-care center, they just roamed around the reserve all night, or until it was safe to return home. . . .
>
> Amanda and her brother, older by one year, were always dirty, always hungry, and were poorly clothed for the harsh winter of Grassy Narrows. Their father was part of the "broken generation," a man in his middle thirties, caught between the old and the new ways of life. He worked intermittently at the sawmill, but most of his income came from welfare and unemployment insurance. He was one of the heaviest binge drinkers on the reserve. His house was bare of furniture, and most of his money went to buy liquor and rides to town in taxis. When he felt rich, he ordered a plane to fly him the sixty miles to Kenora. . . .
>
> Amanda died on the same day that her father refused to buy her a new pair of rubber boots. In temperatures that dropped to −30° and −40°F, she was still wearing an old and torn pair of sneakers. In the Hudson's Bay store, she approached her father while he was cashing his welfare check. She begged him for new boots because her feet were freezing. In a conversation widely reported around the reserve, he apparently replied, "Get out of my way. . . . You don't

give me anything, so why should I give you anything? I need the money for myself!" Then he went out drinking in Kenora. When he returned to the reserve, his daughter was dead. She had killed herself with an overdose of tuberculosis pills.

Like other forms of violent death, suicide by children and young teenagers is a recent phenomenon. Prior to 1970, no suicides were recorded at Grassy Narrows. In contrast, between 1974 and 1978, four people, aged twelve, fourteen, seventeen, and thirty-six, took their own lives. Although the actual number of suicides may not appear to be significant, in this community of only 490 people (1977 data) it represents an average annual rate of 204.1 per 100,000 population. By the same calculation, in 1974 the overall suicide rate for Canada was only 12.1; for the registered Canadian Indian population in 1976 it was 30.1.[2]

Indian reserves generally show a dramatically higher rate of attempted suicide by drug overdose than do nonnative communities. This is revealed by the 1977 record of admissions for drug-overdose cases kept by the Lake of the Woods Hospital which serves the town of Kenora, the surrounding townships within a fifty-mile radius, and the twelve Indian reserves in the vicinity (table 1.3). Although the data are limited to the cases that actually arrive at the hospital, and also to those individuals who are first-time admissions for attempted suicide, they show that Grassy Narrows has the highest rate of attempted suicide in the entire Kenora region.

## Alcoholism and Illness

The data on violent death and suicide at Grassy Narrows suggest that alcohol plays a crucial role in terms of the circumstances under which fatal "accidents" occur. And indeed the widespread and pathological use of alcohol in the community began in the mid-1960s, after the people were moved to the new reserve and connected to the town of Kenora by road. Thus, deaths of infants from acute physical neglect on the part of drinking parents were first recorded in 1969–70; deaths from alcoholic poisoning first appeared in 1973. While mortality may be the most salient effect of heavy drinking in a community, alcohol abuse obviously has extremely destructive impacts on public health and human relationships. Thus a very high incidence of alcoholism and alcohol-related illness in a population usually points to a deeply troubled and demoralized society.

The search for information on the extent of alcohol abuse in any particular Indian community, and on the severity of medical and social problems associated with it, is frustrated by three factors. In the first place, most official statistics for Ontario are available only on a regional basis. In other instances, the provisions of the Ontario Human Rights Code pro-

Table 1.3    Admissions to Lake of the Woods Hospital for Attempted Suicide by Drug Overdose, 1977

| Locality | Number of First-Time Admissions | Percentage of Total Admissions | Rate per 1,000 Popula-tion* | Combined Rate |
|---|---|---|---|---|
| Nonnative communities | | | | |
| Town of Kenora | 41 | 34 | 4.1 | |
| Keewatin and Jeffrey Melick | 8 | 6 | 5.3 | 4.3 |
| Remote Communities | 5 | 4 | | |
| Native communities | | | | |
| Grassy Narrows | 19 | 16 | 44.2 | |
| Whitedog | 23 | 19 | 38.9 | |
| Rat Portage | 10 | 8 | 40.5 | 35.7 |
| Whitefish Bay | 9 | 7 | 20.7 | |
| Shoal Lake | 7 | 6 | 36.4 | |
| Totals | 122 | 100 | | |

*Source:* Based on hospital admission statistics contained in a letter dated February 20, 1978, from Dr. P. Connop, Medical Services Branch, Health and Welfare Canada, to Chief Simon Fobister of Grassy Narrows.

*In order to arrive at a rate per 1,000 population, the population for Kenora and townships was estimated at 11,500 persons. The population base for the five Indian reserves was calculated as 1,893 total population. Demographic data for each reserve were obtained from The Department of Indian Affairs and Northern Development (DIAND). The on-reserve 1977 population was as follows: Grassy Narrows, 430; Whitedog, 590; Rat Portge, 247; Whitefish Bay, 434; Shoal Lake, 192.

hibit the gathering of data on the basis of an individual's ethnic or racial origin. This makes it difficult to make comparisons among Indian communities.[3]

Second, with the exception of program data kept by DIAND, government social agencies that deal with Indian people do not keep files on a reserve-by-reserve basis. Furthermore, the Children's Aid Society and the Ministry of Correctional Services have kept records for only five and three years, respectively. The absence of data over time frames long enough to detect trends and causes, as well as the paucity of comprehensive records on a community basis, makes comparative work difficult.

Third, the data that do exist on alcohol-related problems in the Kenora area are hard to interpret in any case because the population base of Indian reserves is small and other external influences may distort the figures. In spite of the methodological hurdles to be overcome, the available data confirm the fact that alcohol abuse is the most critical and disturbing element in the life of the people of northwestern Ontario.

A 1977 government-sponsored study of alcoholism in Ontario documented the extent of the problem:

> Alcohol consumption rates are higher in the northwest [region] and climbing even faster than the provincial rates. . . . Liquor offense rates are higher in the northwest, alcoholism diagnoses among hospitalized patients are more common, and mortality rates due to accidents, poisonings, and violence are elevated. . . .
>
> The Kenora district is more notable both in terms of higher alcohol consumption levels and indications of consequences of heavy consumption. . . . Native Indians are overrepresented in hospital and detoxication centre populations in the Kenora area, and a high proportion of deaths among natives are due to accidental and violent causes.[4]

Northwestern Ontario not only has the highest per capita consumption of alcohol relative to the province as a whole, but the rate of increase in consumption during 1969–74 was more than double that of the province (34 percent versus 16 percent). Further, alcoholism is a much more common medical diagnosis in northwestern Ontario than in the province generally; it ranks fifth in the Kenora area and twenty-eighth in Ontario generally. At the Lake of the Woods Hospital, the cumulative frequency of patients with an alcoholic diagnosis has been rising rapidly since the mid-1960s. The rate of increase in alcoholic diagnoses has been much steeper for Indian people than for non-Indian people, particularly since 1971. In terms of numbers, the rate of admission for alcoholic patients increased from one Indian female in 1965 to fifty-five in 1974; the corresponding increase for Indian males was from four in 1965 to thirty-nine in 1974. Alcoholic first admissions to the hospital increased at an average annual rate of 34 percent during 1965–74. On the average, one out of eleven discharges from the hospital involved a person diagnosed as an alcoholic.[5]

The way in which Indians use alcohol is at odds with the norms for drinking in our own society. The difference lies in the binge, or spree, nature of Indian drinking, not only in the Kenora area reserves, but in Indian communities across the country. The following notes in my journal depict a five-day period of spree drinking at Grassy Narrows:

> On Friday, March 31, 1978, the band office paid out a total of $20,370.10 in wages and approximately $5,000 in social assistance. That day the people went on a binge. . . .
>
> After very heavy drinking on the weekend, both in town and on the reserve, the people started going back to town on Monday to get more liquor. On that day, April 3, it was possible to observe the number of trips to town being made by taxi or plane. Five planes took off from the community dock; five taxis took

people to town. Some people went to town with the medical van. The total cost of transportation to Kenora for the purchase of alcohol was $1,050 for that day alone. Over the next three days, we observed eight more trips to town by plane (at $120 per trip) and fourteen trips by taxi (at $90 per trip). We estimated that of the $25,000 paid out by the band office, the people spent over $14,000 on alcohol in little less than a week.[6]

A typical binge at Grassy Narrows has certain characteristics that distinguish it from the "white man's way" of drinking. First, the majority of heavy drinkers in the community are not necessarily addicted to alcohol in the sense of a physiological enslavement. Most people can follow a period of very heavy spree drinking with a week or so of abstinence, at least until the next payday. They can also stay sober for weeks while they are on the trapline. The obsessed and driven alcoholic of the Western world, the one who cannot function without a certain level of alcohol in the bloodstream, finds few counterparts in Indian society.

Second, Indian drinking is a social activity; rarely do individuals drink alone. At Grassy Narrows, alcohol is perhaps the only commodity that is shared widely. During a binge, people move freely from house to house looking for liquor and drinking companions. Each clan group has its own drinking network, and drinking is a family affair. If the husband in the family is a heavy drinker, the wife is likely to be one as well. The children in the family will also drink, usually after the adults have become unconscious.

Third, spree drinking is a continuous process; people drink until they become unconscious. Accidents, or acts of violence leading to death, most often occur in the period of alcoholic "blackout." Upon awakening from this state, people will continue drinking until the entire supply of hard liquor, fortified wine, or beer is exhausted. At that point, someone will make a trip to Kenora to buy more alcohol. The trips to town cease when the cash necessary to purchase the liquor is depleted. Plane and taxi operators, however, are more than willing to extend credit for transportation to town, and the Grassy Narrows people thus remain heavily in debt. Indian spree drinking is big business in Kenora.

Fourth, a prolonged binge is like a tornado that tears across the landscape of the community, leaving devastation in its wake. During the binge, infants become dehydrated, children go hungry,[7] women are swollen from beatings, young girls are raped. The consequences of this mode of drinking reinforce the perception of Indian drinking as pathological.

As part of a comprehensive household survey carried out at Grassy Narrows in 1977–78, I sought information on the amount and frequency of alcohol use for each band member between ages sixteen and sixty-four resident on the reserve. The survey data were checked against personal knowledge of individuals and families so that persons could be placed in one of four categories of alcohol use.

**Table 1.4  Alcohol Use at Grassy Narrows by Sex, 1978**[a]

|                                        | Male | Female | Total | Percentage |
|----------------------------------------|------|--------|-------|------------|
| Nondrinkers                            | 23   | 22     | 45    | 22         |
| Social drinkers                        | 17   | 8      | 25    | 12         |
| Heavy drinkers                         | 30   | 34     | 64    | 32         |
| Very heavy drinkers, close to addiction | 40   | 28     | 68    | 34         |
| Totals                                 | 110  | 92     | 202   | 100        |

[a]"Heavy drinkers" are the spree drinkers of the community, those who will drink for an entire weekend after payday but usually be back at work by Monday or Tuesday. "Very heavy drinkers" are those who are closest to alcoholism in the sense of a behavioral, and perhaps physical, addiction. They are alcohol-dependent and will drink whenever they have money to spend on the purchase of liquor. "Social drinkers" are those who drink occasionally.

The findings are shown in table 1.4, and it can be seen that two-thirds of the entire population between ages sixteen and sixty-four are in the heavy drinker or very heavy drinker categories. Furthermore, drinking behavior at Grassy Narrows varies for different age-groups (table 1.5). For example, in the very heavy drinker category there is a substantial increase in alcohol use in persons thirty to forty-four years old, followed by a gradual levelling off as people reach forty-five years and older. This is not entirely surprising, since it is exactly this age-group that suffered most

**Table 1.5  Alcohol Use by Age and Sex, 1978**

|                      | Percentage of Population in Each Age-group | | | |
|----------------------|-------|-------|-------|-------|
|                      | 16–19 | 20–29 | 30–44 | 45–64 |
| *Male*               |       |       |       |       |
| Nondrinkers          | 35    | 22    | 14    | 7.5   |
| Social drinkers      | 42    | 9     | 6     | 7.5   |
| Heavy drinkers       | 23    | 36    | 20    | 31    |
| Very heavy drinkers  |       | 33    | 60    | 54    |
| Totals               | 100   | 100   | 100   | 100   |
| *Female*             |       |       |       |       |
| Nondrinkers          | 32    | 29    | 16    | 12.5  |
| Social drinkers      | 16    | 3     | 3     | 25    |
| Heavy drinkers       | 52    | 32    | 26    | 50    |
| Very heavy drinkers  |       | 36    | 55    | 12.5  |
| Totals               | 100   | 100   | 100   | 100   |

directly from the onslaught on the Indian way of life and the collision of two worlds that followed the relocation of the band in the mid-1960s. Younger persons, ages sixteen to nineteen and twenty to twenty-nine, tend to drink somewhat less than the middle-aged population, but they are often encouraged to drink by relatives living in the same house. The most important finding is that 70 percent of adults in their child-bearing years (20–29 years old) and 80 percent in their child-rearing years (30–44 years old) are heavy drinkers.

The data support the observation that the community is in serious difficulty with respect to alcohol abuse, especially in the group aged thirty to forty-four. Because alcoholism is a widespread medical and social problem in northwestern Ontario, it is important to ask whether the conditions at Grassy Narrows are any worse than those on other Indian reserves in the area.

Available comparative data are scarce; however, some indications of the relative circumstances of Grassy Narrows are to be found in statistics pertaining to admissions to the Lake of the Woods Hospital for alcohol-related traumatic injury (table 1.6). This class of injury includes assault, suspected child abuse, attempted suicide, severe emotional disturbance, and hysteria. The statistics show that Indian communities generally have a much higher population-adjusted rate of hospital admissions for alcohol-related injury than the town of Kenora does: the rate for Grassy Narrows is slightly higher than the rates for other Indian reserves. When days of hospitalization for alcohol-related injury are the standard of comparison, however, the population-adjusted rate for Grassy Narrows in 1975 is about thirty times the rate for the province of Ontario and about five times the rate for the Kenora district.

**Table 1.6   Admissions to Lake of the Woods Hospital for Alcohol-Related Traumatic Injury, 1977**

|  | Number of Admissions | Percentage of Total | Rate per 1,000 Population |
|---|---|---|---|
| Town of Kenora | 70 | 37 | 7.0 |
| Grassy Narrows | 27 | 15 | 55.1 |
| Whitedog | 32 | 17 | 54.2 |
| Whitefish Bay | 16 | 9 | 38.1 |
| Rat Portage | 13 | 7 | 54.2 |
| Keewatin | 11 | 6 | |
| Other | 17 | 9 | |
| | 186 | 100 | |

*Source:* Data supplied by the Kenora district office of Medical Services, Health and Welfare Canada, February 1978.

Given the fact that per capita alcohol consumption is much higher in northwestern Ontario than in Ontario as a whole, it comes as no surprise that the rates of hospitalization for diseases known to be connected with heavy alcohol consumption are also much higher in this region. Health problems likely to be encountered among heavy drinkers include certain diseases of the nervous system; problems with the digestive system and liver, such as acute and chronic gastritis and peptic ulcers; respiratory diseases, such as chronic bronchitis, pneumonia, and tuberculosis; heart and vascular diseases; and certain cancers, especially those of the upper respiratory and digestive tracts. Within the northwest region, the Kenora area has higher hospitalization rates for infective and respiratory diseases than the Sioux Lookout and Red Lake areas, which also have substantial native populations. But within the Kenora area, compared to six other Indian reserves, Grassy Narrows has the highest rate of hospitalization for all illnesses (table 1.7).

The special situation of Grassy Narrows is reflected best in these statistics. The fact that this community has a hospitalization rate about 27 percent higher than the combined rate for five other Kenora area reserves suggests that neither the common historical experience of the native peoples nor the conditions of housing, sanitation, and isolation they share can, by themselves, account for the difference. The Grassy Narrows people seem to be suffering from exceptional stress and experiencing difficulties that go far beyond those that trouble Indian communities in the region as a whole.

Finally, Grassy Narrows has the highest rate of hospitalization for

**Table 1.7   Days of Hospitalization at Lake of the Woods Hospital for All Illnesses, 1976**

| Area | Number of Days | Number of Days/ 1,000 Population |
|------|----------------|----------------------------------|
| Five reserves in the Kenora area, excluding Grassy Narrows and Whitedog | 3,709 | 3,811.7 |
| Grassy Narrows | 2,225 | 5,174.0 |
| Whitedog | 1,941 | 3,278.7 |
|  | 7,875 |  |

*Source:* Data supplied by the Kenora district office of Medical Services, Health and Welfare Canada, February 1978.

pneumonia and upper respiratory infections (189.8/1,000 population, as compared to 31.8 for Ontario and 132.7 for the Kenora district). Young people make up the majority of patients with respiratory problems. In 1976, the percentage of total cases of pneumonia in the zero to fourteen age-group recorded for Grassy Narrows was almost double the figure for the region as a whole: 82.3 percent versus 45.2 percent, respectively. When cases of upper respiratory infection are added to cases of pneumonia in children in the same age-group, the figure for Grassy Narrows is more than double the figure for the Kenora region: 85.6 percent versus 41.0 percent. The high incidence of respiratory illness among the young at Grassy Narrows is another reflection of the more general problem of child neglect in the community.

## Public Disorder and Criminal Offenses

In our society, high offense rates are widely accepted as an indicator of deteriorating social conditions. Physical violence directed against persons and the destruction of property are offenses subject not only to moral disapproval and informal sanctions but also to certain rituals leading to judgment and retribution by the justice system. In the Indian community, however, "the law" is "the white man's law." Indian people often do not share the prevailing notions of what classes of behavior constitute offenses against the social order. In particular, they reject the concept of guilt and punishment for behavior influenced by alcohol, and they grant little legitimacy to the regulations that fall under the Liquor Control Act of Ontario. Thus, problems arise when law enforcement agencies apply their notions of law to people who do not believe that they are guilty and who are not condemned by members of their own community for their actions.

Furthermore, Indian people see that the denunciation, stigmatization, and sanctions attached by the white society to an alcohol-related offense often stem not from the nature of the act itself but from the social position of the individual who commits it. The greater the social and economic worth of the offender, the more muted is society's condemnation of his actions. In the case of an Indian person, conviction for an offense is a confirmation of his social worthlessness; whereas in the case of a white person of prominent social status, an offense is regarded as an expression of his human fallibility.

These observations qualify the interpretation of official statistics on criminal offenses by Indian people in the Kenora area. The information produced by the police, the courts, and the government correctional bureaucracies is relevant to the description of deteriorating social conditions on Indian reserves, but we must recognize that the justice system is grounded in the interests, perspectives, and values of the dominant white society. Other factors also have a bearing on the statistics relating to the extent of public order problems.[8] Moreover, it goes without saying that statistics represent only what has been placed on record, not necessarily what exists. In the Kenora area, official records probably underestimate the number of offenses, since many occurrences of unlawful behavior do not result in charges.

In the light of what we know about the extent of alcohol use in northwestern Ontario, it is to be expected that this part of the country has the highest overall rate of public order offenses in the province. Over half of all the charges brought by the police in this region are for liquor offenses, whereas these account for only 10 percent of all charges in the province as a whole. The Kenora area not only has the highest proportion of liquor offenses versus all charges brought by the police, it also shows the fastest growing rate of increase in such offenses in the province.[9]

In the town of Kenora, 75 percent of all charges made by the police in any single year are for liquor offenses. On the average, about 82 percent of these offenses are for displays of public drunkenness. Other liquor offenses, such as having or consuming liquor in an illegal place, selling liquor illegally, or driving while intoxicated, form a much smaller proportion of offenses in the Kenora area than they do in the province as a whole.

Although information on the racial origin of persons charged by the town police is not available, we know that the vast majority of people the police send to the Kenora Detoxification Centre are Indians. The Kenora Detox Centre opened in September 1972 in response to protests by the residents of the town against the visibility of the alcohol problem ("the drunken Indians lying on the streets"), which they believed was hurting the town's image and its tourist trade. Between July 1973 and December 1975, 83 percent of all new admissions to the center were Indians. An ever increasing share of admissions is now made up of recidivists—people who keep being readmitted—and more and more of them are young Indians. Although the center has only forty beds, about 5,400 persons pass through its doors each year.

The majority of convictions handed down by the Kenora District Court are for liquor offenses. Between 1966 and 1974, liquor offenses made up 66 percent of total convictions handed down by the court; the provincial annual average was only 12 percent. "Intoxication in a public place" constituted about 80 percent of all liquor convictions, versus 45 percent for Ontario. About 90 percent of all convictions handed down to females involved liquor offenses, compared to less than 10 percent for the province as a whole.

Finally, most of the people committed to the Kenora jail are there for liquor offenses. In the period 1966–74, a yearly average of 77 percent of the people in jail were there for liquor offenses, compared to 41 percent for Ontario as a whole. On a population-adjusted basis, the rate of committal to jail for liquor offenses during this period was 49.0/1,000 population for Kenora, 1.5/1,000 for Ontario.

It is common knowledge that native people are overrepresented in the inmate population of the Kenora jail. The process of "justice" as it is administered to an Indian person in Kenora is typically as follows. An Indian person is picked up by the police and charged with an offense under the Liquor Control Act (LCA). He/she is taken to the Detox Centre, stays there for a few hours or overnight, and is released with a summons to appear in court. If the person goes to court and is found guilty as charged, he/she is given a fine or a jail option in default of the fine. Often the person does not appear in court, is found guilty in absentia, and is given two weeks to pay the fine or go to jail.[10] Many Indian people are repeatedly picked up, charged, taken to the Detox Centre, released, convicted, and fined.

Against this background of offenses documented for the Kenora area, it is not difficult to understand the types of problems that characterize "lawlessness" within the Indian community. Prior to 1977, much of the heavy drinking by the people of Grassy Narrows took place in Kenora's bars, parks, and streets, because the reserve was "dry" and no alcohol could be brought into the community except surreptitiously by bootleggers. In the early 1970s, therefore, Grassy Narrows people made up a substantial proportion of the total convictions handed out in Kenora for liquor offenses.[11] The way in which the system typically deals with Indians is illustrated by the record of the Kenora District Court for one woman from Grassy Narrows for the period April 1970 to March 1972 (table 1.8). Clearly manifest here is the pattern of binge drinking every two weeks or so after paydays or the receipt of welfare checks, as well as the predominance of offense LCA 80-2 (Intoxication in a Public Place).

**Table 1.8   Court Record of a Female Band Member of Grassy Narrows, Aged 26, 1970–1972**

| Offense | Date Charged | Disposition |
|---------|-------------|-------------|
| 80-2 LCA | April 11, 1970 | 15.00 ttp 7 days Apr 21[a] |
|  | April 21 | Com 10 days cons.[b] |
|  | May 9 | 1 day time served |
|  | May 26 | Com 10 days |

*(Continued)*

**Table 1.8** (*Continued*)

| Offense | Date Charged | Disposition |
|---|---|---|
| | June 8 | Com 14 days |
| | June 26 | Com 10 days |
| | July 6 | Com 10 days less 2[c] |
| | July 17 | Com 10 days less 1 |
| | September 25 | Com 7 days |
| | October 3 | Com 10 days |
| | October 17 | 15.00 ttp 7 days Nov. 26 |
| | October 19 | Com 8 days |
| | November 26 | Com 7 days cons. |
| | December 14 | Com 5 days |
| | January 4, 1971 | Com 8 days |
| | January 20 | Com 10 days |
| | February 19 | Com 10 days |
| | March 4 | Com 10 days |
| | March 22 | Com 10 days |
| | April 5 | Com 10 days |
| | April 15 | Com Vanier Institute not exceeding 90 days[d] |
| | June 18 | 25.00 ttp 6 days June 25 |
| | June 25 | Com 10 days cons. |
| 373-1 CCC[e] | July 2 | Discharged |
| 42-1 LCA | July 16 | Com 8 days |
| 80-2 LCA | July 26 | Com 8 days |
| | July 30 | Com 90 days |
| | September 27 | Com 5 days |
| | October 4 | 30.00 |
| | October 22 | 25.00 ttp Nov 15 |
| 68-2 LCA | November 15 | Com 15 days cons. |
| 133 CCC | November 19 | 3 months indefinite (sentence not to exceed 3 months) |
| 80-2 LCA | February 14, 1972 | Com 7 days |
| 68-2 LCA | " | 15.00 ttp Com Feb 14 |
| | February 25 | Com 10 days |
| | March 3 | Com 10 days |

[a]Disposition is read as "to pay fine of $15.00 with time to pay (ttp) 7 days, to April 21.
[b]Committed to 10 days in jail.
[c]Committed to 10 days in jail, less two days.
[d]Vanier Institute of the Family.
[e]CCC refers to the Criminal Code of Canada.

The alternation between fines and jail as punishment by the court is also representative of the disposition of justice to Indian people.

In 1975, a special detachment of the Ontario Provincial Police took up residence on a site adjacent to, but not on, reserve land. One police officer admitted that "Grassy Narrows . . . was a community out of control." With the stationing of a police force near the village, we begin to have a record of the occurrences of physical violence and assault against persons, as well as of theft and damage to property. Of course not every occurrence results in a charge, because Indian people are reluctant to press charges against members of their own families.

Nevertheless, the number of recorded occurrences in this small village of only sixty-five frame houses is quite startling. In the first ten months of 1977, for example, the police were called 698 times to investigate some disturbance or threat to persons or property (table 1.9). It is difficult to imagine any other settlement of similar size where police are involved in

**Table 1.9   Record of the Ontario Provincial Police at Grassy Narrows, 1975–October 1977**

|  | 1975 | 1976 | 1977 (Jan–Oct) |
| --- | --- | --- | --- |
| Number of occurrences investigated | 460 | 673 | 698 |
| Number of charges brought | 201 | 295 | 426 |
| Liquor offenses as a percentage of total charges | 67% | 67% | 66% |
| Assault offenses as a percentage of total charges | 12% | 11% | 12% |
| All other charges (break and enter, theft, willful damage) as a percentage of total charges | 21% | 22% | 21% |
| Cases of homicide/murder | 2 | 1 | 0 |
| Percentage of all charges accounted for by juveniles (under age 16) | 7% | 23% | 28% |

*Source:* Based on statistics contained in a letter from K. E. Wilson, Superintendent of the Ontario Provincial Police in Kenora, to Chief Simon Fobister, April 4, 1978. In this letter, Wilson adds the following comment: "From the above statistics, I am sure you can appreciate that the majority of the problems encountered by our personnel at Grassy Narrows is due to the overconsumption of alcohol, drug overdoses, and gasoline sniffing. . . . Our personnel feel that gas sniffing is common to *most* children on the reserve, but it is not being reported to the police."

keeping order almost seventy times each month. At Grassy Narrows, the incidents of assault and other forms of violence are closely correlated with spree drinking among the adults. The incidents of theft, vandalism, and breaking and entering, for which young persons are usually responsible, are also associated with these "black" periods of heavy drinking.

Another source of information about the extent of public order problems in the community is the record of the Adult Probation Branch of the Ontario Ministry of Correctional Services. It shows that, in the period 1969–77, forty persons from Grassy Narrows were placed on probation by the judges of the Kenora district and provincial courts. Their average age was only twenty-four.[12] The majority of offenses for which people received a sentence of probation involved some form of assault causing serious bodily injury; however, 17 percent of all cases involved "break, enter, and theft," and 12 percent were related to the misuse of firearms. Manslaughter, mischief, and causing a fire by negligence made up the remainder of the offenses. For more serious crimes, like homicide or murder, people were sentenced to a penitentiary. Alcohol was involved in three-quarters of all the incidents that resulted in a sentence of probation.

Around Kenora, it is well known that until the late 1960s, the people of Grassy Narrows were minimally involved with the justice system. Chuck Wingfield, who has been with the Adult Probation Branch in Kenora for twenty years, admitted that his office "never had any problems with the Indian people from Grassy Narrows until the government moved them to that new reserve. That's when the problems really started. . . . Now our case load from Grassy Narrows of adults on probation is one of the heaviest in the region, and, of course, everything is tied up with alcohol abuse."

Aside from crimes against persons and property committed by adults, there has been a dramatic increase at Grassy Narrows in the number of offenses committed by persons aged fifteen or under. In 1978, for example, almost one-third of the entire population of children in the community between ages eight and fifteen were on probation for criminal acts. Two-thirds of those on probation were between twelve and fifteen years old.[13] Not one child came from a nondrinking family; all belonged to the heaviest drinking families on the reserve.

The progressive deterioration in community morale is also reflected in police records for juvenile offenses. In 1975, for example, children under the age of fifteen accounted for only 7 percent of the total charges brought by the police; in 1976, this rose to 23 percent; and in the first ten months of 1977, to 28 percent. Juvenile crime most often involves willful damage to property and break, enter, and theft. In 1977, young people were responsible for 96 percent of all the break and enter charges, 100 percent of the theft charges, 66 percent of the offensive weapons charges, 89 percent of the willful damage charges, and 11 percent of the liquor offenses. The police admit that gas sniffing at Grassy Narrows, which is extremely destructive to the central nervous system, has increased dramatically among very young children. Since gas sniffing is not an offense under the law, most incidents are not reported to the police.

But statistics alone cannot convey the full import of what is happening to the children in the community. The terms *assault* and *break and enter,* which are official designations of categories of crime, connote little of the anger that finds expression in such acts of violence. Yet there was a marked qualitative change in the nature of juvenile crime in the late 1970s. In the first place, the damage to community buildings and facilities became much more extensive. During the bleak winter of 1979–80 for example, the cost of repairs to community property that had been vandalized by children was estimated at $50,000.

In the second place, private property of non-Indian persons, once considered out of bounds for vandalism, became a target. During the same winter, three boys under fifteen years of age burned down a tourist lodge on Grassy Narrows Lake. In just two months, young people went on a rampage of teachers' houses twelve times. The kind of wholesale destruction that takes place in a case of break and enter is illustrated by the following incident, based on notes from my diary. "Peggy" is Peggy Halcrow, the supervisor of the Grassy Narrows day-care center.

On the evening of January 17, 1980, I stopped by Peggy's house. The hinge of her back door was broken, and the screens of her kitchen windows had been ripped apart. Pushing the door open, I stepped into a mass of garbage, broken glass, and earth from the plants that had been pulled out by their roots. As I maneuvered my way through the corridor, I saw a bunch of kids jump from the front door into the snowbank below. One child, about ten years old, was either too terrified or too stoned to make his escape.

The house looked as if it had been hit by a tidal wave. Everything that could possibly have been destroyed was lying in pieces on the floor. Peggy had an Indian foster child with her; all the toys were ruined. Her stereo equipment was broken and the records shattered; the pictures on the wall, cracked; her special collection of china dolls, smashed. Garbage and clothing were scattered on the floor amid empty beer bottles and broken glass. Cans of grape juice had been thrown against the wall until they burst. In the bedrooms, all the closets and dressers had been emptied of their contents, trampled, and the clothing stained with grape juice and mud. The walls were covered with graffiti written with lipstick and magic markers. Dirt from the plants littered her bed, her furniture, and the floor.

In the kitchen, the kids left empty beer and liquor bottles. They had also been sniffing magic markers and glue. Empty packages of frozen vegetables, bacon, and meat were left on the table; they had been eaten raw. Someone had drunk a bottle of facial astringent mixed with milk.

Next day, it took six people working steadily for five hours to bring order from the chaos. There was one moment of relief when Peggy found her camera in the snow.

There is yet another disturbing element in the recent pattern of violence carried out by young persons. During the same winter, some children set their grandmother's house on fire and burned it to the ground. In another incident, a fifteen-year-old boy held his entire family hostage with a loaded shotgun. He narrowly missed killing a band constable and was finally smoked out of the house with tear gas. The year before, on the first day of the winter carnival, a boy shot one of his younger brothers through the heart and fatally wounded another brother in the head. He critically injured a third brother by a shotgun blast through the chest and ripped off the hand of a girl who was spending the weekend with the family.

These examples speak to the intensity with which young persons are turning their rage against members of their own families, particularly against those who are even more helpless than themselves. The children who repeatedly get into trouble say that no one cares about them. They pass from childhood to adolescence without guidance and without love. Gone are the elaborate rituals of puberty and transition that were practiced on the old reserve. To substitute for the family, the children of heavy drinkers organize themselves into gangs.

The gang leaders also come from alcoholic families, and their leadership is almost never of a benevolent nature. In the youngest female gang at Grassy Narrows during the period of my residency, the leader used to force her adherents to sniff gas. She would not sniff herself but used this ritual to assert her power over the members of the group; anyone who refused to do so would get beaten up and expelled. The approximately twenty children in this particular gang were all under the age of eleven. The male gangs in the community were responsible for a number of incidents of rape, following the pattern of gang rape that takes place during adult drinking parties. In February 1980, a twelve-year-old girl was raped by four members of a gang aged twelve to fourteen. She was also beaten so badly that she had to be rushed to the hospital in Kenora. In April, another group of boys gang-raped a ten-year-old girl. These incidents were not reported to the police and thus do not show up on police records of juvenile crime.

It is important to realize that in this community where children belonging to alcoholic families have neither emotional nor physical security, the only sense of belonging comes from membership in a gang. It is not unusual to see children huddled together like orphans, seeking warmth, companionship, and direction from others not much older than themselves. When their families are drinking, these children band together. They roam around the reserve all night if necessary, waiting until the adults lose consciousness. At that point, they will slip back into the house and finish the remaining liquor. I have seen children of five and six intoxicated, swaying from one side of the road to the other at two and three o'clock in the morning.

Residents of the community have different interpretations of the roots of the problem with the young. The teachers, who are recent victims of the violence, blame the vandalism on "the system" of economics and "the system" of justice, which offer no disincentives to juvenile crime. One of the teachers at the reserve school put it bluntly:

> At Grassy Narrows, the kids see their parents getting everything for nothing; the government provides welfare money; the government provides jobs; the government gives free houses. There's no rationale *not* to get into trouble, and some good reasons to do exactly the opposite. Why keep your house in good shape when you can break the windows during the summer and then get paid during the winter to fix them? Why keep the siding on the band store when maybe your father will get the job of putting the siding back on and a fat paycheck, and maybe you'll get a new pair of jeans out of it?
>
> Why not wreck the school? Somebody will fix it. You won't get into trouble for it; you may go to court, but then maybe your mom will finally buy you a new shirt so that you'll look nice in front of the judge. . . .
>
> And there's no punishment. At one point the judges decided to give community work orders to the kids. But so far, out of approximately fifty work orders handed out, not one has been enforced. Nobody on the reserve wants to take the trouble to supervise them. Sometimes you think that the band really doesn't care about the kids and the vandalism. For example, last winter [1979] the kids destroyed their own skating rink. Just demolished it. The band didn't press charges, so the police couldn't do anything either. The same thing happened when the gangs got into the school and smashed up several classrooms. No charges. No punishment. And probation is just a joke.

Some children work out their powerlessness to change things by using violence and vandalism as means to an end. Their route of escape from the intolerable conditions of reserve life is through crime.

> Young Jordan, for example. He would get high on gasoline and then come into the school to destroy what he could. Then he would go to the police and say, "I did it. Now get me out of this place." But the police weren't smart enough to do that. So Jordan broke into the school and vandalized it five times before they had had enough. Finally, the judge ordered him to be sent to training school.
>
> It gets so desperate for the kids here that sometimes they just have to get out for a while. Like Jordan. He just went crazy after his sister killed herself with an overdose of drugs. Even the kids in grades three and four say they "want out."
>
> The fact is that there's hardly a family on this reserve that hasn't got some tragedy to live down. We know children who say they would rather die than live at Grassy Narrows.

Within the community, no blame is attached to acts of violence committed by children. One sixty-eight-year-old band member was beaten so viciously by a gang of children that he required lengthy hospitalization. Yet he did not press charges. When asked why, he said that he was very ashamed that the old way of life had gone, "because this would never have happened on the old reserve . . . the kids, they had been drinking, and when a person is drinking, he is not himself." Most people forgive the youngsters, even for atrocious offenses, because they know that their violence is both a symptom of the general disorder in the community and an effect of the breakdown of the Indian family.

## Failure to Thrive

One of the signals of a society in disarray is when an entire generation fails to realize its inherited potential for development of the intellect and the spirit. At Grassy Narrows, the vast majority of the young are thwarted in the drive for growth. Not only have most parents apparently lost their capacity to provide physical care for their offspring, but the society as a whole seems to have abdicated its responsibility for the intellectual and moral formation of succeeding generations.

The situation is compelling. Caught in a void between two cultures, the children in this community are learning neither the basic skills of the mainstream society nor the traditional skills of the Indian way of life. With very few exceptions, they are not being taught how to trap or hunt or survive in the bush. And they no longer have the opportunity to learn the moral and symbolic rudiments of their culture from the elders, who used to communicate such knowledge through stories and legends. The young have now been disinherited from the accumulated knowledge of earlier generations; at the same time, they have been dispossessed of the physical and emotional nourishment prerequisite to cognitive development. In any case, schooling seems to be an anomaly in the context of reserve life. As a result, the children can thrive in neither the old world nor the new. They are effectively trapped in a vicious web of stunted growth and lack of opportunity for learning and discovery.

The records of school attendance and educational achievement at Grassy Narrows strip away all doubts about the long-term consequences of the demoralization that has enveloped the community. Let us take a look at just one school year. Table 1.10 shows the number of students who dropped out of school in 1977–78 because of poor attendance. Any child who missed more than 70 days out of a school year of 170 days effectively lost the year. The data show that an astonishing percentage of children, in some cases the majority in any one class, dropped out of school. Overall, across all grades, including those children who did not even register for

**Table 1.10   School Dropout Rate at Grassy Narrows, 1977–1978**

| Grade | Number of Dropouts | Class Size | Percentage of Class |
|---|---|---|---|
| Kindergarten | 10 | 20 | 50 |
| 1 | 3 | 16 | 18 |
| 2 | 7 | 24 | 29 |
| 3 | 9 | 17 | 53 |
| 4 | 7 | 17 | 41 |
| 5–8 | 10 | 24 | 42 |
| 4–6 (special class) | 10 | 25 | 40 |

*Source:* Based on the records of attendance at the Grassy Narrows Federal Elementary School.

school, 46 percent failed to complete the school year.[14] One can hardly conceive of any nonnative community in Canada where almost half of the entire population of school-age children would be allowed to withdraw from school.

Poor attendance virtually guarantees that children will fall further and further behind in terms of grade progression. If a child never fully masters the basic concepts of language and the arithmetic skills that are normally learned in kindergarten and grades one through three, he or she becomes discouraged by the inevitable repetition of lower grades and eventually quits school permanently. This is exactly what happens at Grassy Narrows. Most children reach grades four or five and then never go back to school again.

It is to be expected, then, that very few students reach high school. In 1977–78, of the sixty-nine young people in the fifteen to nineteen age-group, only nine were enrolled in high school, and four of these dropped out by the end of the first quarter.[15] Yet the high school years are usually the years of intense preparation in a person's life for a career or a chosen line of work.

Band members admit readily that the dropout problem is the result of parental alcoholism and the sharp deterioration in family life:

> The kids don't go to school because the parents are too busy drinking and the kids are not taken care of properly. I was that way too when I was drinking. We never had time to wash the kids' clothes. We never made sure that they got up in time for school. If they managed to get there by themselves, that was good. But when they got home, though, they forgot what they'd been taught 'cause the home was a wreck, or maybe there was nobody home and nothing to eat. . . .
>
> And another thing. If you're drinking all night, then you sleep in the day-

time. If there's drinking in the house, the kids don't go to sleep either. They sleep in the daytime too. So how can they go to school? And another thing. If the parents are drinking, the older kids have to take care of the young ones. So they can't go to school with those kinds of responsibilities.

Of the thirty-four families at Grassy Narrows to which the dropout children belong, only four do not drink heavily and regularly after each payday. The drinking parents do not nurture their young; they give them no encouragement to develop intellectually; they often deprive them of food, shelter, and clothing; and sometimes they abandon them altogether to go drinking in town. The crux of the problem is that the majority of adults in their child-bearing and child-rearing years are heavy drinkers, who are themselves caught in the cultural disorientation of the past fifteen years. And so the circle closes. Tragically the parents condemn their children to the same fate, to the same entrapment in the hiatus between two worlds.

But there is more to be said on the structural impediments to educational achievement at Grassy Narrows. The very nature of the reserve economy offers little incentive for young people to break out of the mold of stunted intellectual growth. The teacher of the senior class at the school speaks to this point:

> One of the basic problems in education here is that there's no pat on the back for success and no negative feeling about failure. There's no incentive to go to high school. From the kids' point of view, they see that none of their friends are going to high school. They see their parents on welfare. They know that when they turn sixteen, they can go on welfare, or get a job, work for six months, and collect unemployment insurance just like everybody else. Getting an education at Grassy Narrows is an ambition that is soon exhausted, because it cannot attach itself to any role or function in this society.

The cumulative impact of the annual dropout rate at Grassy Narrows, as illustrated by the 1977–78 school records, can be seen in data on educational achievement over the decade of the 1970s. In schools across Canada, most educators think in terms of a "cohort" or "class" of students that start school together and move through succeeding grades together. At Grassy Narrows, since the federal day school opened on the new reserve in 1971–72, it is difficult to think in terms of a cohort. The majority of children do not move from grade to grade in any regular progression. Their educational reality is distinguished by failure, repetition of grades, and ultimate discouragement from learning.

The data speak volumes about the failure of the young to thrive. Of the total of 117 students who entered kindergarten during the seven-year period between 1971–72 and 1978–79, only 19 (16 percent) passed every year and were registered in the grade appropriate to their age. Of the thirty-seven students enrolled in grade one in 1971–72, only two (5 percent) made it to grade eight, eight years later.[16] The fact is that over the decade of the 1970s, about 40 percent of all the children who entered kindergarten repeated their kindergarten year at least once. About 12 percent spent three years in kindergarten, and 30 percent repeated grades one and two. The rates of grade repetition diminished for higher grades simply because fewer students reached these grades.

The educational record of some students is so erratic that they cannot even be included as part of a class in any given year. Of the 107 children who fall into this category and who were registered in school at some point during the decade, only 11 (10 percent) achieved partial grade progression. Almost all of these children came from the heaviest drinking families in the community.

In short, less than one-fifth of the entire population of children enrolled at the Grassy Narrows elementary school achieve regular grade progression. Almost one-quarter of the students are one year behind their expected grade level. Nearly one-fifth are two years behind, and one-tenth are three or four years behind. The norm for this community is grade repetition, discouragement, and permanent retirement from school at the lower grades.

This extraordinary waste of human potential brings no cries of protest, no voices of alarm, from the larger society. The Department of Indian Affairs, which is responsible for Indian education, remains mute on the subject. Yet it is difficult to imagine that the trustees of our own children's future would tolerate such a situation for very long. Although information on educational achievement in Ontario does not exist in a form that would make comparison with Grassy Narrows possible, it is nevertheless true that in the province as a whole grade failure is relatively rare, cohorts are the rule, and grade repetition is an exceptional occurrence. Moreover, students with learning difficulties are removed from regular classrooms and placed in special education classes. Yet the attention and priority given to the training of the next generation in our own society have no parallel when it comes to the development of human resources in the Indian community.

The Grassy Narrows people realize that their future is at stake if this trend of learning failure continues. For this reason they appealed to DIAND to consider the establishment of an Indian-run boarding school off the reserve. This kind of intervention would at least allow some children a means of breaking out of the void of powerlessness and despair that is today their only inheritance. But so far DIAND has ignored the proposal and taken no action that offers any hope of a reversal of the dismal prognosis for the formation of succeeding generations.

## Child Neglect, Abuse, and Abandonment

In describing the failure of parents at Grassy Narrows to care for their offspring physically, emotionally, or spiritually, it has been especially difficult to maintain emotional distance. For as anyone who has lived on the reserve for an extended period of time will confirm, in addition to the knowledge gleaned from witnessing events, one builds up a reservoir of anger provoked by adults who seem to have lost their humanity.

Perhaps the way to begin is simply to present the official statistics on child neglect. The Children's Aid Society (CAS) is the government agency that intervenes in cases of serious child injury or ill-treatment; its social workers take the abused child into care until the court decides whether the child should be returned to its parents, temporarily placed in a foster home, or permanently assigned as a ward of the state. According to the Society's records for the Kenora district, Grassy Narrows has the highest number of children in the care of foster homes in the entire region. In 1977, for example, out of a total of 108 children taken into care by CAS social workers from 10 Indian reserves around Kenora, 56 (52 percent of the total) came from Grassy Narrows.[17] In some years during the 1970s, a third of the entire population of children between five and fourteen years of age has been in foster homes outside the reserve. But it has not always been this way. Like all other forms of self-destructive violence, child neglect is a phenomenon associated with the new reserve.

There are several reasons why children are taken into care. Conditions such as overcrowded housing, lack of income, parental/child illness, and child behavioral problems often lead to temporary placement; the last two in particular are likely to be statistically similar in native and nonnative communities alike. But the specific reasons of parental alcoholism, desertion, abuse, and neglect are associated with social pathology and family breakdown. It is significant that at Grassy Narrows, three-quarters (73 percent) of all the children taken into care are apprehended for reasons of desertion or neglect caused by parental alcohol abuse.

On a population-adjusted basis, statistics on children in care in the Kenora district in 1975 (the last year for which comparative data are available) reveal a rate for Grassy Narrows that is dramatically higher than the rates for other Indian communities. The rate (22.5 per 1,000 population) is almost three times as high as that for the Whitedog reserve (8.1) and four and six times as high as the rates for the Indian communities of Whitefish Bay and Shoal Lake (5.5 and 3.4), respectively.

Impressive as the statistics are, they do not reveal the full extent of the problem. Only a proportion of the actual cases of neglect find their way into CAS files. In recent years, fiscal restraint and budget cutbacks have necessitated reductions in the Society's staff and operating costs. Social

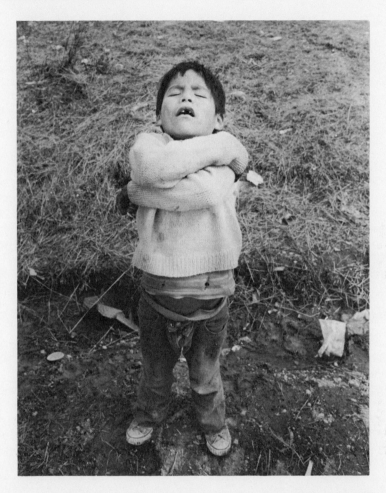

workers, reluctant to add to their case loads, try to deal with only the extreme cases. In the community, however, teachers confront what they feel is child neglect on a daily basis. Inevitably, their own background and upbringing influence their perception of the problem. But as the following conversation with the first-grade teacher and the day-care supervisor also illustrates, the way children are treated on the new reserve has its roots in the disorientation accompanying exceedingly rapid cultural change.

> I would say that most of the children on this reserve are very poorly taken care of, and over half are really neglected from the point of view of their physical well-being.
>
> It may have something to do with the fact that at the age of about four, the mother suddenly cuts the child off from care. I have seen a mother completely

change her attitude to a child. . . . She will protect and nourish the infant, but at a certain point, she'll shove the child out of the nest. Then the kids are on their own. The parents leave them to do whatever they want to do—fall asleep wherever they can, eat whatever they can find, and so on. Even the parents that don't drink that much seem to have no concept of putting the child to bed at a certain time or having a meal at a certain time or knowing where the child is.

Probably all this is related to traditional child-rearing patterns. In the old way of life, you ate when you were hungry and went to sleep when you were sleepy. The women used to prepare the kind of food that could be eaten whenever anyone was hungry: fish chowder, meat stew, things that would sit on the wood stove all day long.

The big difference on this reserve is that women no longer prepare this kind of food. Yet they don't feed their children either. They buy cans of spaghetti, cans of meat stew, Kraft macaroni dinners, and a lot of junk food. The adults will eat, but very few people sit down to supper as a family. The kids have to fend for themselves. If there are any groceries left, they'll make a hole in the can of spaghetti and put the can on the stove, or they'll eat it cold. Most of the time, they live on potato chips, candy, and Coke—things they can buy at the store.

This new way of life places a terrible strain on the children of alcoholic families, because often there are no groceries to be eaten and no place to sleep. So you'll see very small children wandering around the reserve at night. They are hungry, helpless, and sad. Little Wanda, for example, she's only five years old. She's a ragamuffin . . . she has no home. She has only her older brothers and sisters to protect her. They'll get the food, and if there's no food at home, they'll break into somebody's house and steal it.

When Jimmy, who is only nine years old, was kicked out of his house, he slept with five dogs to keep himself warm. And this was in the middle of a horrible winter. He hid underneath someone's house for five days before the police found him. His parents had been drinking for one full week, and that's before his mother went to the hospital to have a baby. Sure enough, the baby was born a fetal alcohol syndrome baby, alcoholic at birth. Afterwards, his mother wouldn't feed Jimmy. She said that everything was for the baby, so Jimmy went begging for food. And this case is not at all unusual.

I have kids in the day-care center who are so hungry that they will sneak out of the playroom to see what crumbs they can find on the kitchen floor. Others will eat lunch ever so slowly, so that when everybody else is finished, they can eat what's left on the plates. I also have kids who haven't had their clothes changed since Christmas [almost a month before] except by me.

The old people told me that they see a big difference in the way people raise their kids on this new reserve. They say that parents never used to desert their kids like they do now. On the old reserve, children were important and valuable. They had responsibilities—to haul water, set snares for rabbits, chop wood, and help on the trapline. Now they have no responsibilities, no chores. People used to have children to help them, and to take care of them when they got old. Now they have children because they get drunk and have sex. There is no respect for children any more. And there is no respect for the old either.

This has something to do with the fact that in this type of economy, both are "useless" except for bringing in the family allowance and the old age pension.

The problem is not that there is no love, for everyone knows that Indian people love and indulge their children. It's a paradox. The Grassy Narrows people would do anything for their children if they knew how, but they are caught between what they know how to do and the conditions of life on this new reserve. . . . In some ways, the kids are spoiled. For example, they'll have the fancy skates that are advertised on TV. They'll be given lots of money to spend on Cokes and candy. They'll have a color TV in the house. But they won't be fed properly, and they won't have proper winter clothing. These children lack the most basic things: security, shelter, food, and love that is demonstrated. It's these things that are tragically absent. Or at least the kids don't have them on a regular basis. No one sits down to tell them stories, no one talks to them about their problems. The kids feel uncared for and unwanted. And how can they respect parents who won't feed them and will beat them when they're drunk? The love is there and it's powerful, but it is unspoken and undemonstrated, on both sides.

This interview has been quoted at some length because it offers a vivid glimpse into the reality of reserve life for children. The point is well made that, aside from the pathology of alcoholism and its effects on family life, certain appearances of neglect arise because traditional child-rearing patterns have become dysfunctional under the fundamentally changed conditions of the new reserve. Furthermore, the emphasis on the "big difference" in child care between the old reserve and the contemporary community reaffirms the fact that pervasive child neglect is a recent phenomenon associated with the new reserve.

Spree drinking, which intensifies and sharpens the contradictions arising from the collision of two ways of life, takes an almost unbelievable toll on the lives of children at Grassy Narrows. To evoke a sense of its specific horrors, here is a quote from my diary pertaining to a typical five-day period following a payday in June 1979.

*Friday.* My neighbor comes over to tell me that last night, just before midnight, she found four-year-old Dolores wandering alone around the reserve, about two miles from her home. She called the police and they went to the house to investigate. They found Dolores's three-year-old sister, Diane, huddled in a corner crying. The house was empty, bare of food, and all the windows were broken. The police discovered that the parents had gone to Kenora the day before and were drinking in town. Both of them were sober when they deserted their children.

It's going to be a bad weekend. The police also picked up an eighteen-month-old baby abandoned in an empty house. No one seemed to know how long it had been there. . . . The milk in the house had turned sour. The baby was severely dehydrated and lying in its own vomit and accumulated excrement. Next door, the police found two people lying unconscious on the floor.

My friend J. is very angry with his younger sister. This isn't the first time she's left her two small children and gone drinking in town. But her parents used to leave her alone when they went drinking, so the pattern just repeats itself through generations.

*Saturday.* Ten o'clock. Peggy calls me through the window. Duncan (one of the police officers) has just given her a nine-month-old baby to care for. I go out and see that the child's head is deformed. He has obviously been hit or kicked or thrown to the floor earlier in his infancy. His face, neck, arms are covered with sores, and the area around his ears is deep red from coagulated blood. He's got bruise marks all over his body. Duncan says he found the baby locked up in a room after he took everybody else in the house to jail because they were drunk and fighting. The mother has been drinking solidly for the last three days. Somehow this child is still alive. Her older child was nearly crushed to death and is now a ward of the state.

*Sunday.* Peggy has another baby in her care. Old Annie called her about a child crying in the bush behind her house. So Peggy went to see what was wrong and found an eight-month baby who had been abandoned. The infant was covered with mosquito bites. The parents left the child in the care of older siblings and went drinking in town. But the girls who were supposed to look after it felt like sniffing gasoline. So they took the baby and threw it in the bush.

Today, from my window, I saw an incident that could easily have ended in death. A bunch of people who had been drinking staggered into a boat at the dock. As the boat was pulling away, I was startled to see an infant left behind and now crawling toward the edge of the dock. It would have drowned in a matter of seconds, but a passerby saw what was happening and ran to save it. It took the mother three days to remember that she had a child missing. Her first one died from acute physical neglect at the age of six months in 1974.

11:00 P.M. There is a loud banging on the door. The kids are shouting for help. A nine-year-old girl is in desperate trouble, and another is hysterical, after sniffing gas. The girls had been sniffing all weekend while their parents were drinking in town.

*Monday.* I saw Mary today. This child is having a severe reaction to the medicine she is taking for impetigo. Her beautiful face has been so scarred from the infection that she has had it sanded twice. She's only seven years old. She and her sister are always in and out of foster homes. The teachers plead with the social workers to keep her away from the reserve, so that the sores of her face and body have a chance to heal. But the social workers say they can't keep her, and the court keeps sending her back to conditions of abject privation and squalor.

In the evening, two more cases of gas sniffing. A girl, eleven years old, is screaming and raving. Her younger cousin is in the same state. Both sets of parents have been drinking in Kenora since Wednesday.

*Tuesday.* It's after midnight. I am called out by a group of kids and taken to the back of the recreation center. A girl, about fourteen, is crumpled up by the wall, unable to keep her balance, unable to speak; her eyes are rolling around grotesquely, and I smell gas. I borrow a car. She offers no resistance as I get her into the car and take her to the police. The family is drinking in town. Her mother and brother were burned to death in a house fire last March during a drinking party.

*Wednesday.* Late last night, more screaming at the back of the house. A gang of teenage boys brutally beat up a twelve-year-old girl and raped her. For the entire week, there was hardly a single night unbroken by the sounds of children crying in the dark.

The events described in this fragment are not unusual; the incidents are real and were recorded as they happened or as I heard about them. In microcosm, these five days reveal many of the elements that make up the pattern of child neglect in this community. For example, of the eleven incidents that came to my attention, seven were cases of desertion in one form or another. Three incidents involved gas sniffing, and one was a serious case of child abuse and desertion combined. Fourteen children were affected by the binge drinking of parents, and five were under the age of two. Significantly, only three of the eleven incidents were reported to the Children's Aid Society. The pattern that emerges, on the basis of my experience or that of others close to me during such a five-day period, shows desertion to be the most common form of child neglect when adults choose to drink, followed by negligence in feeding and caring for the young. Such negligence includes failure to maintain personal hygiene and cleanliness in the environment and failure to treat sores and infections arising from squalid physical surroundings.[18] Specific cases of child abuse are rarer but not unknown, and child rape is not uncommon. The teachers know that sexual abuse exists because the children talk about it in school; they just say, "My daddy did this to me," without being aware of the implications of what they are saying. Another kind of child abuse is described below:

S. and J. (both less than six years old) will come into the day-care center with cigarette burns on their arms. At first, they used to tell me that those were mosquito bites, but when I asked, "How come those bites got so big so fast?" they finally admitted that "It's daddy. . . . When he's drunk, he wakes us up with his cigarettes. If we cry because it hurts us, then he puts us out in the bush, and then the mosquitoes bite us."

I know that these two kids are abused in that house. It's no wonder. They have a stepmother who's only eighteen years old. She has those two kids, plus a baby that will be two years old in June, and one that will be one year old in July. And on top of that, now she's pregnant and due in May. When there's drinking in that house, as there often is, all hell breaks loose.

The ways in which children learn to live with the cruel circumstances of childhood, the coping mechanisms that they use to resist or escape from reality, have far-reaching consequences. I have already mentioned the formation of gangs, which are substitutes for a family, and also the conscious utilization of criminal behavior as a means of getting out of the reserve. In desperation over their powerlessness to change things, some children decide that death is better than life. And they kill themselves. Others mimic their parents by "getting drunk and having sex," usually with their siblings, as a way of coping with an emotional void. Although a tight lip policy is practiced by Medical Services personnel, venereal disease is a serious and widespread problem among young children. Alcohol, sex, and a desire for death form a typical response by children to soul-searing neglect. One of the teachers provides an example of the syndrome:

> Stewart is ten years old. One night he was being beaten up by other kids because he had stolen a 40-oz bottle of rye and had drunk it all by himself. We took him home and stayed with him all night because he was close to alcohol poisoning. He thrashed about in a wild frenzy and kept screaming that he needed "to have a fuck!" As he began to sober up in the morning, he said he wanted to die. He was serious and calm and determined to kill himself.
>
> At seven that morning, his mother burned her house down. She had been drinking all night too. She lit a fire in the bedroom and one in the kitchen and then went outside and watched the house burn to the ground.
>
> Here we were. We had Stewart wanting to die and watching his house go up in flames. The worst part was that in her stupor, his mother suddenly remembered that maybe one of her other children was still inside the burning house. It was a nightmare to watch the police go through the burning ashes looking for a body.

Perhaps the most insidious form of coping is the use of gasoline to get high. Sniffing gas is a form of escape from reality that is widely used, especially by the children of heavy drinkers. Like drinking for the adults, it is a social activity. Several children have already been severely burned by lighting cigarettes while sniffing, but the risk of immolation has not been a strong enough deterrent against this practice. The risk of physical burning of the body by accidental ignition of the gas has a parallel in the popular use of the word *burnt* to describe the permanent destruction of brain cells by lead poisoning. The following story describes what happens to children when they become burnt through gas sniffing. This child is only six years old, and the story is related by her first-grade teacher.

> Alicia started sniffing gas when she was three years old. She's burnt now, and the brain damage is permanent. In class, she can't concentrate, and she's lost her retention ability. She has lost her sense of balance. She sways all over the place and topples over in her chair. She falls down sixty times a day, like a Raggedy-Ann doll. She has constant bruises on her arms and legs just from falling down on the floor all the time.

Now, there's a child for whom there is no hope and no future. If she can't walk, if she can't keep her balance, if she can't think and can't reason, what hope is there for her?

Alicia is going to be just like Pamela, whose father gave her gas so that she would sleep with him. She did, and now she's burnt too and always in trouble with the guys. All the boys gang-rape her because they know she's a "wipe-out." It's going to be exactly the same for Alicia and for many other girls like her.

The incidence of gas sniffing is not recorded in official documents for it is considered to be neither a crime nor a disease. Within the community, few seem to have noticed that so many children are slowly poisoning themselves. Alicia is the only one in first grade who is burnt, but other children are sniffing. Of the twenty-four children in grade two in 1979, ten were sniffing heavily and showing signs of mental disorientation. Over half the children in grade three were sniffing gas. Grade four had a class of twenty children, six of them in an advanced state of intellectual and emotional derangement due to mixing gas with alcohol. The damage to the brain as a result of gas sniffing can be swift and fatal, as the following example, again provided by one of the teachers, illustrates:

Marlin was such a nice, bright kid. We all had great hopes for him, and we thought that just maybe he would make it to high school. But last summer he started to sniff gas. In just one summer, he got burnt. He lost his concentration and his balance. The change in him was not only physical but emotional and mental. He seemed to have aged ten years, although he was only thirteen years old.

Then, one night in December, over the Christmas holidays, Marlin went out on the lake and froze to death. No one asked any questions when he died. No one cared enough to do anything about it.

One of the most depressing things about this kind of child neglect is that, as a result, the kids have no concept of life and no concept of wanting to live. It is beaten, it is starved, it is kicked out of them. And it seems that the parents and the community care only after the child is dead. Or maybe they care, but they sure don't show it. The important thing is that the kids think that their parents don't care.

To a normal child, if you say, "Don't go out on that ice because you'll fall in and freeze to death," the child will think twice. But the kids at Grassy Narrows, they'll say, "So what? I don't care!" Here, the kids don't know exactly what death is, except that they know it's a lot better than what they've got.

## Family Breakdown

Not so long ago, before the people moved from the old reserve to the present settlement, the Grassy Narrows family was an extended family, bonded by strong totemic affiliations and guided by an unwritten code of respect and tolerance for each person. There were strong taboos against incest, promiscuity, and marriage between close relatives of the same bloodline. A man and woman "belonged to each other" only after a period of courtship during which the man offered proof that he could support a family. The family transmitted to the young the values of the Indian way of life, organized the productive contribution of each member, and guided proper social relations. It was the warp of the fabric of community.

Today, the bonds of the Indian family have been shattered. The deterioration in family life has taken place with extraordinary swiftness. Of fundamental importance has been the change in the moral standards and circumstances surrounding sexual relations. The apparent disregard for the healthy continuity of the species, the breakdown of once strict culturally defined taboos, and the lack of concern about how new life begins—these conditions point to a society that seems bent on its own destruction.

The collapse of traditional Indian codes of behavior in the practice of sexual relations has gone hand in hand with the explosion in spree drinking. The drinking party during the binge is almost always composed of family members belonging to the same bloodline. During such a binge, the taboos against incest or sexual relations between close relatives are dissolved. The old people of Grassy Narrows lament the fact that children are often conceived during the drinking parties. Because of the blackout period, the woman sometimes cannot remember who the father is. The same blurring of paternity and confusion in bloodline structures occurs when children are conceived during gang rape.

The old people look upon the incidents of gang rape with incomprehension and despair, for this behavior was unknown on the old reserve. Gang rapes, however, have been happening with increasing frequency in recent years. Not all of them are spontaneous events that can be explained or legitimized by the fact that the men had been drinking. According to a former chief:

> Indian people used to use tobacco to communicate with the spirits, but they never learned to use alcohol with respect. Alcohol was the white man's poison, and now it's ours.
>
> Look at what happens during the drinking parties. You think it's just because of the alcohol, but I tell you, it's just a cover-up for a lot of angry, hurt feelings. The gang rapes . . . a group of men will sometimes conspire to ask a young girl to a drinking party. They will give her drink until she passes out. They they will each have sex with her. If the girl is not quite passed out, the experience can be very bad for her, especially if her father is involved in the gang rape. There have been cases where the girl tries to commit suicide after that experience.

The connection between gang rape and attempted suicide by young women is no secret in the community, or outside it. Medical authorities and police continue to deny the seriousness of the gang rape problem, in spite of its now public disclosure.[19] But one has to wonder why young females predominate in the statistics on attempted suicide. The chief explains: "Girls blame themselves when they find out they've been raped while they were drunk, especially when raped by members of their own family. It's a great shame to them."

The community as a whole, aside from a number of concerned individuals, seems to be indifferent to the problem of gang rape. There are no sanctions for those who participate in it and no reproaches for promiscuity.[20] People forgive acts committed under the presumed influence of alcohol. Still, there is no doubt that there has been a marked degeneration in the cultural precepts and enduring standards by which men and women at Grassy Narrows used to conduct their lives when they were still on the old reserve. This can be illustrated by two generations of women in the same family.

Vivian is in her early forties. Her mother is a traditional Indian woman in her late sixties; she's now a widow, but in her time, she had ten children, all fathered by one man, her first husband. Vivian, on the other hand, has nine children. The first two are by a man she lived with before she was married and carry her maiden name. The next three are by the man she married and carry her married name. Each of the next three children, however, has a different father, and all three were conceived during alcoholic binges and are of uncertain paternity. The last child is by the man Vivian is now living with. This situation of nine children by six different fathers would have been unthinkable under the code of behavior on the old reserve.

The young people of the reserve have no role models to follow. They see their parents' indifference to sexual taboos designed to protect the species from deformity and genetic weakness. They see the adults' behavior during drinking parties. And they note that the old precepts of courtship and marriage are not relevant to social relations. As a result, the traditional Indian idea that a man and woman should constitute a "family unit" prior to consummating their union through sexual relations is no longer an operative principle.[21] Today, the young girls desperately want to conceive, because a child gives them something to live for and someone to love; they don't care about the conditions of its conception. Young people engage in sex at an early age, and girls just beyond puberty bear children. In 1979, sixteen babies were born to girls under the age of sixteen, outside the context of a family or a stable relationship.[22]

The lack of concern for the conditions under which a new life begins has profound and long-term consequences for the community. An ever increasing number of children are born with birth defects and symptoms of mental slowness.[23] An increasing number of infants are showing the fetal alcohol syndrome at birth. In 1979, there were four medically diagnosed cases of infants born alcoholic. One such child, now four years old, is mentally retarded, has difficulty in movement, and is in the care of institutions with special programs. Those who are not certain of their father's identity often suffer maltreatment and abuse later in life. Other infants just don't live long enough to experience the trauma of childhood. According to Medical Services personnel, Grassy Narrows has the highest number of infant deaths in the Kenora area. About 22 percent of all deaths in the community are infant deaths, compared to about 4 percent for the white population of Kenora.[24]

There is, moreover, an even darker side to the statistics on infant death. Until 1975, the death of children under one year was recorded simply as "infant death." Since then, deaths caused by proven maltreatment have been recorded as "infant death/neglect." Death by neglect has now reached such unprecedented levels at Grassy Narrows that the police are beginning to bring charges against the parents for manslaughter/ homicide. The situations vary. One mother passed out on her baby while she was drinking and smothered it to death. Another threw her baby on the wood stove, and the child died from first-degree burns. A third dropped her baby in the snow, and the child froze to death. A fourth abandoned her baby in an empty house, and the child died from dehydration and hypothermia. The most common form of infant death from neglect is through suffocation and abandonment. In a five-year period, 1974–79, eight infants died by suffocation, and four were abandoned. This is a formidable record in a community of only 249 persons over the age of fifteen.

The community forgives parents whose children die of neglect. One parent expressed this as follows: "I can't explain it to you, because I can't explain it to myself. The only thing I know about alcohol is that alcohol is a stronger power than the love of children. It's a poison, and we are a broken people. We suffer enough inside, and therefore we understand each other."

One does not have to look very far for evidence that social disintegration has occurred at Grassy Narrows in a very short space of time. Almost every family has a history of profound hurt and anguish. The intergenerational manifestations of suffering are vividly portrayed in this story of one family:

Mary Kay is a sixty-seven-year-old woman and the grandmother of thirty-five children. She used to drink when she was younger, but it's been a long time now since she's had a drink. She can't afford to lose control; all her children are among the hard-core drinkers in the community, and now she alone has to protect her grandchildren from their parents.

Twenty-seven of her grandchildren have at some time or another been in the care of the Children's Aid Society. Over half have long records as juvenile delinquents. Five have attempted to die from an overdose of drugs. All of them are drinking and sniffing gas, even the youngest ones. During one such bout, Mary's own grandchildren burned her house down, and this was not the first house-burning incident in her family. She remembers that, in her time, babies used to die from illness or tuberculosis. Yet she has been a witness to the discovery of one of her grandchildren smothered to death, one who was found frozen in an empty house, and two who died from acute physical neglect. She is bewildered that everything can change so fast, that her own children don't care any more, that the community doesn't care any more about its own survival. And she feels powerless to change things, to turn them around.

So every few weeks, after she gets her old age pension check, she quietly disappears from the reserve. She takes the taxi to Kenora, then boards the bus for Winnipeg. In the city, she goes directly to the wrestling matches, and there she screams and screams and lets go of all the accumulated sorrow and rage that she says is eating her inside. That's her way of coping with the life she has.

There may not be a viable solution to the present crisis at Grassy Narrows. No proposals for remedial action, however, will have much impact unless we can arrive at an understanding of the forces that pushed the people to such denial of their own humanity. Is there a validity to their behavior? Parts II and III of this book try to answer this question by examining the events and forces that combined to rend the community apart.

# PART II
# EXODUS TO EXTINCTION

. . . they lost their pride
And died as men before their bodies died.
  —W. H. Auden, "The Shield of Achilles"

In the summer of 1963, the Indian Affairs office in Kenora initiated a process of relocating the people of Grassy Narrows from their old reserve of islands and peninsulas on the English-Wabigoon River to a new site five miles southeast, adjacent to the Jones logging road. Government officials justified the move on the ground that the new location, with its access by road to the town of Kenora, would make it easier to provide the Indian people with some of the benefits of modern life: an on-reserve school, medical attention, electricity, water, and sewage. As a matter of public policy, it was thought that the time had come to redress the historic disparity in standards of material well-being between Indian and non-Indian communities. It was also the moment to break the cultural and geographic isolation of those bands that had resisted past governmental efforts at assimilation.

Up to the time of resettlement, contact between the Grassy Narrows people and white society took place on the basis of the Indians' active participation in the regional economy as expert trappers, guides, harvesters of wild rice and berries, and commercial fishermen. Their relationship with government officials was confined to semiannual visits by doctors from the Indian Health Service and annual ceremonial visits by the Indian Agent and an officer of the Royal Canadian Mounted Police (RCMP) on Treaty Day. This limited contact with white society and its officialdom did not undermine the traditional Ojibwa ways of life; there was still some stability and continuity with ancient patterns. The people of Grassy Narrows continued to live within the protective boundaries of their ancestral lands; they preserved their clan-based extended family as the basis of social organization; and they maintained their seasonal pattern of migration from the winter trapping grounds to the summer community of the old reserve. In this way, they were able to preserve much of their culture, much of their self-sufficiency in terms of material provisions, and much of their freedom.

The exodus from the old reserve was a turning point in the history of the Grassy Narrows band. By 1970, old social ties had snapped. Men and women gave up traditional roles and occupations when they ceased to trap as a family, and the special relationship of the people to the land, which had cushioned all previous crises, was severely undermined by the imposed economic, political, and spatial order of the new reserve. All the people date the beginning of their time of troubles from this event. They say they live in crisis because they were uprooted. And before new roots could be established, they were faced with another blow: mercury poisoning of the English-Wabigoon river system.

The importance of the relocation in the life of the people of Grassy Narrows is the subject of this part of the book. The reader should try to imagine the time when the people of Grassy Narrows, in the upheaval of their exodus, were cast adrift from their moorings in time, space, and way of life.

# 2 • THE WAY OF LIFE OF A PEOPLE

## Journal of History

The Grassy Narrows people like to say that they have always lived on the English River in northwestern Ontario. They feel an intimate attachment to this river and this land, and their roots in this territory are deep. Although some historians believe that the ancestors of the present inhabitants occupied the same area at the time of the first contact with Europeans, in the early seventeenth century, others insist that there were no peoples who could be categorized as northern Ojibwa at this time.[1] The latter interpretation is favored by historical evidence indicating that the aboriginal Ojibwa inhabited only the north shore of the upper Great Lakes[2] and that a major migration of the people took place westward and northward of Lake Superior into the area now known as northwestern Ontario only in the late seventeenth and early eighteenth centuries.[3]

Throughout the eighteenth century, the life of the Ojibwa was characterized by mass migrations, population growth, and the segmentation of the once large corporate kin groups called patrilineal clans into much smaller and highly mobile clan-designated family groups.[4] The functional importance of the large patrilineal clans diminished during this period, presumably because their size prevented them from becoming effective trapping units. The smaller family groups, of about twenty to thirty-five persons, could be much more mobile in their search for furs and for the best price for their pelts. Thus, they could take advantage of the competition between the Hudson's Bay Company and the Northwest Company to trade on the most advantageous terms. As these smaller groups came to exploit game resources more fully, they became localized in certain regions, especially after trading posts were built in the interior. Adaptation to the new conditions of the fur trade involved not only this change in social organization but also a realignment in patterns of resource use. The hunting of large game animals for subsistence became less important as the economy became more oriented to trapping and trading. Although some items of barter such as guns and powder afforded the Ojibwa better technological control over their environment, the Indians also "became increasingly reliant on the Hudson's Bay Company for muskets and shot, for clothing, and certain items of food. . . .

New appetites were created, which could be fed only by the Hudson's Bay Company, new subsistence techniques were developed, based upon the old, but for which Hudson's Bay equipment was necessary."[5]

The process of population growth, clan segmentation, and ecological adaptation continued into the nineteenth century until, under the pressure of much changed environmental conditions, specific bands of Ojibwa became associated with specific trading posts. Three major factors apparently accounted for the sharply curtailed mobility of Ojibwa groups and their seasonal settlement around trading posts. The first was the amalgamation of the Northwest Company and the Hudson's Bay Company in 1821, a development that reduced competition between fur buyers and also minimized the potential advantages of travel among trading posts in search of better prices. The second was the disappearance of large game animals from northwestern Ontario. This constriction of the food supply had the effect of bringing the Ojibwa closer to the trading posts, where they could get food and supplies on credit. The third was the general decline in the European demand for furs. Although the Ojibwa were still able to hunt and trap, they gradually congregated around specific trading posts and began to rely on fishing as their principal means of subsistence. Thus, many of the original Grassy Narrows families assembled in the spring and summer at the main Hudson's Bay trading post, at Lac Seul, and at smaller outposts on other lakes in the region of the English River. As a loosely knit confederacy of small family groups under the hereditary leadership of Chief Sah-katch-eway, the Grassy Narrows people entered into treaty negotiations with the Dominion of Canada in 1871.

On October 3, 1873, Chief Sah-katch-eway and seventeen other chiefs of the Saulteaux Indians of the Lake of the Woods signed the North-West Angle Treaty, or Treaty No. 3, with the queen of Britain and Ireland.[6] To this day, the Grassy Narrows people consider this treaty the foundation of their relationship with the government and people of Canada. Because of its historical importance and its contemporary relevance to the issue of aboriginal rights, it is worth reviewing the treaty's main provisions:

1. The Indian chiefs agreed to "cede, release, surrender, and yield" to the government, forever, all their rights, titles, and privileges to 55,000 square miles of land, from the height of land west of Lake Superior to Lake Winnipeg, and from the American boundary to the height of land north of the English River.
2. The government agreed to lay aside reserves for the benefit of Indians, to be administered and dealt with for them by the government; these reserves would not exceed one square mile for each family of five.

3. The government agreed that the Indians would have the right to pursue their traditional occupations of hunting and fishing throughout the tract of land surrendered, subject to "such regulations as may from time to time be made by government and saving or excepting such tracts as may, from time to time, be required or taken up for settlement, mining, lumbering, or other purposes" by government.
4. The government agreed to "maintain schools for instruction," to encourage farming among Indians by supplying them with agricultural implements, seed, and cattle, and to give them ammunition and twine for fishnets.
5. In "extinguishment of all claims" by Indians against the government, each Indian person was given the lump sum of $12, with the promise of $5 more every year. The chief and councillors would receive a salary of $25 and $15 per year, respectively; every three years, they would also get a suit of clothing, a flag, and a medal.

In 1882, the government complied with its promise by delineating two reserves for the Indians represented by Chief Sah-katch-eway, one at Grassy Narrows, comprising 10,224 acres, the other at Wabauskang, comprising 8,042 acres.[7]

From the signing of the treaty to the time when the Hudson's Bay Company established a trading post on the site of the old reserve of Grassy Narrows, in 1911, it seems that the people continued their seasonal migration from winter trapping grounds to summer base camps around trading posts. One band member describes his family's movements this way: "My family . . . we used to put down camp in the summertime wherever the Bay had a trading place. . . . In the old days, the Bay had a post at Pekangekum, One Man Lake, Minaki, Wilcox Lake, and of course, at Lac Seul. Then the Bay moved from Wilcox Lake to Oak Lake, and from Oak Lake to around Ball Lake, and from Ball Lake to the site of the old reserve. I think the Bay bought their island on the old reserve from a free trader called Bush. . . . The people, they just followed the Bay around."

The people's quasi-nomadic way of life, based on hunting, trapping, and fishing for subsistence, seems to have been unaffected by the population boom and the resource development activity that followed the coming of the transcontinental railway sixty miles south. The completion of the Canadian Pacific Railway line in 1881 through Rat Portage (now Kenora) permitted the expansion of white settlement. It also provided the essential infrastructure for the logging operations that sprang up in the Lake of the Woods area and for the mining industries that followed the gold rush of the 1890s. By 1920, a pulp mill had been built in Kenora and about thirty small gold mines had been established within twenty-two miles of the town. The Grassy Narrows people, however, had no real place in the rapidly developing society on the new frontier. Their resources were not yet terribly important to the white economy, and their contact with the outside world continued to be limited to fur traders and missionaries.

The first missionaries to the people of Grassy Narrows, according to a band elder, "were French people, Roman Catholics. . . . They came by canoes, following the routes of the traders." Although the names of these early missionaries may have been forgotten, the people of the English River remember Father Lacelle, who ministered to them for twenty-six years. I asked him about the early days of missionary activity.

> The Oblates started doing missionary work among the Saulteaux in the nineteenth century. The first small mission was started at Whitedog in the 1840s, and then our missionaries moved further north. Our mission at Whitedog was sold to the Bay Company, but the Bay sold it to the Anglicans, who became much more active at Whitedog than the Catholics. . . . This was not true of Grassy Narrows. An Oblate priest was already visiting the Grassy Narrows people in 1905, and in 1910–15, Father Clement was the priest at Lac Seul, and therefore knew the people of the English River very well. . . . The people moved around a lot in those days, you know, so you had to catch up with them around the trading posts after the trapping season.

The influence of the missionaries before World War I was felt mostly by those Grassy Narrows people who were taken to boarding schools called "residential schools." In 1909, the Canadian National Railway (CNR) completed a line about midway between the reserve of Grassy Narrows and Kenora. This line, which intersected the Jones logging road connecting the two settlements, afforded much better access to the northern Ojibwa. Says a seventy-six-year-old band elder: "Every summer . . . the priest would come in on the CNR railway and stop at Jones. Then he would paddle up the river and look for the children that should be in residential school. . . . I went to St. Mary's school in Kenora, around the First World War, I think. The school was called St. Anthony's then. The priest came to Wabauskang to pick us up. My father would walk from the reserve to Kenora to visit us, after Christmas. Took him more than one day to do that, but maybe he camped halfway to rest. . . . But I was only in school for four years, because my father needed me on the trapline."

In 1919, a massive influenza epidemic broke out on the Wabauskang site and spread quickly to the small groups of Indians around Maynard Lake, Indian Lake, and Ball Lake. Over a thousand people are believed to have died.[8] Father Lacelle recalls: "Wabauskang was a big reserve once, but it was wiped out during the epidemic. . . . This was a big catastrophe for the people because they couldn't explain it. They were scared of it and took it as a kind of spiritual punishment." From the time of the epidemic, the Wabauskang reserve became associated with a curse. The medicine men were powerless to cure the sickness and advised against continued settlement on this territory. Charles Pierrot, who succeeded his father, Chief Sah-katch-eway, in 1888, decided to relocate the band to the site of the old reserve of Grassy Narrows, because that site was believed to be sacred ground. Today the people think of themselves as the descendants of the ten families who were north on their traplines when the epidemic hit Wabauskang. "It was the survivors," say the old-timers, "who moved to the old reserve after the epidemic." Since the epidemic and the move from Wabauskang in the mid-1920s, the Grassy Narrows people remember no other major disasters until the mid-1960s, the time of the relocation from the old reserve to the present site.

### Journal of Memory

When one is describing the way of life of a people, one is really talking about culture, about those ways of knowing, imagining, and doing that people learn to regard as natural. According to Kai Erikson, "To speak of culture is also to speak of the elements that shape human behavior—the inhibitions that govern it from the inside, the rules that control it from the outside, the languages and philosophies that serve to edit a people's experience of life, the customs and rituals that help define how one person should relate to another. To speak of culture is to speak of those forces that promote uniformity of thought and action."[9]

The way of life at Grassy Narrows before the relocation is now a kaleidoscope of images in the minds of those people who lived on the old reserve. These highly subjective recollections contain not only memory of what was but also desire for what ought to be and nostalgia for what is no more. The actual and the ideal elements of traditional culture are inextricably interwoven in people's reflections on the past. In spite of the difficulties presented by this mixing of memory and desire, however, there is no evidence more powerful than that drawn directly from what people say in their own words about their life experience. Therefore, I have chosen to present the life story of one woman, Maggie Land, as she told it to me in a series of conversations over a number of years. From the resonance of her autobiography emerges our first impression of what life was like on the old reserve of Grassy Narrows.

Maggie Land was born in 1916. She was one of two children from a liaison between an Indian mother, from an old Wabauskang family, and a white father, manager of the Hudson's Bay Company trading post. In 1920 her mother married a man from Grassy Narrows and had four more children, two of whom survived infancy. Three years later, Maggie, aged seven, went to residential school at McIntosh,[10] where she stayed for twelve years. In 1935, at the age of nineteen, she married into one of the most prominent and powerful clans of Grassy Narrows. Her husband, Jerry Fobister, was thirteen years her senior and the direct descendant of Chief Sah-katch-eway, who signed the treaty. She had eight children by him, five of whom died in infancy. After Jerry's death in 1950, Maggie lived with his brother, Charlie, and had three children by him. In 1959 she left the old reserve and went to live with her son, who was working on the railroad at Jones. Four years later, she met Isaac Land and married him. Since he also worked on the CNR railroad at Dryden, McIntosh, and Favel, they travelled together from place to place before returning to the new reserve in 1972.

Today, Maggie Land has twenty-five grandchildren and, at last count, five great-grandchildren. Like others at Grassy Narrows, however, she is no stranger to pain: her twenty-four-year-old daughter Margaret was brutally murdered in the vicinity of McIntosh in 1969; her last child, Patrick, seventeen, died from shotgun wounds after a drinking party on the new reserve in 1974. Yet Maggie is an energetic, lively, hardworking, and generous woman. She is the undisputed matriarch of her large extended family and a person to be reckoned with in the community. In her own words:

> I was brought up by my grandparents, my mother's parents. In those days, most children were brought up by grandparents. . . . I still remember the stories my grandmother told me. Some were about white people. Some were about wars with other Indians. We still fought with the Sioux in my great-grandmother's time.
>
> My grandparents and the old people said that everything was going to change in our Indian ways. I don't know how they knew about the future; they had no books, they couldn't read, they had no Bible. But they had their ways of knowing what was going to happen. They said, if we lived long enough, we would see that what they said was true. My grandmother used to tell me that I'll see something in the skies. I think she was thinking of an airplane. She said that the white man will take over the land, and that is happening too. She said there will be many killings on the reserve. When these killings began here, sudden-like, I remembered what she said. . . . I don't know how they knew these things. But my grandmother told me this: the old ones they know what's going to happen, they fast for ten days and ten nights, and then they dream about it. She used to tell us to fast like that too.
>
> When I was around seven years old, I went to residential school. I was one of the first in the school at McIntosh, which was run by the Oblate Fathers and Sisters. Grassy Narrows was the closest reserve to McIntosh, as the crow flies. At first, people were lonely for their kids, especially if it was the first one to go to school. But then they got used to it. People came by water, in canoes, to be close to their kids. They camped on the other side of the lake. Visits were permitted

on Sundays. I was in school twelve years, until I was nineteen. I was still in school when my husband came and picked me up and we got married in the church at McIntosh.

I never knew where babies come from. We were told that "babies come by snowshoes." Soon I had my first baby, and he died from fever. People lost many babies in those days. My second son, Andrew, was born the next year. Then Evelyn came. Then John. John died when he was four, from fever. I don't know what fever it was. Margaret was born at the end of the Second World War. But my three youngest, Roy, Robert, and Jeanne, died from fever while they were still babies. After my husband died, I lived with Charlie, and Steve, Sharon, and Patrick were born. But by then, babies didn't die from fever as much.

On the old reserve, there weren't too many jobs, so almost everybody worked on the trapline. Each family had their own trapping area. They would stay there all winter, coming back to the old reserve only at Christmas time. That time, they went to McIntosh to visit their children in residential school. Trapping started in late fall and continued until spring. In the springtime, everybody trapped for muskrat. That's the thing I miss. We all went out, by families, in March before the ice broke. Sometimes we used to meet each other at one place, but everybody went, even the kids. The women skinned the muskrats. We ate muskrat meat, boiled or roasted. We caught fish and beaver and ate it with bannock. Around the end of spring, everybody came back to the old reserve. The old reserve was our summer camp. Around May, we started to clean the yards and plant gardens.

On the old reserve, every family had its own place. And the people lived far from each other. The old reserve was a beautiful place. You could see for miles. We were not crowded there. Your neighbor was about half a mile away. . . .

When I was growing up, we didn't meet white people very much. I still remember Charles Pierrot. He said that according to the treaty, the reserve was just for Indians. For as long as he was chief, Charlie never let white people come into the reserve. The chief was not afraid to talk to white people, but he didn't want them on the reserve. Anyway, in those days, the Indian Agent came only once a year, on Treaty Day. The Indian Agent came with a doctor and the RCMP all dressed up in uniform. They came by canoe. As soon as the people saw the flag of the Union Jack coming, they started a gun salute. The white people went to Treaty Hall, where they shook hands with the people gathered to meet them. All the councillors and the chief wore the uniform given to them by the Indian Agent. The rest of the people wore their best clothes. Treaty Day was a big celebration for us. There was usually a pow-wow and dancing and the beating of drums . . . sometimes even a square dance, with everybody participating.

The Indian Agent paid treaty money to the head of the family. If a young girl got a baby and she was not married, she had to appear before everybody and say who the father was. She couldn't get treaty money if she didn't say that. It was very strict. This is what the Indian Agent wanted. Also the Indian Agent used to make people who lived with another man or woman—not their husband or wife—come together again. He would make the man take his old lady back. The chief and councillors were strict too. One time when Alex Fobister, my husband's dad, was chief, one man tried to go away with another man's wife. The chief and three councillors took a gun and canoe and went after them. They brought them back. In those days, there was more family discipline. The chief and council wanted children to have a mother and father living together. It was like this until the time of Hyacinthe as chief [late 1940s], when things became less strict.

Still, for as long as I can remember, people couldn't marry of the same totem . . . cousins couldn't get married. Today, everything has changed. Even cousins marry, and this is not good. Also, when I got married, a man had to have a house and be a good trapper and a good hunter and be able to provide for his family. All this has changed too. Now, kids just shack up young, at thirteen or fourteen. There is no more discipline, no more family life.

Treaty Day was first in June, long time ago. Then in May. After Treaty Day, some people went to work as guides or cabin girls in the fishing camps. My husband had a job with the Bay hauling supplies from the Jones Road, where the CNR railway came in, to the old reserve. . . .

In the middle of July, blueberry picking started. All the families, except those working in the tourist camps, went picking blueberries. We set up tents in different places each year—like Redditt, Brinka, Quibell, Farlane. Somebody would always go first to look around where blueberries were the best and tell the others. At the place where we camped, you could see lots of tents. That's what we are missing now, the way it used to be, the good times when we all picked berries. . . . We made money selling blueberries, and with this money we bought what we needed for the winter—flour, lard, tea, sugar, salt, raisins, canned milk. We didn't need too much else, because the men hunted for meat whenever we needed meat, and we also had fish from the river when there wasn't enough meat.

We came back to the old reserve around the end of August. We dried blueberries and raspberries for the winter. Then it was time to pick vegetables from the garden. Every family had its own garden. We had potatoes, corn, onions, pumpkins. There was also a community garden planted with potatoes. There was lots of work for everybody.

Wild rice began about the first or second week of September. At first, we didn't pick rice to sell it. I remember the first time we sold rice, after it was finished [processed]. Andy was just a baby that time . . . so it must have been forty years ago. The first time anybody sold rice, it was down the Wabigoon River, between Dryden and Quabelle. We were picking blueberries there too. That time, we could pick rice wherever we wanted to. White people didn't know about wild rice like they do now. . . . Also, we had no licences for hunting either. The men could go out any time. And traplines, they started making traplines after the war, the Second World War. So things change. We finished rice ourselves, in the old way. I don't remember when people started to sell rice green. I still keep some of my rice, and I still finish it the old way. I don't sell all my rice. The time of rice picking was another time when people came together, when they had a feast. It was a happy time.

After rice picking, men went hunting for moose and deer. Women worked hard to dry fish and meat for winter. There was lots of moose and deer around the old reserve. Enough for everybody. That time, people shared more than they do now. Especially with the old people.

In the middle of October, people got ready to go to the trapline. At first, we had dog teams, but later, we could fly out by plane. The Bay helped trappers with credit, grub stake. Sometimes the Bay helped pay for a plane for people who had traplines far north. Men trapped for beaver, muskrat, mink, otter, lynx, and fox. But mostly beaver and muskrat. Women skinned animals and stretched skins. We sold furs and ate beaver and muskrat meat. We made clothing from deer and moose hide—moccasins, mukluks, jackets. There was always something to do. The children set snares for rabbits.

Except for a week or so at Christmas time, families stayed on traplines all winter. They came back to the old reserve after spring trapping. In those days, we didn't live all bunched up in one place all year round. I think we were happier the old way. There was no hunger, and sickness was cured by the medicine man.

My grandfather was a medicine man. The medicine man healed the spirit of a person, not his body. If a child was sick, it used to be that a medicine man held a kind of rattle over the body. I was afraid when I heard the noise of that rattle echoing off the walls. When he came to the place that was sick, he knew what was wrong by the sound of the rattle. He took a piece of bone that had a hole in it, like a straw, and he sucked all the sickness from the body. When he was finished, the child got well. There is no one on the reserve today that knows about these things. The old people, they used to know a lot about medicine from trees and plants. I had a bad bleeding once after my baby was born. I nearly died. My grandmother made me a drink from the bark of a tree, and she stopped the bleeding. Every family had someone who knew about these things.

The last time I saw a shaking tent ceremony was on the old reserve. The men built a strong tent and put the stakes deep in the ground. A medicine man was inside the tent. People who wanted help from him asked him many things. Maybe their relative was far away on the trapline, and they wanted to know if he was all right. The medicine man called for the spirit of the person. The tent began to shake. The spirit came, and it looked like a ball of fire. I heard the medicine man talking to the spirit. After that, you had to give the medicine man something, a kind of gift for his work.

Life on the old reserve was hard. But people were happier then. I think it was better to live the way we lived before. If only we could have been left alone. But maybe it's too late. It is too late. We can't bring back the past. There is no choice. The young people try to become like the white people, and the ones in between don't know who they are. Maybe we have to join the white society, but I will not join it.

Through these images drawn from her experience, Maggie Land touches upon almost every dimension of life on the old reserve. She describes aspects of both the material and the conceptual world. On the one hand there is the quest for food, the seasonal cycle of economic activities, the constancy of work, the division of labor among all family members, and the mix of play and work at different times in the annual cycle. On the other hand there are "those ways of knowing and imagining," the knowledge available through dreams, and the special power of healing and divination granted to the gifted. Maggie Land also talks about the inhibitions from the inside—the taboos governing sexual relations and marriage—and the rules from the outside—the sanctions imposed by the Indian Agent and the chief and council in order to preserve the social order. She characterizes community life on the old reserve as the ebb and flow of separateness and togetherness, as a movement of family groups between the isolation of their winter trapping grounds and the sociability of the summer camp on the old reserve.

Throughout her story, one can sense that everything is related to every other thing: religion, social organization, political life, economic system, and spatial order—these are all interconnected, all part of a larger whole, and subject to the forces of nature and the spirits of the universe. One can also sense the rhythm—the seasonal movement through time and space—and the repetition of everyday life in slow cycles from one generation to the next. Thus, life on the old reserve mirrored much of what was left in the traditional culture: trapping as a way of life, economic self-sufficiency on the part of clan-based family groups, and close ties with the natural world.

# 3 • WORLDS IN CONFLICT

Perhaps one of the most important elements given to the human personality by culture is the orientation to space and time. Because this orientation involves such a fundamental dimension of our experience and is so central to the ordering and coordination of human activity, we often take it for granted and assume that people with whom we come into contact share our own spatial and temporal perception. Yet variations occur among people of different cultures with respect to the selective emphasis given to the spatial relations and attributes of things and the degree of complexity and refinement in the concepts employed for time.[1] It is also true that cultural precepts assist in determining not only how a people will think and act but also what they will imagine, and hence what they will create, in the realm of the arts, fantasy, and myth.

As a result of the move to the new reserve, certain aspects of the Ojibwa way of knowing about the reality of time and space ceased to be useful in structuring individual and social experience. It is these aspects in which I am most interested, although I recognize that other features of the Indians' orientation to time and space were not directly affected by resettlement.[2] I have also limited the discussion to ideas and themes that figured most prominently in my conversations with the people of Grassy Narrows about the changes in community life following their relocation.

## Space and Order in Human Settlement

Perhaps the most striking feature of the way in which the traditional Ojibwa dealt with the concept of space is that they did not limit their experience to the attributes that could be perceived by the physical senses or to the qualities deemed important solely at the level of pragmatic action. Their perception of space allowed for cosmic values as well as practical applications. Indian people admitted the probability of a "reality" hidden behind the phenomenal world and governed by an order not subject to conventional laws of space and time. They believed that human experience in the physical world took place and was interpreted within a very narrow range of possibilities, defined by physiology, psychological structure, and culture. No doubt they would have agreed with the proposition that we see things not as they are, but as we are.

Although the Western cultural tradition has yet to incorporate fully the idea of the relativity of space and time, Christian mystics and contemplatives, among others, have written extensively about the ability of the human soul to transcend boundaries imposed by the physical body and the social construction of reality. We have also been reminded of the confining nature of our thinking by Carl Jung. He writes:

> Our concepts of space and time have only approximate validity. . . . We cannot visualize another world ruled by quite other laws, the reason being that we live in a specific world which has helped to shape our minds and establish our basic psychic conditions. We are strictly limited by our innate structure and therefore bound by our whole being and thinking to this world of ours. . . . We must face the fact that our world, with its time, space, and causality, relates to another order of things lying behind or beneath it, in which neither "here and there" nor "earlier and later" are of importance.[3]

Jung was an empiricist and a scientist, yet he spent a lifetime probing the unconscious mind through daring personal confrontation with the unknown, the "other reality." Ultimately he concluded that alternative concepts of time and space, such as those proposed by the Ojibwa, were no more or less real than the more generally accepted ones. The difference was to be found in the root assumptions upon which ideas of existence were based.

Up to the time of the relocation, the Grassy Narrows people relied on two sources for the perception of space. The first is familiar to us because it involves the use of the physical senses and intersensory cooperation to distinguish size, shape, extension, direction, locality, and distance. Mediated by culture, this way of knowing is indispensable for the ordering and coordination of human activity over a certain territory. Like people in every other culture, the Indians have used this mode of spatial perception to develop certain ideas about how much space is required to maintain social order among neighbors and how much territory is necessary for the satisfaction of practical needs. Thus, on the old reserve clan-based family groups were separated by unspoken, yet well understood, distances, and definite territories were allocated to them by custom and usage for trapping, hunting, and gathering.

The second source of spatial knowledge is less familiar to us because it rests on the inner senses, or inner perceptors, of man. Whereas the physical senses lead one to translate all experience into physical perception, the inner senses open up the range of perception and allow the interpretation of space and reality in a freer manner. It is not that physical reality is a false reality; it is just that the physical image is only one of many significant ways of perceiving. In this frame of reference, there is no objective reality; reality is that which is created by human consciousness.

One can easily understand how the Ojibwa dealt with spatial relationships in everyday life. The first impression of the old reserve as one approaches it by water, for example, is the direct relationship between customary social organization and spatial form. In spite of the lack of a concept of private property among the Ojibwa, one cannot fail to observe distinct areas of the old reserve that once belonged to individual clans. The old people of Grassy Narrows explain:

> On the old reserve, every family lived together. We weren't all bunched up and mixed together like we are today. . . .
>
> On the old reserve, the families were far apart from each other. We lived beside the Fobisters, about a half mile apart; in between us were the Lands. John Loon and his family lived on that island, up the English River. The Assins were more on the Wabigoon side of the river. The Hyacinthes all lived together on one shore . . . the next point belonged to the Ashopenaces . . . then the Fishers, then the Necanapenaces. . . . The Taypaywaykejicks had a different spot too. It was traditional for all the clans to live separately from each other. That's the way they have always lived. It was much better that way.

Clan territoriality certainly played an important role in reinforcing the identity of the group and its place in the order of things. The sense of place was very strong for individual members of the group as well: "On the old reserve, you knew your place. It wasn't private property, but it was a sense of place, your place, your force around you." A large clan, moreover, may have had more than one house on the old reserve; it could form a minicolony of people, spatially, economically, and socially independent of the rest of the band: "My family's house on the old reserve was very good, made from logs. It had two stories. All the Fobister brothers, they were carpenters and helped build it. Each brother, Jerry, Dennis, Tom, Father, and I—we had our own houses, but in the same clearing. Five log houses, the whole clan, together. The family would all help one another. It was better to be scattered, to live far apart from other people."

The wide distances between family groups reflected also the sparseness of their social interaction and their preference for community life only on special occasions like Treaty Day and the feasts around Christmas and the start of the wild-rice harvest. Other social occasions, such as the naming ceremony for children, were confined to members of the clan and only rarely involved persons who were not relatives.

The form of settlement on the old reserve was thus characterized by a clan-based residence pattern, with a wide margin of privacy and space separating the clans from one another. From the air, one can still observe a form that used to be circular rather than linear, a kind of clustering in space around the center, which was the Hudson's Bay island. Equality of access to the river was evidently a very important consideration, because the river was not only the main artery of transportation but also a source

Cabin on the old reserve.

Cabin on the old reserve.

of life-giving water and food. In addition, a critical element in the layout
of the old reserve was the need to have sufficient warning of the approach
of strangers. According to Father Lacelle:

> There was no way to get to the old reserve without someone knowing that a
> stranger was coming. There was, you see, a very clear line of vision to protect
> against unwanted visitors. I would also say that each house had a line of vision to
> the water as well, to know who was coming to visit. It was very important to the
> people of Grassy to have this security, and all the houses on the old reserve were
> located strategically.
>
> Of course, it bothers them a lot on the new reserve that not every house has
> access to the lake, and that the whole reserve is not laid out in such a way that the
> approach of strangers can be noticed.

In short, space and social order, with attendant considerations for privacy, security, and equality of access to water, were inextricably inter-
twined in the settlement form of the old reserve. While unspoken boundaries protected the residential areas occupied by individual clans, there
was also communal space: "Yes, we did have space that everybody shared
on the old reserve. That was where the Treaty Hall was. Nobody made
that area his home. That belonged to everybody, and everybody worked
on it. Everybody helped build the Treaty Hall too; we cut the logs, we put
it up, and we shared the cost of the windows and the stove."

Other areas were communal in the sense that every family had the right
to pick berries or harvest wild rice in these areas. Hunting territories were
held in common as well. There were certain areas around the old reserve,
however, that were particularly favored and therefore habitually exploited by the same families year after year. Specific trapping grounds, on
the other hand, were inherited; more precisely, the right to use these
grounds was inherited, for there was no concept of individual ownership
of land among the Ojibwa. Trapping grounds might be used by one
extended family for several generations or for several years. The productivity of the territory and its accessibility affected the desirability and
continued use of the trapline, but sentimental ties affected its transfer.

In 1948 the government of Ontario initiated a system according to
which registered trappers were allocated exclusive trapping rights to specific areas of Crown land. This meant that no one could trap without
having a registered trapline or permission from the holder of the trapline. These rights were renewable at the discretion of the Department of
Lands and Forests (now the Ministry of Natural Resources), subject to the
provision that the holder of the trapline had to harvest an annual agreed-
upon quota of fur from each species, particularly beaver. These quotas
were imposed on all trapline holders but were less strictly enforced for
Treaty Indian trappers. The boundaries of the registered traplines corre-

The old reserve.

The new reserve.

New reserve interior.

sponded roughly to the areas that had been traditionally used and occupied by Grassy Narrows families.

While the clan-based residence pattern and customary trapping
grounds were very important elements in the way of life on the old reserve, the Indians considered them part of their material, everyday existence. Yet, as Hallowell has written: "What appears to be particularly
significant in our human adjustment to the world is that over and above
pragmatic needs for orientation and without any pretense to reliable
knowledge of regions of space outside their personal experience, human
beings in all cultures have built up a frame of spatial reference that has
included the farther as well as the more proximal, the spiritual as well as
the mundane, regions of their universe."[4]

The people of Grassy Narrows, in their beliefs about the true nature of
space and reality, were no exception to this general observation. The
prediction of the old people, that the move to the new reserve posed the
gravest danger to the life of the community, was based on what could be
perceived by the inner senses, the "eyes of the soul." The new site, they
warned, was not spiritually suitable for human settlement:

> In the Indian religion, there is good land and land that is bad land. The land is
> not good for people to live on if the people who lived on it before did not use it
> right, or did not use their spiritual power in the right way. The old people used

to preach that when a person dies, his spirit leaves the body and travels. If you are a bad person on earth, the spirit has trouble leaving the earth for the long journey into the other world. Instead, it stays in the same place where the person lived before and wanders about restlessly. So there is no such thing as empty space. All space is filled with spirits, but one cannot see them. Land over which troubled spirits travel is not good for people to live on. . . .

But there are other spirits too, and they live in certain places. These are different from the ones that have trouble reaching the "happy hunting ground." They possess certain spots, and you have to be careful not to disturb them. This land where we are now [the new reserve], this spot is unfit for people to live on because it is already owned by a bad spirit. Maybe this is why there is so much trouble here.

The old people of Grassy Narrows hold tenaciously to the belief that because other forms of consciousness inhabit the same space as man, it is essential to know the properties of space. A woman now in her late seventies, whose father and husband had both been chiefs of Grassy Narrows, told me that the old people have known for a long time that "the new reserve is a very bad place, spiritually." She said that both her father and her uncle, at different times, saw someone surfacing at Garden Lake. This was considered an extremely ominous warning that the territory around the new reserve was off limits to human habitation. "This was an evil spirit at Garden Lake, for sure, the opposite of the Great Spirit. This was the sign of the presence of Machu-Manitou. . . . The old people, they knew that the land around the new reserve was no good for our people, but nobody asked them, nobody listened to them."

The spirit beings of the Ojibwa world not only existed in the same space as man but occupied a characteristic spatial locale associated with a natural feature of the terrain, like a set of cliffs or a body of water. They were not all evil, of course, and some were helpful to man. The Grassy Narrows people were very familiar with the abodes of the spirits and with their nature. As one elder explains:

Our people used to believe there is a spirit that dwells in those cliffs over there. Whenever the Indians thought something like that, they put a marker. And you can still see these markers on the old reserve. Sometimes you see paintings on rocks. These mean something; they were put there for a purpose. You can still see a rock painting when you go up to Indian Lake. It's on the left-hand side of the cliffs. And as you go towards Maynard Lake and Oak Lake, there's a channel. You see a painting there too.

The rock paintings mean that there is a good spirit there that will help us on the waters of the English River. You see a cut in the rocks over there; that's where people leave tobacco for the good spirit that inhabits that place.

On the old reserve, they used to gather at the rock formation—"Little Boy Lying Down," they called it. From there they sent an echo across the space. They could tell by the strength of the echo if the land was good. Good echoes meant that the land would give people strength, that they could live well and survive there, that the land would support them.

Another way to tell whether the land was good to live on was by the light that comes off the land. The old people used to be able to see this light. The place where the new reserve is, it is not a good place. It is not a place for life.[5]

It is, of course, not accidental that land chosen for its spiritual value was never deficient in its productive capacity. The land of the old reserve, for example, had fertile soil; it was rich in game; its waters were abundant with fish; and rice grew wild along the shores of the river.

Because space to the Ojibwa was never empty but was filled with spirit beings whose existence was not dependent upon physical form, some places were better than others to settle on, to build houses on, to live in. There were certain points in space where the health and vitality of people would be strengthened, where, other things being equal, all beneficial conditions for life would seem to converge. By turning off the physical senses and focusing the inner senses, certain gifted individuals could see the reality beyond three-dimensional physical space and locate those points in space that would support life.

The Ojibwa considered all the objects of the natural world to be animated with the same life force as man, a life force whose source was the Great Spirit. To the Ojibwa people, rivers, even rocks and stones, as well as trees, plants, and animals, had life. They were all formed by minute particles of consciousness bound by the same energy field as the atoms and molecules of the human body. As the spirit beings could not be perceived by the physical senses, so too other objects in space required another source of perception in order to distinguish their true reality and their special attributes and powers that could be helpful to human beings. For the Ojibwa Indians generally, and for the Indians of Grassy Narrows in particular, there was not only no such thing as empty space; there was also no such thing as dead matter. All matter was related to the energy of the universe, and both man and nature were endowed with life by the Great Spirit.

Just as the choice of a site for human settlement on the basis of spiritual criteria was critical to the collective survival and well-being of the band, so certain special places were of extraordinary importance to individuals. These "places of power" were intensely personal spaces, often distinguished by some physical configuration like a clump of trees or a certain rock pattern. Often they required a special effort to reach and were known only to a single individual. Around the old reserve of Grassy Narrows, there were apparently many places like this where individuals went to be alone, where they could meditate, where they could most easily focus the inner senses. These micropoints in space can be thought of as amplification points for human psychic and spiritual energy, and perhaps this is why they have been called places of power. It is significant that there seem to be very few places of power in the immediate area of the new reserve.[6]

## Time and Consciousness

As with space, the Ojibwa knew that a valid reality of time could also be captured through the inner senses. They believed that direct personal experience of this reality was fundamental to understanding one's self and one's place in the universe. Notwithstanding the transcendental experience of great mystics, we in Western culture have come to assume that there is one natural and absolute temporal order in the universe. We believe that the units of time as we know them follow a cyclical pattern measured by the time in which the earth completes one revolution in its orbit around the sun with respect to the fixed stars. Our sidereal year consists of 365 days, 6 hours, 9 minutes, and 9.54 seconds of solar time; then we progress to sidereal months, weeks, days, hours, minutes, and seconds, with hardly a thought of the fact that our temporal bearings are products of our culture. Time becomes a commodity that can be bought and sold, saved or spent, wasted, lost, or made up. Above all, it can be measured and its components aggregated. We also assume that other people will not waste time and that speed will have the same value for them as it does for us. In our world, time is certainly not just "a clock with a set of mechanical gears" but something God-given and natural, an animating principle of the universe that we take for granted.

It therefore seems rather odd to us that only forty years ago, the people at Grassy Narrows still went by the "time of the moon." A woman, now seventy-three years old, recalls that: "We had a calendar, and it went by the moon. My dad kept it. It had animals to symbolize the months, and it was a good way of telling time."

The *moon* to the Ojibwa was not a division of continuous time; rather, it was a recurring event. The moons were differentiated by names that referred to the seasonal appearance of certain animals or to the condition of plant life during a particular season.[7] The cycle of the seasons was probably the most important means by which the Ojibwa people kept themselves adjusted to the solar year. Further, the year was not a temporal unit of continuous duration that could be reduced to smaller measurable units but simply an interval of time between the recurring events of the seasons. It always began with the onset of winter. In short, the reference points for the perception of time by the Ojibwa were the seasons, because to them were tied all the economic and social activities of the annual cycle; within seasons were the moons, which established certain regular intervals of time also tied to visible changes in nature. Then, within moons were other temporal units, days and nights measured not in standardized units of hours but rather by alternating periods of light and darkness caused by the movements of the sun. For the purposes of every-day life, time was always related to chosen natural phenomena and their predictable recurrence. No other yardstick was necessary as long as the Ojibwa obtained a living from the land.

A major change in the temporal orientation of the people of Grassy Narrows occurred during the lifetime of people now in their sixties and seventies. The old people at Grassy Narrows say that their entire way of life, including their ways of thinking about time and of structuring their daily activities, changed with the relocation.

> Now, on the new reserve, we have to work from eight in the morning to four in the afternoon. They give us coffee breaks and a hour to eat dinner. I tell you, this is hard to get used to, and it makes no sense. Indians don't live that way. We eat when we're hungry. We eat when there's food, maybe somebody catch a fish. We're used to working when there's work to do . . . like we set fishing nets at night and lift them in the morning. There is always work to do, but there is a time to do it. We used to live this way on the old reserve, but not any more. Now they [government people] tell us what to do and when to do it.

Night, the period of darkness alternating with the period of light, was also once a convenient point of reference for the work of the day:

> Early in the morning, before the sun came out, my grandmother would get me up. She believed that the sun was some kind of spirit. When the sun got up, then it was time for people to get up. It was time to start working. And when the sun went down, it was time to rest, to sleep. That's the way I was brought up.
>
> But now, on the new reserve, you can see the kids running around all night. They sleep in the daytime. People have been mixed up. They don't know any more what's day and what's night. Everything has changed since we moved to the new reserve.

The hours of the day as such were of little practical importance to the Ojibwa. There was not much need for sophisticated coordination of human activity by means of time, because family groups were relatively independent, and on the rare occasion of social gathering, the precision of the hour was irrelevant. The "moccasin telegraph" would inform the people of community meetings on the old reserve, and they would start when everyone was there. Similarly, other social occasions, like dances or celebrations, would start when the people were ready, although certain religious ceremonies had to take place at sunrise, and most conjuring activities were done after dark.[8] It appears that there were no occasions on the old reserve when the collective attendance of any group of people was demanded at a certain hour.

On the whole, the temporal rhythm of life on the old reserve was elastic and gentle, flowing in response to physical necessity, external circumstances, or just whim. Time conceived in an abstract fashion, time assumed to be autonomous, time thought of as infinitely divisible, time perceived as linear or sidereal, time treated as a commodity—these means of temporal orientation were alien to the Ojibwa culture. Western time perspectives became a dominant mode of individual and social orientation at Grassy Narrows only after the move to the new reserve. Among adults, Western time perspectives went hand in hand with the shift to on-reserve wage labor and government-sponsored employment projects. Among children, however, orientations to time were profoundly influenced by television. The day-care supervisor put the matter plainly:

> The kids here at Grassy Narrows have no concept of time. They can't tell time. The only way they know time is through TV programs. They will say, for example, "Come to my house when Fonzy's on," or, "We'll do this . . . after Mork and Mindy's over." If I ask them when they went to bed, they'll tell me that they went to bed after Johnnie Carson. If I say, come over at 7 P.M., they'll just stare at me blankly and ask, "Is that before or after Mary Tyler Moore?" It has always amazed me that their entire concept of time is related to TV, and yet the people only got electricity on the reserve in 1975. . . . You sometimes wonder how the kids ever managed to tell time before they got TV sets. But then, of course, things were altogether different. The way of life was Indian.

In short, the orientation to time on the old reserve was largely dependent upon the seasons and the alterations in the sun and the moon, events which were guides for vital social and economic activities. All these means of perception were limited in their application to activities in the immediate future or the immediate past, within the range of observation by the physical senses, and thus part of people's everyday experience.

As in their conceptualization of the reality of space, however, the people made a distinction between time as it could be perceived by the outer senses and time as it could be known through the inner senses. To the Ojibwa, spirit beings that coexisted with man in the same space were not subject to physical time; they did not age, for example, and neither does the spirit in man. Knowledge of the other reality of time was just as important to human life as knowledge of the separate reality of space. Time could be experienced as psychological time if conventional definitions of sequence and duration were suspended. The Indians considered that personal awareness of this kind of time was fundamental to an understanding of the true nature of the self and personal identity.

I've chosen two examples from what the people of Grassy Narrows told me to illustrate the psychological implications of the perceived relationship between the inner mode of temporal perception and self-awareness in individuals. The first example speaks to the recollection of time past in time present that stretches the limits beyond which we think reliable accounts of personal experience can be recalled. The second illustrates the ability to know time future in time present with respect to one's own life path.

Simon Fobister, now in his early twenties, became chief of Grassy Narrows at the age of nineteen. From November 1976 to March 1980, he guided the community through three turbulent, violent, and exhausting years. He is a remarkably gifted young man, with an unusual intelligence, an inner strength, and a sense of purpose in life granted to him in the following manner:

> When I was just a very small baby, maybe eight or nine months old, my mother put me to sleep near a window in our log house on the old reserve. When I was left alone, I saw a very old, old woman quickly open the window and take me away with her to where she lived.
>
> When she entered her house, she put me down. Then she touched my eyes and said that I would see. She touched my ears and said that I would hear. She began to speak in words I could not understand; I could not understand her speech. But then I understood. She said that she was giving me a blessing so that one day I would be a leader of my people.
>
> Much later in life, I remembered this happening to me. I remembered what that woman had said. At first I thought it had all been a dream, but one which had left a very strong impression. So I asked my older sister whether she knew if I had ever been abducted as a baby. "Yes," she said. "When you were a baby, an old woman took you away." Then I knew that this was not a dream, that I remembered a real event in my life, one which had an important message for me.

Simon Fobister's story, his conviction that it happened, illustrates the point that the phenomenal reality of self-awareness may be independent of time as we know it. After all, we think that very early infant experiences cannot be recalled as such because the infant has not yet become an object to himself and because he has not yet incorporated any operational temporal sense making it possible to differentiate very early experiences from later ones. In the context of the importance granted by the Ojibwa to phenomena that are not bound by conventional means of perception, Simon's recollection would naturally be accepted as valid. Further, such self-related experiences need not be true according to anyone else's standards of truth or reliability in order to be psychologically significant for the individual in understanding who he is and what role he is to play in society.

The second example illustrates the possibility of consciousness of the future in the present. A very common type of experience that has always been important to the Ojibwa as a source of knowledge about the self is dreaming. In dreams, time and space as we know them are suspended. Hallowell suggests a link between the reality of dreams and the reality of the spirit beings in which the Ojibwa believe. He notes that the very fact that the Ojibwa can experience an enormously broadened mobility of self in space and time while dreaming is one reason for their extending the same ability to mythological creatures in their own environment. "In the case of the Ojibwa," he writes, "human beings share such mobility with the nonhuman selves. . . . Experientially, the world of the self and the world of myth are continuous."[9] Like Ojibwa people everywhere, the Grassy Narrows people also believe strongly that dream experiences are the experiences of the inner man and that therefore there is no inherent discontinuity between what is phenomenally real in dreams and what is real in waking life. Dreams always carry significant messages from the unconscious part of the self, messages that should be incorporated into the experience of daily life.

The other category of time-suspended experience, similar to the dream in its source but different in the sense that conscious preparation is required, is the vision. On the old reserve, the people still practiced the tradition of encouraging young men to seek visions at the time of puberty.[10] The puberty vision quest was considered fundamental to gaining knowledge of one's self, one's identity and purpose in life, and one's special powers. Naturally, the perceptions acquired and the experiences undergone by the individual during the vision quest might far transcend those of ordinary waking life with respect to spatial and temporal orientation. In the following story, told to me by a man in his early fifties, there is for one moment a wondrous perception of the other reality of time: time indivisible into past, present, and future; time simultaneous.

> My father once told me this story. . . . It was the custom of our people to send boys out in the bush to prepare themselves for becoming a man. They had to be alone, and to fast, usually for a week. . . . It was in the middle of winter when my father went into the bush. One day, after many days, he went out in the middle of a frozen lake. He was very cold and very hungry, and he felt alone. Suddenly, he saw a whole bunch of people around him. Some were tall, and others were just little. Some he recognized, but many he did not know. The people, they just stood around him, and he saw their faces clearly. Then, as suddenly as they appeared, they disappeared.
>
> Many, many years later, my father knew who those people were. They were us, his sons, and our children. He had seen all his family, four generations, his children, and his children's children. . . . And he told me something I never forgot. He told me that all the past, present, and future is within all of us, now.[11]

Thus, in their belief in a reality separate from that which can be perceived by the physical senses, the Indians challenge our assumption that an objective world exists independently of our own creation and of our perception of it. In their conviction that this reality contains important information for ordering human settlement in space or for guiding indi-

vidual experience in time, they extend immensely the range of possibilities open to them. Yet, in practical terms, their conceptions of time
and space also satisfy certain everyday requirements in the pursuit of
livelihood and in the preservation of the social order.

Although some people still believe in dreams as a source of knowledge
about the self, the vision quest is no longer practiced on the new reserve.
There appears to be a sharp discontinuity between the old and the new
reserves regarding Indian ways of teaching the young about the nature of
the world around them. The relocation disrupted the way of life, and
under the fundamentally changed conditions imposed by government
planners the traditional Ojibwa orientations to time and space lost their
basis and their value. The young people of Grassy Narrows are now
caught between Western ways and the old ways of seeing and believing,
with no moorings in either camp.

# 4 • RELATIONSHIPS IN TRANSITION

When the people of Grassy Narrows speak of their society on the old reserve, they invariably begin by describing their close ties to the family—the grandparents, parents, aunts, uncles, and cousins who formed the community of residence on the winter trapline and in the summer encampment. This is not surprising. In the way of life based on trapping, the family took on an importance unlike anything known in less isolated settings. During those long, dark winter months, the family group, for all practical purposes, was a community unto itself: it was a factory, a school, a hospital, a shrine. The bonds of family were very close because the extended family had the responsibility of providing for the physical survival of its members, educating the young, sheltering the dependent, curing the sick, and transmitting the moral and spiritual values of the culture. In a society with very few public institutions and no formal associations, membership in a family unit was the individual's primary source of identity and support. The family was the point from which one fixed one's place in the larger universe, visible and invisible.

In the summer months on the old reserve, when the trapping families settled into their customary clan territories around the shores of the English-Wabigoon River, the community of Grassy Narrows took on the appearance and shape of a larger collective unit. Certain powers and responsibilities related to the welfare of the band as a whole were exercised by the institutions of the chief and the band council. The clan-based family groups, however, retained their autonomy, comprehensive functions, and fierce independence. Theirs was a life of minimal interference from external authority until the time of the relocation.

These observations of the human relationships and family life characteristic of the way of life on the old reserve are organized around themes that surfaced over and over again in my conversations with people about their life experience. This is not a comprehensive account, because it pays too little attention to the complex and unique kinship system of the Ojibwa.[1] Rather, the themes developed here are significant in terms of the social changes at Grassy Narrows following the relocation and the massive intervention of government in community life.

For those who lived on the old reserve for most of their lives and for those who spent their formative years there, the new reserve is certainly a different and scarcely comprehensible place. It is a world ruled by the haphazard and capricious whims of government bureaucrats, a world beyond their influence or control. People hardly ever speak of the way of life on the old reserve without some reference to their present condition. When they do speak, it is always with a great deal of emotion, because they feel that they have lost their most treasured institution, the Ojibwa family. And so they have. Outside the context of the trapping economy, the extended family could not possibly survive in the same form. Its structure, its functions, the roles and responsibilities of each family member—all have had to change and adapt to new conditions. In the process, many of the rituals practiced by the family to mark the stages of life, the passages in the cycle from birth to death, have simply disappeared.

## The Bonds of Family

The Ojibwa had a very broad notion of family. The very term, *nin-tipe.ncike.win*, was sometimes used to refer to any group involving a leader and followers.[2] In everyday life, the concept of family always related to the community of residence on the trapline, composed of those who worked together and were bound by responsibility and friendship as well as by ties of kinship. Ideally, the family might consist of several males and dependent females, patrilineally related under the leadership of the eldest male. The core of this group might be two or more brothers and their families or a man and his sons and their families, in addition to single persons attached to the group. The size of this family averaged twenty to twenty-five persons.[3] In this group, there was continuous economic cooperation and sharing. The men hunted and trapped together, and certain tasks, like house building or repair, were performed cooperatively. Sharing and mutual aid were always expected and delivered within this group. The extended family was both the largest unit of economic cooperation and the primary system for the socialization of children. The important social activities, like the naming of a child or a feast for the dead, were arranged by this group. On the old reserve, there were very few social occasions during the year that were organized by the band as a whole.

Not so long ago, then, the extended family functioned as an all-encompassing institution in the life of the individual at Grassy Narrows. From all accounts, life on the old reserve was primitive, but families showed a remarkable degree of competence in ensuring the survival and well-being of their members. Indeed, each family group had to be fairly self-sufficient in terms of the skills it needed to survive in the bush. The bonds of family were tight, because they were welded in the foundry of economic interdependence and respect for what each member had to

contribute to the entity as a whole. An eloquent statement about the changes in family life since the move to the new reserve is given by a forty-one-year-old band member who describes himself as a man "caught between two cultures . . . two ways of life," with a foothold in neither the old ways nor the new. Like most men and women of his generation, he has had to struggle with prolonged periods of depression and alcohol dependence.

I was born on the trapline, and I grew up in the bush. Trapping was our culture. Trapping kept the family together because everyone in the family had something to do; the man had to lay traps and check them; the woman skinned the animals, cooked, and looked after the kids. The grandparents helped with the kids; they taught them manners, how to behave, and told them stories about our people. The kids, if they were old enough, had work to do. They had to set snares for rabbits and chop wood.

Now, on the new reserve, we can't trap as a family any more. The woman has to stay home 'cause the kids are in school on the reserve. The man has to go out on the trapline by himself. But he gets lonely there and doesn't like to do all the work by himself. So he comes back to the reserve and tries to find a job or he goes on welfare. At least in the days of residential school, we could still trap as a family, but no more. You can see that only a few people are trapping nowadays.

What happens now is that the men, if they have a job, go to work in the morning, and the women are left in the house alone. They don't share in the

work any more. They buy cans at the store and have nothing to do in the daytime. The kids also don't do chores any more. The old people don't teach the kids how to behave. In my generation, marriages are breaking up. Families are breaking up, and the kids are sniffing gas while their parents are drinking. This is happening because people don't work together any more. Trapping was not just an occupation for the man. It was a way of life for the whole family. With the school on the reserve, we just can't live like we used to. If you divide the family in work, you tear it apart in other ways as well.

The idea that "if you divide the family in work, you tear it apart in other ways as well" is one that Grassy Narrows people often express. The women, in particular, feel greatly diminished as persons as a result of not being able to share in the work of the men. A notable feature of family life on the old reserve, the cooperation and equality of importance of men and women, no longer applies. And I sense that in the traditional Ojibwa family, husbands and wives were bonded less by strong emotional attachments perhaps than by a well-understood code of rights and duties of each partner. It is not surprising, therefore, that the old order of respect between spouses has been eroded as the mutual obligations on which it rested became irrelevant under the changed economic conditions of the new reserve. Today, men and women find it very difficult to determine what their roles should be. They feel adrift, separated from each other. And children are caught in the disorientation of their parents.

On the old reserve, every age had its appropriate tasks. What a parent owed his offspring was clear: the child had to be fed, clothed, and housed; it had to be imbued with beliefs necessary for continued membership in the community. The obligations of the young were equally plain: they were to obey the adults and assist in the labor of the family as a whole. Parents, and especially grandparents, were indulgent with their children, teaching by example and experience rather than by discipline. The role of grandparents in transmitting the values of the culture to the young was extremely important. At Grassy Narrows, many of the generation now in their late thirties and forties attended residential schools but still had the chance to come back to the old reserve and learn the "Indian ways." Recognizing that young people were subject to alien influences in the residential schools, parents and grandparents made a special effort to teach them Indian values and traditional skills. A man now in his mid-forties speaks to this point:

I was only thirteen years old when I lost my dad. I was in residential school since I was seven years old. I was there for nine years. When I got out, I knew nothing of Indian ways. We had to talk English at school and learn how to farm. . . . But old Robert Land, he took me and showed me how to hunt and how to trap. He taught me about our Indian ways. He taught me how to respect people. In the old days, the old people made sure that the kids who came back from residential school knew all these things. They taught from the heart and the kids learnt from the heart, and from watching how other people lived.

We know now that the extended family did not survive transplantation to the new reserve. Given the interlocking of Ojibwa social structure and economic life, neither the structure nor the functions of the extended family could be maintained outside the theater of the trapline and the old reserve encampment. In the words of Father Lacelle:

> When I used to know the Grassy Narrows families on the old reserve, and I knew them well over a quarter of a century, it seemed to me that the clan had much more control over what happens in family life. Within each family, the old people kept a sharp watch over the proper upbringing of the young people, and they were the ones who gave them spiritual training.
>
> Now I see the families breaking up. Marriages aren't what they used to be. Not that people didn't separate, because they did, but there wasn't so much fighting, so much drinking. I believe that all this is because the people no longer work together, like in trapping, and also because the pressures they're under now are just too great.
>
> First of all, the women used to do their share of the work; this has been disrupted. Second, the grandparents used to help raise the children. Now it's all on the mother. She's under too much stress. If there's a problem she can't handle, she doesn't have the support of the whole clan like she used to. Third, the way in which the government put all the houses on the new reserve doesn't help either, because now the relatives are scattered all over the reserve, and it's impossible to live like they used to. And then, finally, there's the man, the husband. If he can't provide for his family because there's no job on the reserve, if he has to go on welfare, well, that surely causes him to lose pride. Indian people like to be able to provide for themselves, like they've always done. So, he begins to fight with his wife, and they both begin to drink.
>
> In this situation, the children are growing up with no training, no guidance whatsoever. You can see that yourself. There is a great permissiveness on the reserve today, and no one cares to teach spiritual values. When the parents drink, the children suffer deeply. There is no question about it. There has been a tremendous deterioration in family life after the move to the new reserve.

Indeed, there now seems to be little connection between the concept of the extended family of the old reserve, based on the winter trapping settlement and the summer family compound, and the nuclear family or household that emerged under the unpropitious physical and economic setting of the new reserve.[4]

People often speculate on whether or not it would be possible for Indian families to return to the trapping way of life, assuming that alternative arrangements could be made for the schooling of their children. A forty-one-year-old informant tells us that the process of disintegration in the beams supporting the economic structure may have gone too far:

Can we go back to the trapline as a family? To keep our culture? I don't think so. . . . Now, I would be afraid to leave my wife and kids in a small log cabin on the trapline while I went out for two or three days. . . . They may take sick, and what do I do? You see, before, our people were much stronger. They were eating a different kind of food, not cans, but fresh wild meat, fish, wild rice. And besides that, every family had someone who knew about medicine, who could heal with bark or roots or herbs and other things, who had the power to help people. So the trapping families made their own medicine and took care of themselves. They didn't need your doctors and nurses.

And now? We are weaker physically from eating your kind of food and not having as much wild meat. So I'd be afraid of leaving my family in the bush. Your kind of first aid wouldn't help us in the bush.

One more thing. When we lived as families on the old reserve, we had our spiritual elders. Every family had a spiritual person, someone who solved all kinds of problems, who helped persons trap better and be more successful in hunting. For other things, there were other medicine men who had even greater power and could help in other ways.

Now, this religion is missing from the new reserve. There is no knowledge to give to the next generation. There are no more medicine men. Now we have nothing. Not the old, not the new. Our families are all broken up. We are caught in the middle . . . between two worlds, two ways of life.

On the new reserve, many of the responsibilities once carried out by the extended family, such as providing for the physical welfare of family members, curing the ill, and sheltering the dependent, have been thrust upon an impersonal bureaucracy. Agencies of the federal and provincial governments now deliver economic and housing programs and medical and social services. In one critical area, however, the role of the family has not been, and can never be, replaced. This is the area of ritual. For many older people, the discontinuity in the practice of certain rituals marking the stages of life is one of the most widely lamented manifestations of cultural breakdown. Although in some degree the rituals of death are still respected on the new reserve, many other ceremonial observances of life's stages have fallen into disuse. Yet no one can deny their importance in the process of identity formation, a process by which the individual in society derives some measure of his/her role and stature as a social being. And there is a sense of loss, of emptiness in life, without the ebb and flow of symbolic observance and the reenactment of ancient myths.

## Rituals and Identity

On the old reserve, the first significant event in a person's life was the naming ceremony. Corresponding in some ways to the baptismal rite, this ceremony usually occurred during the first year of life unless the baby became ill, in which case it was performed promptly. For this ceremony, the parents asked an old man or woman to bestow a name on the child. The chosen person had to be in good health and in good standing in the community as a spiritual leader. The Ojibwa people believed that by granting a name, the old person bestowed on the child the blessings of the *manitos,* or deities, that he or she had received during a long lifetime. They also believed that the old person could share life with the child and thus grant it added duration and strength. Here is a description of a ceremony, provided by a sixty-year-old man, that took place at Grassy Narrows in the late 1950s:

> The ceremony had to take place early in the morning, before the sun was up. On the day of the naming, the old man came into the house just as the light of the day was breaking. Everybody else came in at about the same time.
>
> The old man had a rattle with bear claws and bells. He took the child in his arms, and then the family passed some home brew around. Everybody drank from the same cup until it was all gone. Then they passed tobacco around. The Indians, they used home brew on special occasions, but tobacco always had some religious meaning. After that, the old man began to sing songs and to shake the rattle. Then he kissed the child and said, "I give you part of my life." And then everybody kissed the child. And she got a name like Loud Thunder. Then there was a feast of meat, bannock, wild rice.
>
> The naming ceremony was a beautiful ceremony because the old man breathed life into the child, shared his life with the child.

Apparently the formal naming ceremony was last practiced at Grassy Narrows on the old reserve. One sixty-seven-year-old woman told me that six of her eight children were named in the proper way, but none of her thirty-five grandchildren, all born on the new reserve, has been so named. She says she has a very "heavy heart" on this account.[5]

As the young child moved into adolescence, parents and grandparents prepared the child for the second major rite of passage: the puberty vision quest. Of all the life cycle ceremonies arranged by the family, this one was the most important; it was the cornerstone of the process of molding a child's sense of identity. Like other Indian peoples on the continent, the Ojibwa believed that a human being did not start life with powers and full identity. These came, in the first instance, from the blessings with which the child was endowed during the naming ceremony and, more important, from the powers acquired through the puberty fast, when a young person gained the aid of a manito, or guardian spirit.[6] To the traditional Ojibwa, "All those talents and traits of character which we think of as functions of a total personality are regarded by the Ojibwa as isolated, objective items which may be acquired in the course of life by individuals who are fortunate enough to coerce them from the supernaturals. In Ojibwa thought, there is no original and absolute 'Self': a person freshly born is 'empty' of characteristics and of identity. Consequently, tremendous pressure is exerted upon a young person to pursue the supernaturals and move them to fill up his 'emptiness.'"[7]

In addition to its social value, the puberty vision quest was also an intensely personal religious experience. If the individual was fortunate enough to make contact with a spiritual guardian and obtain special powers, the encounter might form the basis for subsequent spiritual experiences; at least it would establish the channels and criteria for perceiving and judging other than physical phenomena.

At Grassy Narrows, both girls and boys were urged to dream and to remember their dreams, but the institutionalized vision quest does not seem to have been as clearly defined for girls as for boys. According to the older women, their ritual of passage into womanhood placed less emphasis on the vision and more emphasis on seclusion. The Indians believed that every woman possessed a mysterious power at the time of her first blossoming into womanhood, a power that was dangerous to men and that could also ruin crops planted in the spring and berries in the wild. At her first menstruation, the young girl went into seclusion for a week or so, during which she was given very little food and was encouraged to obtain a vision. Here is the ritual, described from personal experience by a sixty-five-year-old woman: "On the old reserve, when I began to menstruate, I was taken away to the bush. I had my own tent. It was summertime. The older women went to pick berries—raspberries, blueberries, strawberries—whatever they could find. They mixed the berries with black ash, and maybe wild rice. I had to eat this, so that I didn't spoil anything." Although the generation of women now in their sixties experienced this ritual and subjected their daughters to it, the custom was not carried over to the new reserve. The last known rite of passage into womanhood was held on the old reserve in 1962.

Not by coincidence, the boys' rite of passage into adulthood was also last experienced by the generation of men now in their late fifties and sixties. We know very little about the puberty fast as it was practiced at Grassy Narrows. Indian people believed that the knowledge and powers granted to the young person during the vision would be rendered useless if the identity of the guardian spirit were to become known and the contents of the vision made public. What we do know about this practice comes from fragments of conversations. According to Father Lacelle:

> The Grassy Narrows people had beautiful ceremonies on the old reserve that influenced their whole lives. The most important of these was the ceremony of "taking responsibility for your life," the ceremony that took place when the young man was ready for a religious experience, the Indians used to say, "when his soul was awakened." This was the time of the fast and preparation for vision. This fast took place over a number of days, perhaps seven to ten, and was held in a secluded place with the spiritual leader of each clan presiding over the ritual.

The people thought that we, the missionaries, did not understand, did not approve. When I think back on those days, I think that maybe we did not understand. Anyway, what happened was that the old people, they just gave up. They stopped teaching and guiding the young, and as I said before, there is no spiritual training at all on the new reserve.

The puberty vision quest, once considered fundamental to a person's identity and spiritual awakening, died out at Grassy Narrows at the time of the present grandparents' youth. From the time of puberty to the time of death, no other events equalled the naming and puberty ceremonies in importance for demarcating life's stages and shaping individual identity.

The rituals of marriage were not thought to be of great consequence in traditional Ojibwa society; the conditions under which marriage took place, however, were matters of considerable importance. Many older Grassy Narrows women cannot understand how, in the span of one generation, the foundation of customary man–woman relationships could be so radically undermined. "The young people today, they just shack up with anybody . . . they do things that used to be forbidden," they lament. Most alarming to the older generation is not the fact that young people are just living together; according to custom, men and women who live together are considered to be married. What troubles them is the disregard being demonstrated for the taboo prohibiting sexual relations with close kin or persons of the same blood. From all accounts of life on the old reserve, it appears that violations of this taboo were rare. Because of the peculiar characteristics of the kinship system, this taboo extended to relations with parallel cousins. Cross-cousin marriage, however, was not only permitted but favored, particularly among the Lake of the Woods and the English River Ojibwa.[8] In an older tradition, which had lost much of its force earlier in the century, the totem clan affiliation precluded marriage among members of the same clan.[9] Incest (sexual relations between mother and son, father and daughter, or brother and sister) was also prohibited by the same taboo that governed relations with kin. Cases of incest on the old reserve were rare exceptions.

Generally, then, there were strict social codes attached to the choice of a marriage partner. There were also certain pragmatic considerations in the process of courtship. It was not unusual for marriages to be arranged by relatives on the basis of certain ideals in the character of the prospective spouse. Industriousness in both sexes, for example, and spiritual power in the male sex were especially appreciated. A woman recalls her experience in these matters:

In my time, it was important that the parents accept the boy. He had to be a good hunter and a good trapper. He had to be able to provide for his family. He had to have a house. And he had to be from a good family.

Also, we did not get married so young, not like nowadays. I was twenty-six when I first got married and my husband was thirty years old. . . . There was no feast when people got married, only sometimes when they moved to a new house. And in those days, most people waited until the priest came, and then they were married by the church.

Both the Chief and Council and the Indian Agent tried to make people stick to their marriages, yet no formalities were ever associated with separation; the disaffected spouse simply walked out of the marriage. "The Chief and Council were closer to the people in those days. One day, I had a quarrel with my husband and I ran away from him. The chief and all three of his councillors went out to look for me. They found me and talked to me and told me to go home again. If something like this happened on the old reserve, the Chief and Council tried to put things right. . . . But if people really couldn't get along, the man or woman would just leave the house and not come back."

The difference between the old and new reserves in the customs and traditions of courtship and marriage is always emphasized in any discussion about family life. To what extent the past is idealized is difficult to judge, although an element of nostalgia undoubtedly exists. What is perhaps more important is that the Grassy Narrows people perceive the difference to be related to the disorganizing pressures of the new reserve environment. The following excerpt is typical of many conversations on the subject:

Yes, the Indian Agent on the old reserve did try to make people stick to their marriages, and so did the chief and council. And most people then were married by the Church, even though they were already married when they first started to live together. And you just didn't change your partner when you wanted to. You had to have a reason, a good reason.

Now look at the situation today. After they moved here, that's when people really started to live common-law and break up whenever they wanted to. In the last twenty years, there's a big difference. The young people are shacking up much younger than before . . . at the age of twelve or thirteen, just after puberty. They don't feel that they need to have any life experience . . . they can go on welfare. Now, before a woman gets to be thirty years old, she may have had two or three husbands and children from each of them. Or she goes with a man when she's been drinking, has a child, and doesn't know who the father is.

This never happened before, and I'm not that old. There used to be some rules in family life. For one thing, it was a kind of crime to have a baby without a definite father. . . . You couldn't get your child registered under the Indian Act if you didn't know who the father was. Now that was a restriction. When I was growing up on the old reserve, I know of only two kids born without a definite father, and in both cases, the chief and his councillors went around and demanded to know who the father was.

In my opinion, if people had been able to stay on the old reserve, and keep living in their own way, well, maybe some of these changes would have happened anyway. But it would have taken much longer, and they would not have happened to the same extent.

The rituals around naming or puberty, the customs around marriage—these ways of knowing and being do not persist in a society unless they work economically, socially, psychologically, and spiritually. Their absence on the new reserve of Grassy Narrows is a measure of the extent to which certain customs and norms of behavior have become dysfunctional under fundamentally changed conditions. It is most revealing that the only rituals that have survived the move to the new reserve more or less intact are the rituals relating to death, which expose most clearly the Ojibwa conception of the nature of man.

The Indians believe that neither human beings nor any other living creatures can exist without a spirit or soul. The soul is sheer energy; as such, it is the one absolutely essential attribute of all classes of animate beings. Since energy can transform itself into matter and take any desired form, the spirit is not locked into any particular physical shape. It follows that all animate beings, including humans, have the inherent potential of a multiform appearance. The very existence of one's self is, by this definition, not coordinate with one's bodily existence in the ordinary sense.

Embedded in this understanding of our human nature is the idea that the soul can detach itself from the physical body at will; it can transcend time and space as we know it. The soul does this at death and during dreaming and visions, and herein lies the conceptual connection between the rituals of death and the rituals of puberty. On both occasions, the soul detaches itself from the body to occupy a different position in time and space. In the case of dreaming or the vision quest, the separation of the soul from the physical body is a temporary one; at death, the separation is permanent. The soul never returns to the physical body but begins the journey to the Land of the Dead. But here lies a crucial article of faith: death does not mean extinction but only a change of form, a metamorphosis. A person cannot die as long as it is assumed that a soul continues to exist. Death claims only the physical body, the external form; the continuity of the self is maintained.

So far this is familiar, for the Christian tradition also holds the soul to have eternal life. The Indian rituals of death, however, are more easily understood if we share the assumption that the spirit has functionally the same generic attributes as the physical self in life. Let me explain. In the Indian world, the spirit of both the living and the dead knows who it is and where it is in space and time; it is conscious of past, present, and future experiences; it has a capacity for volition; and it needs nourishment and protection against more powerful spirit beings. Indian people consider it necessary to guard the spirit of the newly dead for three days and three nights, during the journey to the Land of the Dead. The spirit of the dead is protected from any malevolence from other powers by the beating of drums and quiet chanting. At the funeral feast, food and tobacco are burned and offered to the spirit, and certain objects special to the person in life are buried with the body. These rituals are still largely observed, even on the new reserve of Grassy Narrows.

> After a person dies, it is our custom to sit with the body for three nights. The relatives take turns sleeping, and there is always somebody who is awake. We can't leave the body in case the soul of the person is snatched away by evil spirits before it has a chance to begin its journey. During the night, someone will beat the drum and people sing special songs. The body is guarded during the day as well.
>
> At the burial, everything connected with the funeral has to go into the ground, everything that has touched the casket. People put tobacco and other things into the casket. After the burial, the family gives a feast of wild rice, moose meat, bannock. . . . A little bit of everything that is eaten at the feast is burned. This is food for the spirit of the person who has died. The food gives the spirit strength for the journey.

Whether or not death occurs from natural causes makes little difference in the manner of burial. But the cause of death is exceedingly important in terms of the subsequent experience of the spirit. Like other indigenous peoples on the continent, the Ojibwa believe that the spirit of a person who dies from violence, particularly one who dies young at the peak of his mental and physical capabilities, has great difficulty in leaving the physical world. The spirit lingers on earth; it wanders, restless and disturbed. Not being at peace, it makes itself heard and felt by the living members of the family. And it begs for assistance in its struggle to depart from the territory of its previous physical life and the place of its violent death. The family, in such cases, is usually persuaded to hold special ceremonies until the spirit ceases to make its presence known.

Given the exceptionally high rate of violent death on the new reserve, it is not surprising that this belief is supported and constantly reinforced by events that transcend the objective boundaries of social life. Among other such cases, there has been the recurring appearance of the spirit of a very gifted young man who died violently of shotgun wounds in November 1976. In the year following his death, several persons in his immediate family, and one non-Indian person, claim to have seen him. The recognition was strong enough to be followed by the customary rites. Irrespective of our own prejudices on this subject, it is evident that beliefs in the spirit world still remain an integral part of the psychological field of the people at Grassy Narrows and affect their behavior. It is also clear that the living can continue to be emotionally disturbed by the anticipation of difficulties to be encountered by the soul of the deceased, especially if death follows an act of violence.

It is sad that of all the symbolic observances practiced on the old reserve just twenty or thirty years ago, only the rituals of death have meaning and continued relevance to the conditions of life on the new reserve.

# 5 • TRANSFORMATION IN COMMUNAL ORDER

The preceding pages focused on the Ojibwa family, the warp of the social fabric in the old reserve way of life. Generation after generation, the family assigned rights and obligations to each of its members; it taught values, life skills, and social mores; and it directed the individual's quest for self-knowledge, identity, and status. "Part social hybrid, part residential community, part formal organization,"[1] the extended family functioned as a comprehensive institution in Ojibwa society.

The pivotal importance of the family, however, did not mean that there was no "community" at Grassy Narrows. There certainly was, but the Indian community could not be defined by the notion of year-round residence in a specific village. Rather, the Ojibwa community encompassed the ebb and flow of families over a territory without exact geographical limits, the movement between winter trapping grounds and summer residence on the old reserve, the alternation between times of gathering and times of dispersal, and the shift between the old reserve and new locations during periods of berry picking and wild-rice gathering. This constant movement gave community life its ever changing form and character, while other historic linkages and kinship ties gave it its meaning.

## The Ethos of Community

On the basis of the treaty concluded with the government of Canada in 1873, the people of Grassy Narrows recognized not only their common membership in the band but also their belonging to a definite place called Grassy Narrows. Especially those who were brought up on the old reserve felt a part of it; they knew that other members of the band were also part of it, belonged to it, shared a common history, lived by the same values and sentiments, and participated in the same struggle for physical survival. And in spite of the centripetal tendencies of family life, people knew that they were closely related through intermarriage and that there were wider linkages of blood that permeated the band as a whole.[2] The distinctiveness of Grassy Narrows as a "little community"[3] was certainly apparent to outside observers. It was also expressed in the group consciousness of the people, who were aware of their separateness, as a band and as occupiers of a territory, from all other bands.

The community of the old reserve of Grassy Narrows was a very loosely knit social unit. The way of life there was devoid of the many familiar forms of community life that occur in our own society. There were no social classes, for example, that people could identify. There were no voluntary associations, no societies of any specialized nature, no institutions that demanded a high degree of cooperation. Even in their religious life, individual families undertook ceremonies according to their own schedules rather than according to a standardized tribal or community calendar. Until the advent of the Medewiwin Society in the Ojibwa nation as a whole, there was no standing body of religious leadership.[4] In religious life, as well as in civil matters, Indian people maintained a high degree of personal autonomy. There was little community division of labor or community-wide economic cooperation. And as we have seen, there were only a few occasions in the course of the year when social gatherings encompassed all, or nearly all, of the people. In both their economic and social life, the families of Grassy Narrows maintained their independence, and this feature of their community life was engraved in the spatial form of the old reserve. It is, of course, not coincidental that many other Ojibwa bands exhibited a similar pattern of settlement before the federal government decided to impose year-round, permanent, and highly concentrated Indian reserve communities.[5]

The old reserve pattern of gathering and dispersal, of coming together as a whole community and drawing apart as individual family groups, was determined by the seasonal cycle and mode of livelihood of the people. The occasions of gathering combined work and enjoyment, thus harmonizing multiple purposes in one activity. Treaty Day, for example, was perhaps the most important community affair in the course of the year. Its ceremonial aspects—the gun salute, pow-wow, and payment of treaty money to each band member—commemorated the historic accord between the Indian people and the government of Canada. In addition to having a political meaning, Treaty Day was also a festive time of songs and dances. It followed the period of spring trapping for muskrat and beaver and signalled the beginning of commercial fishing and guiding in the tourist camps. For women, it was a time for planting gardens and settling into a less demanding environment of work than the winter trapline.

Around berry picking time in August, Grassy Narrows families left the reserve and gathered "where the berries were good"; there they set up tents for a week or two. This was a time when the rewards of work were balanced by the pleasures of sociability and merriment. After berry picking, people returned to the old reserve and stayed there until the late autumn provided another opportunity for gathering on the shores of the wild-rice fields. The harvesting of wild rice began with a religious ceremony and a thanksgiving feast. The people burned food for the good spirits and cooked moose meat and wild rice for themselves. Again, social and religious goals were harmonized with economic purpose in the rituals surrounding the harvest.

Finally, in midwinter, most of the trapping families returned to the old reserve with their yield of fur for sale to the Hudson's Bay Company. They gathered to celebrate Christmas and to feast.[6] Then the families dispersed again and went back to the traplines. They did not return to the old reserve until spring, when the ebb and flow of community life began anew.

In this kind of community, with each family looking after its own members and providing for its own subsistence, there was no need for central institutions or complex associations. The very nature of community was perfectly suited to the entire way of life. And it is easy to understand why the bonds of kinship and family would be much stronger affective ties than ties to the band. No wonder that the most effective means of enforcing morality and codes of social behavior rested not with some central government but with the kinship network. Indeed, the chief and the band council had only limited authority to control the actions of community members, although they did attempt to make people stick to their marriages. On the old reserve, the absence of prescribed rules and regulations, the nonexistence of any machinery of government, and the relative isolation of the Grassy Narrows people made indigenous forms of social control necessary.

### Sorcery and Social Morality

The subject of sorcery and magic has caught the imagination of many anthropologists studying Canadian Indian reserve communities. Western-trained social scientists have long been fascinated by accounts of illness and death that resulted from mysterious and supernatural causes. They have recorded cases of sorcerers who harmed their victims by means of small, seemingly insignificant objects that travelled many miles to penetrate the victim's body, causing illness or death. Diamond Jenness, for example, has described death-inducing rituals practiced upon an image or effigy of the intended victim.[7] Edward Rogers devotes almost an entire chapter in his book on the Round Lake Ojibwa to a description of the use of supernatural power in interpersonal relations and interfamily feuding.[8] The level of detail in these descriptions is remarkable, because Indian people generally are extremely reluctant to discuss "bad medicine," the use of power or magic to cause misfortune. At Grassy Narrows they will admit only that "it happened on the old reserve" between feuding families. Thus, much of the information on the use of sorcery as a

means of settling interfamily quarrels comes from outside observers who
knew the Grassy Narrows people well. Thus, Father Lacelle:

> These Indian ceremonies had something to do with the very foundation of
> religion. Some aspects of the Indian religion were very good, for example, the
> use of herbs for healing; but other aspects had nothing to do with medicine. We
> found that some medicine men would usurp power and say, "With my power, I
> can do you harm, I can make you sick." We felt that with that kind of power they
> were in opposition to Christianity, that the use of that power was wrong.
>
> Now, at Grassy Narrows, people lived as clan groups, and every major group
> had their own medicine man or healer. In the band as a whole, there might also
> be one who was more powerful than the rest. . . . Some of these clans, they have
> used their medicine men against each other. That has been said. People have
> told me that. I know there is something there, and to them it is real. I don't think
> we [the missionaries] ever came close to breaking that down. They don't let you
> witness these things, and they don't talk about them too much either.

The Mennonite missionaries, who came to the old reserve in 1958 and
have been residents at Grassy Narrows ever since, have also referred to
several cases of mysterious death and illness that seemed to be caused by
bad medicine. One of these missionaries, a nurse by training, was a witness to the deaths of a number of adults and children that the community
explained as the result of "a curse sent by someone." Personal skepticism
notwithstanding, she admitted that she could not explain these deaths in
any other way.

Other long-term observers believe that if bad medicine was practiced in
communities with which the Grassy Narrows people had a close and
historic association, it must also have been practiced on the old reserve.
This speaker is a man who has worked with the Department of Indian
Affairs for most of his life:

> In my view, there was a much closer connection between the Grassy Narrows
> people and the people northward than between Grassy people and people
> along the English-Wabigoon River, like the Whitedog people. For instance, you
> notice that many old women at Grassy wear tams. This comes from Pekangi-
> kum, where the women also wear tams. You will also notice a preference for
> bright colors among the Grassy women. This is true in Pekangikum as well.
>
> The northern connection is simple to explain. Many Grassy Narrows families
> had their traplines north of Red Lake, next to the Pekangikum people's
> traplines. They intermarried. The Grassy people say they are friends with the
> Pekangikum people.
>
> I was at Pekangikum for eleven years; I started with them twenty-five years
> ago. The Pekangikum people practiced Indian medicine. They had shaking
> tent ceremonies.[9] Many were very good people; I knew one well who was a
> medicine man. He still used to go out in the bush alone and fast for six days
> when he needed something, some special power. Now, he used his power for
> healing, but there were those who used the same power to hurt others. This bad

medicine was all over the place, and it must have been at Grassy too. In some places, the Indian people say the abuse of Indian medicine continues to this day.

A respected elder in Grassy Narrows (now deceased) once told me that perhaps the terrible violence and cruelty of the new reserve are "a punishment, sent by the Great Spirit, for the curses and bad medicine used by certain families on the old reserve."[10]

I include these observations on the practice of sorcery on the old reserve not only because the use of supernatural power is intrinsically fascinating but also because sorcery appears to have been an important instrument for regulating social conduct. In a community without formal laws, without courts, judges, or police, the fear of supernatural power probably played a crucial role in maintaining certain standards in the conduct of relations among family groups. In a subsistence society, for example, where there was an ever present possibility of starvation, people had the supreme obligation of sharing with members of the group. If they did not, their behavior had to be punished, because it violated an ethical principle and endangered the survival of the group. Under these conditions, moreover, no man could be allowed to interfere with the livelihood of others, by stealing equipment, by interfering with trapping, or by impeding the pursuit of game. When faced with such transgressions, the Ojibwa seldom engaged in open expressions of anger or face-to-face confrontation; instead, they retaliated by covert means, namely, by the use of sorcery and magic to punish those who violated social norms.[11]

Aside from justifiable provocations for the use of sorcery, Indian people often attributed human vicissitudes to a "curse sent by someone," whether or not the misfortune was produced by a curse or by chance or accident. They believed that impersonal forces were never the real causes of events; somebody had to be responsible. Over time, the expectations that sorcery was probably involved in the inevitable hazards of life, like illness, misadventure, or death, led to feuds among the Grassy Narrows families. From all accounts, these feuds were an ever present characteristic of the way of life on the old reserve. Indeed, fear and suspicion of covert malevolence from other clan groups continue to operate to this day. "In the last analysis, almost everyone still believes that it is possible for another person to harm him by covert means. . . . Sorcery can emanate not only from individuals of other clan groups, but from one's own relatives. . . . It is reasonable to assert that the major factor which was at the root of the latent suspicion and distrust that colored interpersonal relations of the Indians of earlier periods still operates today. . . . This is the psychological explanation of the 'atomism' or individualism of Ojibwa society."[12]

Even on the new reserve, the possibility of sorcery is real, because
people continue to act as if it were; thus, older attitudes toward the nature
of the phenomenal world are constituents of present-day thought, feeling, and social behavior. A contemporary illustration speaks eloquently to
this point. The speaker is Hiro Miyamatsu, a Japanese photojournalist
who lived at Grassy Narrows from October 1975 to the end of 1979:

> One day, someone brought an old Medewiwin scroll to the reserve. It had been
> found by a commercial fisherman in a crack along the cliffs of the English-
> Wabigoon River. The scroll found its way into my hands.
>
> It was made of birch bark which I forced open. It was about eight feet long,
> composed of about nine individual pieces held together by carefully crafted
> leather bindings. Inside were pictographs etched into the bark, very well pre-
> served. This scroll would have belonged to an individual of significant spiritual
> power, a man of some standing in the community.
>
> Uncertain what to do with it, I took it to the chief, who was visiting the house
> of a friend. As I entered the house with the scroll in my hand, the chief immedi-
> ately got up, began shouting at me, and rushed outside. At the same time, his
> friend jumped up, ran into the bedroom, and from there shouted in Ojibway to
> take the thing back where it belonged. I was very surprised at the obvious panic.
> But this man, Tony, was also in the house at the time. He wanted to see the
> scroll. He wanted to touch it.
>
> Later in the afternoon when I returned home, I received an astonishing
> message. Tony, thirty-five years old, was reported to have had a stroke. I
> rushed to his place. He was lying on a sofa, with one leg paralyzed and the pupils
> of his eyes dilated. Somehow, we managed to get him into my van, and we
> rushed down the Jones Road to Kenora. An ambulance, previously arranged by
> telephone, met us halfway.
>
> When I returned to the reserve, people were eyeing me with great suspicion.
> They thought that I had deliberately exposed Tony to the power of bad medi-
> cine. They believed that the scroll should not have been brought into the re-
> serve, that it was the personal property of a medicine man, and that therefore it
> could cause harm to those who were exposed to it.
>
> I decided to let the strong reaction simmer for a few days. Fortunately Tony
> recovered and came back to the reserve the next day. I realized the power of old
> beliefs and the fear that still exists among the people. The fact is that outsiders
> are always suspect. And once the trust of the people is lost, it takes an extraordi-
> nary effort to recover it.

This example underlines the continuing power of beliefs in sorcery and
the fear and anxiety surrounding any artifacts that might have belonged
to a user of supernatural power. Whether or not the stroke was real and
caused by exposure to the scroll is not the issue. The victim believed it was
real and caused by the Medewiwin scroll; members of his family also
believed that this was so. Indeed, one has to wonder how the people of
Grassy Narrows can ever achieve a high degree of mutual cooperation

and trust when their outlook continues to be colored by the expectation of covert malevolence from other clan groups whose artifacts are still in existence. Such attitudes obviously have a bearing on the nature of politics and government in the Indian community.

## The Eclipse of Self-Government

The community of the old reserve of Grassy Narrows, which consisted of about a dozen clan groups and a total population of not more than two hundred persons, was nominally governed by a chief and his council. From the time of the treaty, in 1873, when the people were formally recognized as a "band," to 1933, the position of chief was hereditary and passed along the male line of descent: "Long ago, chiefs were elected for a very long time, a lifetime. . . . Sah-katch-eway signed Treaty No. 3, and then his son [Pierrot] succeeded him and was chief for many, many years. After he died, that's when things began to change. Our chiefs stopped being hereditary, even though that's the way it's supposed to be. After Pierrot, the government told us we had to elect chiefs for a term of three years."

The chief was expected to set an example for his people in all areas. In times of scarcity, he had to be a good hunter and trapper to ensure the survival of those in need. He had to be spiritually knowledgeable and faithful in his personal comportment to community norms of behavior. He also had to come from a large and powerful clan group. All the qualities that determined his recruitment—his character, connections, and ability—also helped to maintain his incumbency, for there were no formal means by which he kept his job.

The position of chief entailed certain obligations and responsibilities. But because the chief's powers were limited, his duties were not onerous. He was expected to receive delegations from other communities, to deal with the Indian Agent over the security of treaty rights, to ensure that all band members had equal access to life-supporting resources, and to settle interfamily disputes, particularly over hunting and trapping territories. Above all, the chief was expected to keep in close touch with his people and help them with their problems.

In conversations with me about band government on the old reserve, the older people of Grassy Narrows invariably lament the changes that have taken place since the relocation:

> The way in which the Chief and Council worked on the old reserve was different than now. . . . The chief was like the head of all the councillors. Each councillor had something to do. One councillor was like a policeman; he had to keep the peace and look after complaints . . . but we didn't have as much trouble on the old reserve as we do now with people who do bad things. If the problem was

something the chief couldn't handle, he'd wait until Treaty Day for the RCMP to solve the problem. Another councillor looked after the distribution of nets, ammunition, and other things issued by the Indian Agent.

Whenever somebody was sick or couldn't provide his family with food, the chief appointed a councillor to go around and collect tea, snuff, sugar, lard, flour. Everybody had to make a contribution. Also people used to hunt by families, and meat was never wasted. It was dried, smoked, made into a powder and added to stew or soup. Sometimes meat from a big hunt would be shared with other families. It was the job of the councillor to distribute the meat; it was the job of the chief to make sure that people had enough. That's how people helped each other, because we didn't have welfare on the old reserve, and only very old people got rations from the government. Today, people just don't take care of each other like they used to.

The chief was supposed to be a man who set a good example in trapping, in family life. . . . He'd go around and make sure that people were trapping. If they weren't, he'd talk to them, find out why. I also remember that he wanted every family to have a garden. He got the tools and seeds from the Indian Agent and then got maybe a dozen men with picks and hoes to go around and help with the gardens. There's no help like that today.

On the old reserve, the chief appointed a kind of spokesman, someone who could explain to the kids about the Indian way of life. He was an old man, like a teacher. And there were other old people who were like advisers to the chief, who helped him make decisions.

The Chief and Council never decided important things alone. They had a meeting. They called everybody to come to the community hall on the old reserve. Now, the chief and council have a meeting and it's private. They lock themselves up in a room and make decisions for everybody else. That's not the way it used to be. That's not the way it should be.

One of the things I really miss is that on the old reserve, the chief and councillors went from house to house. Sure, people didn't live so close together. They had to come far to visit me, but they came. Do you know that since I moved here [to the new reserve], the chief didn't come to my house? Now they have cars, yet they don't stop to talk to their people. All the chiefs today, they spend too much time talking to the outsiders; they spend too much time dealing with the white society. Now, they are government people, just like white people.

The themes of being closer to the people, of more open decision making, of the division of labor within the council, of the obligations to encourage economic self-sufficiency and to ensure a certain minimum in the standard of life—these themes come up again and again in conversations. The older people of Grassy Narrows wanted to make me understand that the political life of the band was quite different on the old reserve. The description of present-day chiefs as "government people, just like white people," reveals their perception of the direction of change in band government. They feel strongly that the Chief and Council no longer satisfy the traditional Ojibwa criteria of good political leadership; rather, they now serve the interests of the white society and the agencies of government. The people blame the relocation for the change; they say that "it broke the isolation barrier and made us vulnerable to ever increasing government interference in our affairs." Yet, similar changes in the political life of Indian reserve communities occurred elsewhere in Canada as a result of Indian administration policy.[13] In the case of Grassy Narrows, relocation was simply the physical event that captured, symbolized, and manifested government policy in action.

The full extent of government intervention in the affairs of the Grassy Narrows band will be detailed in subsequent chapters. At this point, it is appropriate to outline the impact of government policy on traditional Ojibwa self-government. First, there has been a definite change in the roles and responsibilities, qualifications, tenure, and authority of the political leadership. Second, certain sanctions on social behavior and forms of self-help, once internal to the community, have been replaced by a system of paternalistic controls and administered social assistance, external to the community. Third, government policy set in motion the conditions for the emergence of a class society. Social inequality developed as a result of the fact that family groups no longer had equal access to resources, which became controlled by the federal government and administered for the government by the Chief and Council. As people began to compete for scarce jobs and other government-sponsored privileges, they created fiefdoms of power and influence exclusive to members of their own kinship group. Latent and historic interfamily tensions have sharpened and intensified in the process.

Some of the changes in the character of the institutions of the Chief and Council have already been alluded to. It is clear that the old reserve council was a more informal group of advisors to the chief. Each councillor seemed to be chosen on the basis of kinship relations and natural ability for the specific duties and responsibilities assigned him. The chief exercised his leadership through this council, inasmuch as he had no other means of enforcing his wishes unless the leading men and women in the band endorsed them. It appears that the degree of authority vested in the chief was itself a matter of his personal character and ability rather than of the status ascribed to the position. If he was a superior human being to begin with, as he had to be under the traditional leadership criteria, then he would have little difficulty in exercising authority over the band. From a list of chiefs at Grassy Narrows since the time of the treaty, we know that many were also quite prominent medicine men as well as heads of important clans. All were reputed to be superb hunters.

Until the year 1962—a watershed in the history of political leadership of the Grassy Narrows band—all the chiefs were men who epitomized the "ideal" person, combining religious, economic, and kinship roles in the exercise of leadership. Beginning in 1962, the role of chief began to be purely political. The new chiefs were all relatively young men, distinguished not by their hunting skill, religious powers, or kinship affiliation but rather by their ability to speak English and relate to the Department of Indian Affairs.[14] On the new reserve, the chiefs no longer exhibited the traits of character and the linked roles that had previously strengthened their position as leaders; further, they lost the sanctions that maintained their position. In that they became, in practice, an extension of the bureaucracy of Indian Affairs, they ceased to command moral authority and respect among the Grassy Narrows people. Their one recognized source of political power now rests in their relationship to government. Today, the chief is simply the dispenser of the rewards of the system: jobs, housing, and other programs whose funding has steadily increased since the 1960s. With the development of a community economy based on government subsidies and a sense of privatization in the goods and services to be secured from government, the chief's role in encouraging self-help, sharing, and communal efforts to care for the sick and the needy has, in effect, been made irrelevant. Similarly, his traditional role in maintaining social order has been replaced with paternalistic controls by social agencies of the government.

On the new reserve, the chief and councillors lack the authority, the necessary personal qualities, and moral stature to control social behavior and enforce community standards. The Grassy Narrows families now deeply resent any interference in their lives, and the chief can no longer mediate interfamily disputes. Under rapidly changing social conditions, the once widely held codes of social behavior have given way to conflicting norms and expectations. However the chief acts, there are always people who will disagree with him and condemn him for his actions. The attempt to balance discordant attitudes as to what constitutes proper social conduct generates what Chief Simon Fobister once described as "cruel pressure." The chief becomes a symbol and a scapegoat for the people's discontent, insecurity, and alienation. The result has been an almost complete surrender to standards of social order imposed on the band by non-Indian social workers and government personnel and enforced by the laws of the white society.

At Grassy Narrows, moreover, people have almost completely abandoned their traditions of sharing and mutual help. They have abdicated to the very institutions that maintain their dependence on external sources of life support. The old people say that the new reserve is a much poorer place in spirit than the old reserve ever was. And indeed this is manifest in various ways. If a child has been abandoned by parents during a drinking spree, for example, neighbors will generally not take the child into their home. Instead, they will call the Children's Aid Society or the police to solve the problem. People will not feed anybody else's children unless they are related to them, even if they know that the parents have been on a long binge. Abandoned children are forced to scavenge in garbage cans or break and enter homes or the school to find food. Again, social workers or police are called in to provide help. Such behavior would have been inconceivable on the old reserve. Predictably, however, the "white man's system" for helping people solve their problems doesn't work for Indians:

> You white people, you divide everything up. If we have a family problem, we now have to go to six different government agencies: one for getting a job, one for getting welfare, one for taking care of children, one for curing and medicine, and so on. And no place exists to help the family as a whole.
>
> What I am trying to say is that when we lived on the old reserve, our people had their own ways of solving "social problems," if that's what you call them. Now, these procedures don't work any more. On the new reserve, we are supposed to use your laws to protect ourselves, but you can see for yourself that your laws don't work for us. We can't use your laws to stop the fighting between husband and wife. We're not in that situation yet where we can sue each other in court. And we can't use your social workers to help our families stay together. So, we are caught in the middle. We can't work out our problems ourselves, because our families are broken up, and the chief and council don't work like they used to. . . . For you, for the white society, we Indians are the problem.
>
> And all this, what I am telling you about, all this happened in the last twenty years. In my generation. You know why we can't live any more? Because we are a broken people. When everything changes so fast, we can't even help ourselves.

Finally, changes in the stability of tenure in the office of the chief of Grassy Narrows offer compelling evidence of the pitiless disorganizing pressures of the new reserve environment. Under the "cruel pressure" of events following the relocation, the political leadership of the community collapsed. Elected chiefs rarely lasted for more than a year, because very few could cope with the lightning speed of social and economic change. Accustomed to electing a chief for a long period of time on the old reserve, the people witnessed an extraordinary turnover of chiefs in the decade following relocation. For almost ninety years, from 1873 to 1962, they had been governed by only nine leaders. In the fourteen years after relocation, however, they saw eleven chiefs attempt to govern. Many resigned because they could not handle the stress of the job. Simon Fobister, who was only nineteen years old when he became chief in 1976, proved to be of stronger mettle. He was chief for three years and guided the community through a tough period. Still, he was not immune to harsh criticism by the people for his inability to speak the Ojibwa language fluently, and he could not stop interfamily feuding over the allocation of jobs, houses, and other benefits of the new economic order. Because he was also considered an outsider to the powerful clan structure of the reserve, ultimately he fell victim to the competition between two other powerful clan groups for political leadership.

These changes in the institutions of Chief and Council since the move to the new reserve have touched all aspects of Grassy Narrows society and culture. As the government began pouring money into Indian reserves to bring them up to the standards of the white society, wage jobs and welfare began to be distributed at the band office by people trained as band administrators. The much more egalitarian society of the old reserve, whose customary law dictated that every family had equal rights of access to land and natural resources, shifted in a matter of a few years to a class society. A hierarchy of status, power, and influence developed to administer the financial and employment benefits of government programs. But belonging to the "new class" was not related to traditional hunting or trapping skills or to customary social relationships. Spiritual knowledge meant nothing, and once powerful family groups could no longer compete on the basis of traditionally recognized achievements. Rather, the good jobs at the band office and the good wage jobs now became spoils to be fought over by those who could speak English and who had some schooling. The very rapid shift in the social and political structure of the new reserve created divisions between the haves and the have-nots in the community. Those who are at the bottom of the ladder of economic opportunity are frustrated and angry. This speaker is a forty-five-year-old man whose family has been left out of the benefits of the new order:

> The real trouble between families started when they moved us to this new reserve. Well, we still have strong loyalties to our own family, but the real hard feelings among our people are more recent, I would say in the last fifteen years. This is because our people are all mixed up, and they live much too close together. But another reason is that there aren't enough jobs. The good jobs are only for educated people that can speak your language.
>
> The old families of Grassy Narrows, the original families, they are all left out of these good jobs because they are still more Indian, more traditional. . . . How many of these families have the good jobs in the band office? None of them. They are all on welfare. Sure they drink a lot. What else can they do? There is a lot of resentment against the people in the band office.
>
> Before we moved to this reserve, our people were more equal. Everybody made their living like everybody else.

Under a situation of competition for steady, well-paying jobs, the Grassy Narrows people have developed their own system of social differentiation. There are the "old families of Grassy Narrows" and the "outsiders." The outsiders are not only the white people living on the reserve but also Indian people who do not really belong to the original families—

those who have become band members through marriage, who have only one parent originating from Grassy Narrows, or who fall between the cracks of the clan system. The greatest resentment is reserved for those Indian outsiders who are perceived to have taken away the good wage jobs from the original Grassy Narrows families. This man, sixty-three years old, comes from one of the original families that has been defeated in the struggle for status on the new reserve:

> On the old reserve, everybody had to work hard to make a living on the land: trapping, fishing, hunting, guiding, you name it. And people were more independent. They had to make their own living, take care of themselves.
>
> Now take a look at the band office. Even those who do not belong here get wages for doing nothing. Many of those who make money off this reserve are not even from Grassy. They come from other reserves or they're not even treaty . . . they just married girls from here. And these outsiders get all the good jobs.
>
> There are also too many white people on this reserve. As far as I'm concerned, that's a broken treaty promise. Reserves are supposed to be only for Indians. On the old reserve, we were left alone. Now we are run by white people who don't belong here, and by other Indian people who don't belong here either. We are run by young kids who don't know anything, who can't trap, who don't know our Indian ways, but who are running the band office! I may be an old man, but I don't like what's happened since we moved here.

Not all outsiders of Indian blood are fortunate enough to be members of the "new class." Most are members of the new underclass of the "occasionally employed and on welfare." These people constitute the lowest stratum of society on the new reserve, for they cannot depend on clan strength to exert political pressure on the band office for the allocation of houses, jobs, or special favors. Not coincidentally, almost all these people are extremely heavy drinkers. They feel trapped in their own society. Here is an able-bodied young man, with a young family, who is eager to work. The system, however, has relegated him to welfare and intermittent menial labor. He is an alcoholic. When I interviewed him, I was moved by the anguish he expressed:

> Even though my mother was from Grassy, I am treated as an outsider. The chief tells me to go find a job outside the reserve. I've always been treated this way, and it hurts. Grassy people have become very selfish.
>
> The big division in this reserve is between people with steady jobs, like the people in the band office who don't do anything anyway, and everybody else who is trying to make a living. . . . But those people in the band office, they don't care about us, they only care about themselves, their paychecks, and their own relatives. They don't care about nothing.
>
> So, some people have a lot of money, and others, like myself, have nothing. Right now, I am trying to commercial fish. But it's hard. In the winter, I go cut

pulp, but the prices per cord are too low to support a family. . . . There's nothing for people like me and my family. I'm thirty years old and I have children to feed. So I eat fish, because there's nothing else to live on. I have no future here at Grassy Narrows.

This situation of inequality arising from a shift to wage labor from traditional land-based occupations is a breeding ground for nepotism and patronage. The old system of social sanctions through sorcery and magic doesn't work any more, not just because the norms defining an act of aggression (for example, trespass on another's hunting ground) do not apply to the new economic order, but also because almost all the people with knowledge of magical power have died. Nevertheless, the fear of retaliation for some transgression and the expectation that others have malevolent intentions are still deeply embedded in the collective consciousness of the Grassy Narrows people. Today, the constant competition for favored economic positions for members of one's own kin group occurs silently, in the absence of overt face-to-face confrontation. The old norms constraining trespass on a hunting ground have simply been translated to new norms constricting trespass on a family's established sphere of influence or economic territory. A specific example of the new fiefdoms characterizing interfamily relationships on the new reserve, from an interview with Hiro Miyamatsu, brings this point home:

> When the band first started the school lunch program, we needed someone dependable. Because this one woman was the only nondrinking woman on the reserve at that time, she was offered the job of providing hot lunches for approximately sixty students a day. Right away she hired two women to help, both from her own clan. Although getting reliable helpers to come steadily has been a constant problem, she continued to hire only from her own clan. She refused to consider all others, and until she retired the lunch project was literally run by her family. Her seven children and [almost three dozen] grandchildren provided a labor pool. . . . I was in charge of the budget, and my head would spin trying to keep track of who worked what hours. Yet the lunch program was an important source of steady income and employment, so it was understood that it belonged to this one family.

The establishment of a certain degree of control over opportunities for employment is most notable in on-reserve projects, which are most amenable to influence. The band administration, for example, is for all practical purposes usually controlled by one or two family groups. Most janitorial work on the reserve, which is highly desirable because of its regularity and steady income, is in the hands of a single family. All construction is supervised by a former chief, and he ensures that members of his family have good jobs. Still another kinship group is protected from anxiety over employment because their man is in charge of band work programs. In fact, those families who have established themselves in positions of controlling economic influence are often well represented in the political body of the band council. But these family spheres of influence extend beyond the boundaries of the reserve. In the summertime, for example, guiding provides steady and high-income employment. Different family groups have therefore carved out positions of influence at different fishing lodges in the area. Each family jealously guards its contacts with the white society, on and off the reserve, because a favored relationship with bureaucrats as well as lodge owners is an important channel for socioeconomic mobility and membership in the new class.

All these changes in the political and social order of the Grassy Narrows community are the products of a public policy whose main thrust has always been, and continues to be, the assimilation of Indian people. Without the relocation of the reserve, without the new road access to Grassy Narrows by government personnel, these changes might have come more slowly, with perhaps less devastating impact on the spirit of the community. But the eclipse of self-government at Grassy Narrows is not unique. In a study of Indian communities in British Columbia in the early 1950s, social scientists came to the conclusion that "no customary actions, elements of belief or attitude, knowledge or techniques have been transmitted from earlier generations to the present without major alteration. In other cases, the social inheritance has undergone radical alteration, even inversion."[15]

Other scholars, observing the absence of a minimal level of social interaction and internal sanctions within present-day Indian communities, go so far as to challenge the relevance of the concept of "community" to contemporary Indian reserves. The strongest such statement comes from R. W. Dunning, who studied the Pine Tree Ojibwa:

> For the Pine Tree Ojibwa, government recognition and control is the essential basis of community for the people, rather than any internal organization or indigenous expression of ethnic unity. If this is valid, then the collectivity of persons recognized by government as Indians in Pine Tree is an artificial one. These persons who appear to have lost the essence of their traditional culture, and who themselves would have been lost in the larger population but for government protection, might be termed Indian Status Persons rather than Indians.
>
> The Indian Status Person is the person who lives and depends on government grants in various forms to support his marginal subsistence level of living. Occasional wage labour increases his income, but the solid, one might almost say overwhelming, basis for security appears to be not the group of interrelated families sharing a common history, culture, and residence, but the land itself with the implication of a paternal government in the form of the agent who will not see him starve on land.[16]

This is an icy appraisal and desolate view of the nature of the Indian community in the contemporary setting. Yet the same processes have taken place at Grassy Narrows as a result of government policy. The changes have come much later there than in other Indian reserves in the country and have been much more concentrated in time. A sixty-seven-year-old former chief of Grassy Narrows speaks eloquently about the rate of change in the way of life of his people: "It seems to me like two centuries have passed, and yet I know that we were moved only twenty years ago. For the older people, it has meant living in two worlds. . . . They have seen in ten years what most people won't see in a hundred."

# 6 • RELATIONS WITH THE OUTSIDE SOCIETY

No community, however primitive or isolated, can be entirely free of influences from other communities and external institutions. For this reason, our portrait of the Grassy Narrows people must contain a discussion of their relationship, over time, to white society.

This relationship can best be described with reference to three distinct historical periods. The first, from the time of the treaty to the end of World War II (1873–1945), is characterized by the primacy of the Hudson's Bay Company and the missions in Indian life and by minimal state interference in community affairs. The second period, from the end of the war to the time of the relocation (1945–63), is marked by the beginning of provincial government involvement in land-use and resource-use regulations, the extension to Indians of certain universal federal government programs, and the beginning of a movement of Indian people off the reserve and into private sector wage jobs. The third period begins with the relocation to the new reserve and encompasses present-day Indian–white relationships. It is characterized by massive federal government intervention in band affairs, a sharp decline in the traditional mode of production, a surge in Indian alcoholism and social pathology, and an intensification of racism directed against Indian people in the town of Kenora.

## From the Treaty to World War II: 1873–1945

From the time of the treaty to the end of World War II, the Indians of northwestern Ontario were peripheral to the interests of the government and the white society. Even as resource development and white settlement expanded in the area of the Lake of the Woods, the Ojibwa did not participate in the booming economy of the new frontier.[1] They continued to live on or near their reserve lands and trapping territories, and their traditional means of livelihood, based on hunting, trapping, and gathering, remained largely unthreatened. Their economic activities were not yet endangered by significant competition from white people for resources or by government regulations over land and resource use. The state as a whole, represented by the governments of Ontario and Canada, played a marginal role in their daily lives.

In contrast to the state apparatus, the Christian missions and the Hudson's Bay Company were institutions of paramount importance in the life of the Grassy Narrows people in the first half of the twentieth century. In the geographically isolated regions of the north, the Bay found in Indian people a captive market for its goods and established a monopoly in the trade of furs. In many small settlements clustered around Bay trading posts, the Hudson's Bay Company played god with the Indian people. The Bay's tenacious hold over Indian trappers through their state of permanent indebtedness to the company is well-known; there is no need to elaborate on the basically exploitative nature of that relationship. At Grassy Narrows, however, the people do not speak ill of the Company managers who lived with them on the Bay island on the old reserve after 1911. They remember the time "when the Bay still took care of the trappers and made a feast for them at Christmas . . . and when the only wage jobs available were to haul freight for the CNR or goods and supplies for the Bay, from the Jones Road to the old reserve." They also remember that the Bay managers extended credit for air transportation to those whose traplines were far from the old reserve, that they provided rations in times of need or emergency, and that the Bay was the only source of essential foodstuffs and implements. The record of the Company in other parts of the north may be a cause for shame; but in the minds of the Grassy Narrows people, the Hudson's Bay Company does not touch the raw nerve of historical memory nearly as acutely as the recall of the other controlling force in Indian life, the Christian missions.

Historical accounts of early contact with Indian people are replete with evidence that government representatives and missionaries regarded the Indians as savages. They leave little doubt that the core message transmitted to the indigenous people in the course of their colonization was that their own culture was inferior, even barbaric, and that they should be adopting the more civilized ways of the white society. Christianity was to replace the ideology of the primitive man, just as the missionaries were to serve as the agents of change. The entire process of "civilization" was to be spearheaded by mission-run schools. The attitude of the government of Canada, which was to prevail for almost three-quarters of a century after the treaty, is well summed up in the following excerpt from the annual report of John McIntyre, Indian Agent for reserves in Ontario. He is speaking of the establishment of schools run by missionaries for Indian children: "By methods of this nature . . . the Indian would be gradually and permanently advanced to the scale of civil society; his migratory habits, and fondness for roaming, would be cured, and an interesting class of our fellowmen rescued from degradation. . . . The aim of all these institutes [mission-run schools] is to train the Indian to give up his old ways, and to settle among his white brethren on equal terms and with equal advantage."[2]

Payment of treaty money.

The government relegated social and educational responsibilities to the missions because no "decent white teachers" could be expected to live under the primitive conditions of Indian life: "It is evident . . . that efficient teachers cannot be induced to isolate themselves from congenial society and other comforts of civilized life to undertake to teach schools among savages in remote localities."[3]

The ideology of colonization, of a linear advance "up the scale of civil society," and the alliance of convenience between the government and the Christian missions continued until the early 1950s. In northwestern Ontario, the Oblate Fathers, with financial assistance from the government of Canada, opened the first large residential school in the area at McIntosh in 1924. Young people from Grassy Narrows were boarded there along with Indian children from other northern Ontario reserves. Some

Payment of treaty money.

Grassy Narrows people also attended St. Mary's Catholic residential school in Kenora, while others were sent to Presbyterian Cecilia Jeffreys, located on the outskirts of town. These residential schools became synonymous with Indian education until the late 1950s and early 1960s, when the federal government finally moved to secularize Indian education and bring it under the direct control of the Department of Indian Affairs and Northern Development. For a very long time, however, residential schools were seen as civilizing influences on the young generation of Indians, allowing the young to be educated in the values of the dominant society while the adults continued to live in the Indian way.

The residential schools paid little homage to education. Instead, the missionaries emphasized the virtues of a farming culture, the discipline of manual labor, strict adherence to regular hours, religious instruction, and the exclusive use of the English language. In the following passages, two Grassy Narrows band members, age sixty-one and forty-seven respectively, describe a day in school. Although more than a decade had passed before one followed the other into the McIntosh classroom, the curriculum had obviously changed very little:

In my generation, there wasn't too much resistance to residential school. We had it in our heads, but you couldn't say it out loud. We went along with it. The boys had to get up at 5:00 in the morning to clean the barn before breakfast. At 6:00 A.M. we had to be at Mass, and then we had to milk the cows. Sometimes during the day we had classes in English and arithmetic, but all I remember was the hard work, the chores . . . there was always work to do.

I went to grade two at McIntosh. There was only a couple of hours of teaching in the morning: one hour of catechism, one hour of English and arithmetic. At 10:00 o'clock, I had to go for the mail and returned about noon. Then, in the afternoon, I had to split wood until 3:00 P.M. Then I had to mend socks and do other chores like that. We had to take care of the horses, and the cows, and the garden. I was fourteen years old when I left school, and I know how to read and write just a little bit.

Aside from funding mission-run schools, the Department of Indian Affairs paid little heed to the content of the curriculum. It maintained a superficial and infrequent supervisory presence in the form of an inspector. One of the most revealing statements about the attitude of the federal government to Indian education comes from Father Lacelle, who served as administrator of the McIntosh school:

I remember one time, the inspector was in to inspect the school. We had grade nine. I asked him if he was going to visit grade nine. He says no. He says that as a separate school in Ontario, we shouldn't have grade nine. Then he says that he isn't being paid for visiting grade nine, and then, to my great surprise, he added, "If we let them, the Indian people, go to grade nine, then they'll want to go to grade ten, and then they'll want to go to university. That's what we don't want."

He said that right in front of me, and I told him that I was a witness to what he had said. But then he said, "If you try to do anything different, the higher-ups, they will shut you up. I have a family. I have to do what they say."

What I'm trying to tell you is that there was a lot of pressure on people who worked with Indians not to rock the boat. The Department of Indian Affairs really didn't care about Indian education. We were getting the same grant for an eighteen-year-old teenager as for a six-year-old kid. This was still true in the 1950s. They also didn't care what was being taught, although in my time we tried to upgrade the curriculum. The attitude of the Indian Agents was very poor.

Although the residential school system was supposed to lead to the abandonment of traditional Ojibwa ways, and although every effort was made to denigrate Indian values and repress the Ojibwa language, the system did not have the same impact on every generation of the Grassy Narrows people. The first three generations of students at McIntosh, for example, did not experience the crushing blows to Indian identity that were felt by their successors. The reason for this is not difficult to understand: when these students returned to the old reserve from residential school, they could continue to live in the Indian way. The traditional mode of production was still intact, the social institutions were still functioning, and the elders of each family group made a special effort to reeducate the young people in the values of the Indian community and in the skills required to make a living from the land. The most devastating impact of residential schools on Indian culture and individual identity was felt by the generation that was caught in the transition from the old to the new way of life. This is the group that had neither the integrity of the old traditions and institutions nor the security of the white man's ways to guide it. People now in their mid-twenties represent the last cohort of students educated in residential schools. This speaker, twenty-two years old, feels especially bitter about the cultural deprivation sanctioned by these institutions:

> The missionaries had these big schools where they got paid by government. They took us away from our home life, they showed us their religion, and they brainwashed us in the values of capitalism and the industrial society. This was their definition of education. They forbid us to speak the Ojibwa language. They wanted assimilation. They weren't patient. We were immobilized. It was like a concentration camp.
>
> Then the definition of education was changed, and they put the children into schools on the reserves. But that meant that the parents had to stay on the reserve to take care of the children. There was no choice. You couldn't just leave for the trapline all winter. Everybody was trapped by this educational system. But the goal was still assimilation. . . . That goal was never changed.

The heritage of hostility to the Christian churches and the residue of raw, burning anger at the memory of the residential school experience remain the property of the younger generation of the Grassy Narrows people. The older people held on more tenaciously to their Indian language and identity, but they could not escape the gradual erosion of their culture by the relentless pressures from the state to limit their freedom to use the land.

## From the End of the War to Relocation: 1945–1963

Intervention by the government of Ontario in Indian life increased dramatically after the war, when the provincial government, with its constitutionally enshrined rights over land and resources, began to take a much more active role in the management of fur, fish, and game. The old Department of Game and Fisheries became part of the Department of Lands and Forests in 1946, and a new philosophy of "conservation and management" quickly took hold. Operating procedures included new regulations over access to resources, better record keeping on their use, regular reviews of licenses, and strategies for the scientific management of renewable resources.[3a]

These changes affected Indian people in many ways. In the first place, the government established a system of registered traplines in 1947. Indians in northwestern Ontario received priority in the allocation of traplines, on the basis of historic use; however, they could lose their traplines if they did not meet annual harvest quotas set for certain species, particularly beaver. They also became subject to compulsory reporting procedures on the fur catch. Although these requirements were less strictly enforced for Treaty Indian trappers than for white trappers, Indian people nevertheless perceived them as intrusions on their treaty rights. Furthermore, the trapline registration served to fragment large tracts of territory held by the extended family into smaller individual units, making rotation of trapping areas more difficult and imposing a sense of privatization, of individual responsibility, on areas once managed communally.

The philosophy underlying provincial intervention in trapping was at odds with the Indians' point of view. For the government, the trapline was simply a convenient territorial unit, and trapping was basically a commercial activity. Through sound management principles, the fur could be exploited to yield the maximum return consistent with resource conservation goals. Access to the fur resource, by Indians or any other citizens of the province, was a privilege, not a right, which could be revoked at any time. In contrast, for the Indian people, the trapline was a place to live, raise children and teach life skills, obtain food, and harvest furs to exchange for other commodities. Trapping was not just a commercial activity; it was a way of life. Access to fur-bearing animals was a fundamental right guaranteed by the treaty. This divergence of views, here illustrated by reference to trapping, underlies contemporary struggles between the Indian people and the Ontario government over access to and use of natural resources.

The second area of Indian economic activity affected by the provincial government's postwar concern for resource management was commercial fishing. Licenses for commercial fishing had apparently been required since the turn of the century, but the province did not have an efficient system for controlling the fishery until 1947–48, when strict reporting requirements were imposed and a system of licenses was instituted for fishing specific lakes. In northwestern Ontario, Indian people didn't need licenses to fish for domestic consumption, for that was a fundamental right guaranteed by the treaty. Although the Grassy Narrows people dried fish for the winter, they did not use fish for trade until air transportation made it possible to deliver this perishable commodity to the market reliably and quickly. Thus, commercial fishing began much later at Grassy Narrows than at other Lake of the Woods reserves and was more closely associated with the opening of tourist camps for sports fishing. In 1957, the Ontario government issued a license to the Grassy Narrows band covering "the public waters of Indian Lake, Grassy Narrows Lake, and the waters lying between these lakes and adjacent to the Reserve."

Outside of reserve waters, this license was not valid from April 1 to September 30. According to provincial policy, sports fishing was to be given priority over commercial fishing in the Lake of the Woods and English River areas. The logic applied to the management of the fishery was identical to that governing the traplines: the fishery that yielded the highest economic return per dollar invested was the most deserving of government support. Since the sports fishery clearly generated more dollars per fish than the commercial fishery, its primacy became well established in government policy. Fortunately, the economy of Grassy Narrows in the postwar period had been more closely linked with the sports fishery in terms of the seasonal employment of guides by the fishing lodges. Nevertheless, this policy had an adverse impact on other Indian communities more dependent on the commercial fishery.

The third area of Indian economic activity affected by the new wave of provincial resource administration was the gathering of wild rice. Wild rice had always been an important food for the Ojibwa of northwestern Ontario. It also had a special place in the people's ceremonial and spiritual life. At Grassy Narrows, it was customary for the elders of the band to go into the fields to see if the crop was ready for picking. The fields ripened at different times, depending on water levels, weather, and location. Once the signal for a mature crop was given, the people assembled to begin the harvest with a thanksgiving feast. After the picking was over, the families returned to the old reserve to begin processing the green rice by drying, threshing, and roasting it. Most of the finished rice was stored for the winter. In the early 1940s, the processed rice began to be sold, in small quantities, to nonnative buyers. In the early 1950s, buyers began purchasing green rice directly from the pickers and sending it to processing plants in Manitoba and Minnesota.

As wild rice increased in importance as a cash crop, the Ontario government introduced a system of land-use permits, or "wild-rice license areas." The Grassy Narrows band received a certain block of land reserved for the exclusive use of band members; other tracts, containing actual or potential wild-rice fields, were to be accessible to nonnative harvesters. Indian people perceived this intervention by the state in regulating a resource they considered theirs by custom and treaty right as one more link in the chain that slowly strangulated their freedom to use the land in traditional ways.

More recently, another factor has stimulated government interest in wild rice. In the mid-1970s, the value of green rice quadrupled. The quick money that could be made by picking the rice with mechanical harvesters rather than by the Indian method of canoe and stick attracted the attention of white entrepreneurs. They organized to put pressure on the government of Ontario to open up access to the wild-rice fields, even in the areas licensed to Indian bands. The government prepared policy changes that would have effectively removed wild rice from Indian control. In 1978, however, a Royal Commission on the Northern Environment recommended that a moratorium of five years be placed on any changes to existing license areas. To date the moratorium is still in effect, but the Indian people have reason to doubt that the issue will be resolved in their favor. This issue has inflamed their anger and frustration against the relentless encroachment by the white society on their land and traditional resources.

The postwar period, which began with the registration of traplines and increasing provincial involvement in regulating access to off-reserve resources, also saw a major expansion of social welfare programs in Canada. Since these were based on universality of application, Indian people became eligible to receive regular monthly payments under the Family Allowance Act, passed in 1944. The Grassy Narrows people started to receive family allowance payments in 1946, consisting of $8 per school-aged child per month. In 1951, Indians seventy years of age and older began to receive Old Age Security Pensions. Other benefits administered by the provinces, and formerly available only to nonnative citizens, also began to flow to Indian people. Indians over sixty-five years of age became eligible to participate in the provincially administered Old Age Assistance Act, and blind persons could receive benefits under the Blind Persons Act. By the mid-1960s, Indian people in Ontario became eligible to receive welfare and other social assistance services comparable to those provided for the non-Indian population.

These categorical payments marked the transition from the rations of flour, tea, or lard delivered to widows and old people at Grassy Narrows at the discretion of the Indian Agent to regular transfer payments by check. For the Indian people, who were still largely outside the cash economy, these payments began to constitute an important source of income. Yet they were not of a scale to substitute for or otherwise displace the pursuits of hunting, trapping, and gathering. The corrosive effect of expanded government subsidies and social assistance measures on the traditional mode of production was to be felt in the late 1960s, after the community had been relocated to the new reserve.

At the national level, other winds of change were blowing that were to alter the context of Indian policy in Canada. Perhaps as a token of recognition of the contribution of Indian people to the war effort, in 1947–48 a Special Joint Committee of the Senate and House of Commons was appointed to reexamine the Indian Act, which defines the relationship between Indians and the broader Canadian society.[4] In the course of its deliberations, the committee heard shocking evidence concerning the depressed social and economic conditions on Indian reserves. It then produced a series of sweeping recommendations that were to guide the direction of public policy for the next decade. Among many other proposals, the committee recommended that Indian integration into Canadian society be accelerated; that separate schools for Indians be abolished and Indian education be placed under the direct and sole responsibility of the Indian Affairs Branch; that Indians be included in all "reconstruction" measures dealing with public health, unemployment, and social security; that Indians be accorded the same rights as other citizens with regard to the consumption of alcohol off the reserve; and that greater responsibility and more progressive measures of self-government of reserve and band affairs be granted to band councils.[5]

During the 1950s, the federal government gradually proceeded to take over direct responsibility for Indian health and education. Day schools on Indian reserves in northwestern Ontario were constructed as early as 1951 (at Whitedog, for example), and the Indian Affairs Branch began to be responsible for the selection and appointment of teachers. In 1960, Indian people were finally enfranchised to vote in federal elections. The Grassy Narrows people, however, remained isolated and removed from the mainstream of all these developments until their relocation. Band members working outside the old reserve in the postwar period were more immediately affected by a 1956 amendment to the Indian Act that permitted them to purchase and possess liquor.[6] Thus, the families who stayed on the old reserve for most of the period between the end of the war and the relocation continued a lifestyle undisturbed by interference from the federal government.

In this period, in contrast to the one following, the Department of Indian Affairs confined its relationship with the Grassy Narrows people to annual ceremonial visits on Treaty Day. During his visit, the Indian Agent was supposed to communicate to the people the policy of the department toward them, ensure that their children were attending school, legally sanction marriages, and help the Chief and Council in the administration of justice. An important place in the observance of Treaty

Day was reserved for the distribution of indispensable tools and rations to the old and the disabled. Old people look back to this aspect of the Indian–government relationship and recall a not so distant time when conditions enabled families to provide for their own needs. In the words of a seventy-year-old man:

> On the old reserve, the Indian Agent used to supply us with all the things that we needed to make a living for ourselves—I mean garden tools and seeds, gill nets for fishing, shotgun shells, and things like that. This was good. Why did this stop? Everybody had enough, they could provide for their own potatoes and other vegetables. A lot of families had very good crops, enough to last the winter. They used to build a root house, put straw in it, and keep the vegetables there. People had enough to eat. They didn't need welfare.
>
> Now we can't make a living for ourselves any more. The new reserve is on dirt and rock. We can't have gardens . . . the fish is poisoned, there are not as many moose and deer . . . and our people have to depend on government. This is not good. We used to be a proud and independent people. But everything has changed in my lifetime.

The contact of the Indian Agent with the people of Grassy Narrows may have been infrequent and limited to the transactions described, but the people remember well the attitude of the Department toward them: "At that time, Indians were treated like children. Indian Affairs wanted it that way. Indians had no voice at that time." Although the Indian Act gave the Department of Indian Affairs comprehensive authority to legislate on behalf of Indian people and to control their lives, the Indian Agents seem to have had little interest in "administering" day-to-day existence. According to Father Lacelle, their role in community life up to the time of the relocation was marginal:

> The change at Grassy Narrows had been very sudden. There was very little contact between the people there and the government until the government put them in villages. They resisted the move to the new reserve. That was against their grain. They were tribesmen, trappers, and hunters gathered in clans. Tribesmen, you know, are very independent.
>
> For years, the Department of Indian Affairs didn't know what was going on with the Indians at Grassy Narrows. We missionaries, we had to name people, keep a record of births, deaths, and marriages. The record keeping of Indian Agents was very poor. Also, at that time, the agents couldn't do anything anyway, because all policy came from above, from Ottawa.

The lack of access to the old reserve by road, the time and discomfort associated with travel by portage and canoe, and the expense of air transport served to insulate the Grassy Narrows people from unwanted visitors and even from well-intentioned civil servants. Their isolation alone, however, does not explain the undercurrent of unfriendliness to strangers.[7]

In the words of Father Lacelle:

> The Grassy Narrows people, they used to tell me that they liked to be alone. They didn't like outsiders to get too close, and they most certainly didn't like anyone living on the reserve.
>
> Indian people are certainly not all the same. Each community, even among the Ojibwa, is different. You can be accepted in one place and rejected in the next one. The Grassy Narrows people, they were always more unfriendly to outsiders.
>
> In my opinion, of all the reserves that I ever visited and knew well, the Grassy Narrows people were closer to being primitive, in the sense of not being exposed to the outside society, than any other group I ever knew. They had related, historically, to the northern bands rather than to the Lake of the Woods bands, and they had kept to themselves more. This was certainly true of the group that had never moved outside the old reserve.

Even today, the people of Grassy Narrows continue to resent white people and government officials who come into the reserve. The sentiment of trespass, of violation of rights to domain supposedly protected by the treaty, no doubt has its roots in the extraordinary swiftness with which the protective cushion of isolation was broken down, especially with regard to interference from the state in reserve affairs. A respected elder in the community and former chief speaks to this point:

> You have to remember that just twenty years ago our people saw no social workers, no welfare administrators. No police force was stationed on our reserve; no teachers lived on our reserve. The first white doctors started flying in to treat tuberculosis cases only in the 1950s, just before the Mennonites came.
>
> Suddenly, after we moved to this new reserve, we saw government people all the time. They came to tell us how we should build our houses and where we should build them. They came to tell us how we should run our Chief and Council. They told us about local government, and they told us we had to have a band administration to take care of the money and the programs that were going to come from the government.
>
> Within a few years of the move to the new reserve, we had social workers taking our children away to foster homes.

This statement supports the conclusion that in the period from World War II to the time of the relocation, the limited contact between the Grassy Narrows people and the state did not yet serve to undermine the social, economic, or political bases of the traditional Ojibwa way of life. Aside from the Hudson's Bay manager, the only other white people in the area of the old reserve were the Mennonite missionaries, who arrived in 1958 at the invitation of Chief Pierre Taypaywaykejick. Their influence on the community was a positive one. In 1961–62, they opened a little school on the Bay island and established themselves in the community by providing nursing services. Amazingly enough, the first nurses from the government's Indian Health Service began regular visits to Grassy Narrows only in the early 1970s, after the government recognized the risks to health posed by the mercury poisoning of the English-Wabigoon River. Until that time, medical treatment was administered mainly by the Mennonite nurses. A doctor had accompanied the Indian Agent only once a year, at Treaty time, in order to diagnose tuberculosis cases and send them to sanitariums.[8] The first resident physician, Peter Newberry, came to Grassy Narrows as a Quaker volunteer only in 1974. Contact between the Grassy Narrows people and the state medical authorities was, to say the least, occasional until the early 1970s.

In another sense, however, the absence of government involvement ensured that life on the old reserve was a constant struggle to eke out a subsistence living from the land. Though enveloped in a body of beliefs, customs, and institutions that lent it dignity and meaning, the way of life was not an easy one. So some people left the old reserve and journeyed to places like Dryden, Redditt, Farlane, Red Lake, and McIntosh in search of opportunities for wage employment. Those who wanted to be near their children in residential school settled around McIntosh. The trajectory of movement, and the reasons for the eventual return to reserve life, are illustrated here by the experiences of two families. The first speaker is a fifty-five-year-old man:

> I was born on the old reserve, but my whole family moved to McIntosh in the 1930s. McIntosh at that time was like another settlement for Grassy people. We used it as a base camp and went winter trapping from there.
>
> I went to McIntosh residential school for seven years. After that, I had many jobs. Like other people from Grassy, I worked on the railroad as a section man. I guided around McIntosh for about nine years. I worked at Red Lake in the mines, cut pulp for private contractors, and made a living in various jobs off the reserve. There was no welfare at that time on the old reserve, so some people had to go outside to work. But everyone used to come back for Treaty Day.
>
> I came back to the old reserve in 1959. For two years, I was a commercial fisherman and fished year-round. I also had a trapline near Redditt, guided hunters, and worked on private pulp-cutting contracts. When they started building houses on the new reserve, I worked in construction. And when the training courses started with Manpower, I went on these courses.
>
> When life became good on the new reserve, when people found out that the government was giving jobs and houses, they started coming back to Grassy Narrows.

The second speaker is forty-seven years old:

> For a long time, the only job you could get on the old reserve was hauling goods from the CNR railway tracks for the Bay Company. You had to work hard for $2.50 a day. In 1943, my dad took the whole family and he went to work for the CNR railroad in the summertime. We lived at Brinka, close to Redditt, then at

Farlane, and at Jones. In the wintertime, dad took us to his trapline and there he taught me how to trap. After working outside the reserve like this for seven years, dad got laid off, and we returned to the old reserve. He then got a job guiding at Ball Lake Lodge. I was a teenager then, but I worked there too, first as a cabin boy, and later as a guide.

Most people on the old reserve were very self-sufficient. They found work in trapping, guiding, fishing, or they went outside the reserve and found work on the railroad or in the mines. There was no such thing as unemployment. There was always work to do. But now on the new reserve, there is unemployment and even unemployment insurance.

At the time of the move to the new reserve, I was working for a mining company in Red Lake. I came back to Grassy Narrows, I think it was 1966, because we got a new house, and I heard that there were going to be jobs on the reserve.

Thus, there was a constant ebb and flow of people between the old reserve and the outside, and between seasonal work off the reserve and the winter sojourn on the traplines. Some chose to work outside the reserve in the wintertime and return to guide at the sports fishing lodges in the summertime. A survey of all heads of household carried out in 1977 at Grassy Narrows showed that about 51 percent always lived on or near the old reserve; about 18 percent moved to McIntosh and found work there while the children were in residential school; about 18 percent moved off the reserve in search of employment for periods of more than two years; and 13 percent moved to Grassy Narrows from other reserves.

But the people's migration did not last very long; it gained momentum in the early 1950s and ended in the middle 1960s, when people were induced to settle on the new reserve by the promise of houses, jobs, and welfare. Nevertheless, this brief off-reserve movement was an important aspect of the community's relations with the outside society in the postwar period. It exposed the Grassy Narrows people to the more negative aspects of life in the small railroad communities of northern Ontario. They returned to their community with ideas, conceptions, and habits that were inimical to the way of life of those who had never left the old reserve. Apparently this was particularly true of the people who lived around McIntosh. A former chief and elder of the community explains:

> At one time, the people of Grassy Narrows were really split up. Those who went to McIntosh lived differently than the people who stayed on the old reserve. For one thing, the McIntosh people got exposed to welfare and cash. There was no welfare on the old reserve; only old people got rations, $8 a month in groceries. I think welfare spoils people. At the same time, families at McIntosh, whether they got cash from welfare or from work on the railroad, they learned to drink from the white people. The white people who worked on the railroads, they weren't the cream of Canadian society. There was a lot of violence around McIntosh.

When the Grassy Narrows people came back to the new reserve, they brought with them their way of life in McIntosh. There they got used to being on welfare, and in order to get us to move to the new reserve, the government promised us welfare.

The families on the old reserve, they had continued to live in the traditional way. They still lived an isolated life of hunting and trapping. They were not yet exposed to welfare or to drinking or to violence. This is where the bunching up of people on the new reserve, where the putting up of houses too close together and the mixing of clans, became really critical.

You had no sense of being with your own people any more; you had no sense of being in your own place. It started right after the move to the new reserve, but all the problems of the drinking and the worst of the violence really came in the 1970s.

## The New Reserve and Indian–White Relations: 1963–Present

The third period in the history of the community's relations with the broader society begins with the relocation of the Grassy Narrows reserve in 1963. In general, this was a time of extraordinarily rapid change manifested by a dramatic alteration in settlement patterns, the breakup of the extended family and the shift to nuclear households, the beginning of dependency on social assistance, a change in the nature and functioning of band government, a sharp decline in the traditional mode of production, and the transformation of the economy to one based on the exploitation of government programs. Earlier in this book, we looked at the spatial, social, and political changes that so profoundly affected the customary relationships and institutions of the people; in the next chapter we will focus on the changes in their patterns of livelihood. I propose now to examine an aspect of this third period that bears directly on the relations of the Grassy Narrows people to the broader society: the impact of the road connecting the new reserve with Kenora.

At first glance, Kenora seems like any other community in northern Ontario. Located 120 miles east of Winnipeg and about 300 miles west of Thunder Bay, it is far removed from large urban centers. On every side it is surrounded by a vast expanse of forests, lakes, and bush. This geographic situation provides an identity for the approximately 11,000 people who live there. They think of themselves as "Northerners"—people who can cope with a difficult physical environment, especially in the winter, who love the bush and have prized knowledge of it, who work hard and drink hard too. Kenora is an old town, as northern towns go. It was established with the building of the transcontinental railway in the late nineteenth century. Because of the town's strategic position in opening up the frontier to white settlement and resource expansion, two provinces fought for it. Kenora was first incorporated by the province of

Manitoba in 1882 and then became formally incorporated by the province of Ontario in 1892. Most of its early inhabitants were recent immigrants who worked on railway construction crews: Norwegians, Finns, Ukrainians, Yugoslavs, Poles, Scots, Irish, English, and Chinese. The various ethnic groups settled into little enclaves in the town, developing a definite pattern of residential segregation along ethnic lines. Almost from the very beginning, ethnicity was a tangible and significant facet of community life.

Socially, the character of the community was strongly influenced by the occupational structure and culture of the railroad and the pulp mill, each of which employed different classes of workmen, with different degrees of skill, responsibility, and status. Such differences were translated into social divisions that cut across ethnic origins. This patterning of social structure according to position in the occupational hierarchy was apparently characteristic of many single-industry, resource frontier communities in the Canadian north.[9]

During the first half of the twentieth century, the Indian presence in Kenora was welcomed. Only a handful of Indian people lived in town, simply because there were no real opportunities for Indians to participate in the economy of the frontier. Indians from the reserves around Kenora used to come into town for brief periods of time, primarily to trade or to have a holiday, but also to be educated or hospitalized. They constituted no threat to the social order of the town or to the economic security of its inhabitants. Their productive efforts, their harvest of fish, wild rice, or berries used in trade, were much appreciated by Kenora businessmen; in addition, Indians were "colorful" and "interesting." The memories of this earlier period of Indian–white contact in Kenora are no doubt romanticized, as is evident in this excerpt from a book about Indians by a Kenora resident:

> There were happier days for the Indians of Kenora. They used to come into town on holidays, and sit on the ground with their wares for sale, blueberries, bead work, beautiful art work, and leather work. They would pitch their tents in Ridout Bay and walk to town. Their babies were all decked out in beaded ticanoggans, and the Indian woman would strap the ticanoggan to her back and carry the baby around.
>
> Then when the holiday was over, they would all just disappear. In those days, the white man had respect for the Indian people, and the Indian people had respect for the white man.[10]

Certainly the construction of the Jones logging road in the late 1950s made it a little easier for the Grassy Narrows people to travel between the old reserve and the town of Kenora and thus to come to town more frequently than for special occasions only. However, two more fundamental and interrelated factors contributed to the significant increase in the transient Indian population in town and to the change in the attitude of the whites in Kenora toward Indians. These changes resulted, first, from the diversification of the town's economic base. In the decades following World War II, both federal and provincial governments established district or regional offices in Kenora. New jobs were created, oriented toward bureaucratic administration and service. Government became Kenora's second most important industry, after the Ontario-Minnesota Pulp and Paper Company. Second, this development coincided with the greater emphasis in public policy on providing services to native people in the area. Although the town did not need Indian people for their labor, in many ways it became heavily dependent upon them as various government agencies were established in town to serve the twelve Indian communities in the immediate vicinity.[11] Indian people began to come into town much more frequently for medical treatment, schooling, court, and welfare.

With the provision of social assistance, unemployment insurance, family benefits, and other transfer payments in the form of checks, Indian people demonstrably had more cash to spend in Kenora's retail establishments, restaurants, and beer parlors than ever before. The white population of the town, uninformed about the internal changes in the economy and culture of many reserve communities, reacted only to the external manifestation of the "Indian presence" in town, a presence that rapidly began to be associated with the problem of "drunken Indians lying in the streets." By the early 1960s, a pattern of discrimination was well established in Kenora. Indians were tacitly forbidden to use certain hotels or restaurants, while those places that did accept Indians soon became branded as Indian hangouts. Even at the few bars and beverage rooms that were open to Indian customers, Indians and whites were spatially segregated. On the main streets of the town, Indians became an open target for sneering condescension, verbal abuse, or actual physical assault.

The law dealt unequally and unfairly with Indian people. The police would invariably arrest an Indian man or woman for intoxication in a public place; an equally inebriated white man or woman would receive a reprimand and might even be driven home. In cases of assault on Indians, white people expected no retribution from the law and rarely received it; Indians, on the other hand, if apprehended after a fight with a white person, would be tried and almost always found guilty of assault. Ultimately, the native person was helpless against the violence of the whites. This violence occurred among both adults and the young. Everywhere in town, Indians were confronted with white prejudice and open discrimination. Kenora became a hostile place, a racist community.

This very brief summary of the history of Kenora and of the evolution

of Indian–white relationships in the town sets the stage for a description
of what happened to the Grassy Narrows people after they were moved to
the new reserve and connected to town by road. First of all, in a very short
time, the Jones Road replaced canoe and portage routes as a means of
travel between reserve communities. Indians began seeing each other
more often in Kenora than on their reserves. The traditional orientation
of the Grassy Narrows people to the more northern Ojibwa around Pekangikum shifted southward in a few short years to much closer contact
with the Ojibwa around the Lake of the Woods. This development coincided with the cessation of seasonal migration to the northern traplines.

Second, the Jones Road not only enabled the Grassy Narrows people to
get out of the new reserve but also enabled the more unsavory elements of
white Kenora society to get in. "In the first year after the relocation,
nobody bothered us too much. But then when the Kenora people heard
that there was money, cash, on the new reserve, the taxi drivers became
bootleggers. They started coming in from town bringing a whole load of
liquor in. First they asked you if you were drinking. If you said no, then
they said, "Why don't you try it? Here, I'll give you a bottle free." Then
they started to sell it. We had a dry reserve then, but it's amazing how
much liquor started to get through."[12]

Third, because Kenora became the focal point for meeting Indians
from other reserves and for doing business with government agencies in
town, the Grassy Narrows people encountered the same prejudice and

discrimination in town that faced all other Indians. The white society of
Kenora did not make subtle distinctions between those Indians who had
just come out of the bush, who were therefore perhaps more vulnerable
to acts of overt or covert aggression, and those from other reserves who
had been exposed to the disorganizing pressures of white contact sooner.
"Good" and "bad" Indians were lumped together. Those Grassy Narrows
people who never left the old reserve must have felt acutely the tension
and hostility generated against them in town. In 1964, many of them
came to Kenora to protest racial discrimination. This was the first time in
the history of Indian–white contact in the town that Indians from different reserves organized a peaceful civil rights demonstration. A sixty-
seven-year-old elder reminisces:

> The march of 1964 was organized by Peter Seymour, an Ojibwa from the Rat
> Portage reserve. He called all the chiefs together. He called the Director of the
> Ontario Human Rights Commission because he wanted to do things in a legal,
> peaceful way. About 400 Indian people made the march, about a week before
> Christmas. Six reserves in the Kenora area were involved. At Grassy Narrows,
> about half of all the old people went to this march. It started at the Holiday Inn
> and went by the church and the city council chambers. We made speeches to the
> mayor and his council.
>
> You see, at that time, Indians were turned out of stores and restaurants in
> town. There were very few places where Indians could go. It was time to protest
> the discrimination against our people in Kenora.
>
> Two weeks after the march, the politicians said that the march was organized
> by outside influences. But that's what they said in Georgia too, when the first
> civil rights marches started. Indians in Kenora were in the same position as the
> Negroes in the South in the early 1960s.

Indian–white relations in Kenora were not improved by the 1964
march. Paradoxically, racial tensions intensified as a result of the federal
government's efforts to establish greater equivalence in medical, education, social, and employment services between the two races. The Kenora
people saw only that taxpayers' dollars were going down the drain. They
blamed the Indians themselves, not their status or conditions, and they
blamed the government:

> You Ojibway are just as much to blame for discrimination as anyone. You're too
> busy crying over it to get out and do something about it. Let's see you work for a
> living and build and buy your own homes and pay for your own education. If
> you want equality seriously, then cut your ties with the government and their
> juicy grants and free houses—step out into reality from your dream world. . . .
>
> The blame according to the local [Kenora] people, lays on the shoulders of
> the federal government. The government pays them [the Indians] and pays
> them. It buys them . . . everything, and they still want more. If they hadn't
> given the Indian so much to begin with, the Indian would still retain his self-
> sufficiency, his self-reliance, and most important, his self-respect.[13]

Therein lies the crux of the matter. The Indians exchanged the intangible benefit of independence for the tangible benefits they received from the federal government (housing, schools, jobs, welfare, medical treatment). As the Indians accepted the goods and services offered to them by the government, they progressively lost their claim to being an independent people. Ultimately, they lost the ability to make decisions for themselves, at least within the context of the goods and services they accepted.[14]

The important aspect of this exchange is that the system intensifies the prejudice of the white community against Indians because they are seen not to be participating productively in the economy; rather, they are getting something for nothing, they are not working for a living, and, even worse, they are seen to be abusing property paid for by tax dollars. Thus, the Indians' participation in the system seems to be a total violation of the values and standards of the frontier society: hard work, paying your own way, and controlling your own life. The white people assert their moral superiority over the Indians in this regard, while at the same time they criticize the Indians for failing to live up to their own cultural traditions of self-sufficiency. They believe that Indians are poor because they are shiftless, lazy, unreliable, irresponsible, profligate with money and material goods. At the same time, they insist that Indians are this way because they have given up their old customs and values and have not yet adopted the new ones prized by the dominant society. White people ignore the historical evidence that it is the very geographic, legal, and economic segregation of Indian people from the mainstream society, combined with the erosion of the traditional economic base of Indian culture, that has led to their present dependence on government bureaucracies. They also ignore the fact that the very bureaucracies working to "help the Indians" are contributing millions of dollars and a substantial number of jobs to the economy of the Kenora community. An official of the district office of Indian Affairs ventures an estimate of the Indian contribution to the town:

> I would say that the Indians spend one hell of a pile of money in this town [Kenora]. They keep a lot of businesses going here: supermarkets, car dealers, sports and hardware shops, taxis, clothing stores, you name it. All you have to do is look at one reserve, Grassy Narrows. The money paid out to that reserve by Indian Affairs alone is over a million and a half dollars a year. How much of that do you think stays in the community?
>
> Sure, much of it gets spent on wages, but people spend their wages to buy from the Bay, and they spend an awful lot of money on taxis and airplane trips to town. They spend a great deal on booze, and all that money is spent in Kenora. Most of the money finds its way back to this town. And don't forget, all the construction materials and equipment come from Kenora.
>
> Our Indian Affairs budget in this district, excluding capital but including

staff costs, is about 5.4 million dollars, for Operations and Maintenance alone. Add capital, and our budget for the district may be in the neighborhood of ten million dollars a year. The fact is we have a budget equal to, or larger than, the town of Kenora! Where do you think all that money gets spent? I would say that Indians spend anywhere from seven to eight million dollars in the town of Kenora each year.

And how many white people do you think have jobs servicing the Indians? At one point, we counted twenty-eight different social agencies in Kenora who had something to do with Indians, excluding the Lake of the Woods Hospital. . . . Certainly, many of these jobs would not exist in the community without Indian people in the area. And that's about 600 jobs in total, at least half (and maybe more) of all the jobs in this town. In my opinion, if you took away the Indian reserves, you would close up Kenora.

The tragedy is that the town of Kenora is able to benefit economically from the poverty of Indian people that is ameliorated through government programs and services, but the entire social system of the town, and its social consciousness, in effect ensures that Indian people cannot escape from a life of economic deprivation on the reserves. Not only is it extremely difficult to find housing and employment in Kenora, but Indians are informally excluded from virtually every sector of the town's social life. Indians are valuable to Kenora only if they stay on the reserves and continue their dependence on the government, for only in this case can agencies based in town continue to provide services for them. "Prejudice and discrimination are important to the community, for whether or not the people are fully aware of it, the town as a whole is heavily dependent upon the existence of a separate, unequal, and adjacent native population."[15]

There are no easy solutions to the problem of white prejudice, because the feelings have gone far beyond resentment of the fact that Indians seem to have so much money that is not earned, or that they are spendthrifts and unreliable workers. The majority of whites in Kenora today think of Indians as untouchables, as profane persons. In matters of personal comportment, even cleanliness, whites feel that Indians are a contaminating presence in the town. The diverse manifestations of antisocial behavior exhibited by intoxicated Indians lead white people to generalize this behavior to all Indians. The most ordinary courtesies are neither expected of Indians nor extended to them. All Indians become outcasts; all are incriminated. The very category Indian is equated with a stigma, a moral destitution.

Indians react to their treatment as profane persons in various ways: by withdrawing from white society and seeking a measure of self-respect within the reserve community, by disguising certain essential characteristics of their Indianness, or by capitalizing on their situation to win small gains of money, resources, or services from the white society.[16] In Kenora, the Indians' reaction to the incessant undermining of a morally defensible self-image takes another, more self-destructive form. Rage and anger are turned inward and translated into violence against self or others. Louis Cameron, a young Ojibwa Indian, expresses this very well:

> You know, everybody knows that people have to be free to express human freedom. They have to laugh, they have to yell, and they have to be free to move around. But when you push people into a group like that, a lot of that expression turns inside. It's what you call internal aggression. And as a result of that, Indians live a dangerous style of life. They fight each other, they drink a lot. And the tendency to suicide is higher. . . .
>
> This is the crime, the injustice that is being committed by the government. . . . They are taking one segment of society and pushing it violently inward.[17]

In 1972, young Indians around Kenora decided that the strategy of nonviolent protest advocated by their elders as a means to end racial discrimination in Kenora had to be changed. Led by Louis Cameron, they organized themselves into the Ojibway Warriors Society. In July 1974, armed with shotguns and rifles, young Warriors occupied Anishinabe Park in Kenora and held it as an armed camp, with barricades of barbed wire at the entrance to the park, for over four weeks. Under a poster bearing the following message:

THIS PIECE OF LAND
WE STAND ON,   IS OUR
   FLESH 'N BLOOD
   BONE 'N MARROW
OF OUR BODIES,   THIS
IS WHY WE CHOOSE
TO DIE HERE AT
ANISHINABE PARK

the Indians claimed that the land of the park was rightfully theirs.

In fact, the park had originally been purchased by Indian Affairs as a camping area for Indians travelling between the reserves and Kenora. But in 1959, the town bought the land from the government and developed it as a tourist area, without the permission of the Indian people. Therefore, the Indians claimed the park had been sold to Kenora illegally. In addition, they demanded more job opportunities for Indian people in the town, an end to discrimination by the townspeople, an end to police brutality and harassment of Indians, an overhaul of the operations of the Department of Indian Affairs, and a stronger voice by Indian people in the Department's decision making. According to Louis Cameron, the occupation of the park was a sign that Indian people were prepared to fight violence with violence: "We have to fight that style of life that is detrimental to human beings. So we, the Ojibway Warriors Society, believe that the only way is to bring that internal aggression outwards. It must go out. We must break through the same way we got in. We got in by violence, we must go out by confrontation."[18]

The confrontation in the park was not well regarded by the old people of Grassy Narrows who had participated in the 1964 civil rights march. They felt that the end did not justify the means. They also felt that the situation was influenced too strongly by the leaders of the American Indian Movement (AIM). In the words of one of the leaders of the 1964 march: "Anishinabe Park. We did not feel, at Grassy Narrows, that it was the right thing to do at the time. Not even ten people from our reserve participated in the occupation of the park; it was only the young militants who went to the park. I also feel that the entire thing was too much influenced by Harvey Major and Dennis Banks of AIM, because they had been at Wounded Knee and they had their own ideas about how to do things in Kenora. The occupation of the park got out of control. All that happened was a backlash by the Kenora people."

The Kenora backlash came in the form of the book *Bended Elbow,* by Eleanor Jacobson. She wrote, "the United States have their 'Wounded Knee' but Canada has its 'Bended Elbow,' Kenora, Ontario."[19] Since the occupation of Anishinabe Park, very little has changed in Kenora. The town continues to exclude Indians from its economic and social life. For Indians locked into the reserve system, for the people of Grassy Narrows, the town's racism combined with government policies that sustain soul-destroying dependence may yet provoke a much wider conviction in the community that the Young Warriors were right. The time may yet come when the way out of the entrapment is the way in, when violence is answered by violence.

# 7 • NEW PATTERNS OF LIVELIHOOD

## Changes in the Traditional Economy

In the way of life of the Grassy Narrows people before their relocation, there was a remarkable degree of integration between spheres of activity that we label social, political, religious, and economic. On the old reserve, these things were interconnected, woven tightly into the fabric of every-day life. As one generation followed the next, a certain pattern emerged and was repeated for the better part of a hundred years after the treaty. On a difficult terrain of northern bush and water, the people built a life based on the values of hard work, subsistence, self-sufficiency, and independence.

The primary axis of this kind of life was determined by nature, by a cycle of seasonal activities oriented around the quest for food and commodities for trade, supplemented by occasional wage labor. November, for example, was the time of movement of families from the old reserve to the trapline. Until the mid-1950s, Indian people travelled by dog teams and snowshoes; these were replaced later by small aircraft and snow-mobiles. November and December were months of intensive trapping for fur-bearing animals; around Christmas time, people returned to the reserve to sell their furs, obtain supplies, visit, and have a community feast. Late winter, from mid-January to the end of March or early April, was the most difficult part of the year because of the severe cold, the seclusion of game, and the isolation of the trapline. Yet most families returned to their winter camp and continued trapping, though less intensively than before. Late winter was a good time for snaring rabbits, ice-fishing, and hunting for moose. When the temperature started to rise above freezing and signs of spring appeared, families returned to the old reserve. In spring, the men went trapping for muskrat and beaver, using rifles and shotguns instead of steel traps. Hunting for moose and deer under certain early spring weather conditions ("when the proper crust forms on the snow") was combined with hunting for ducks and geese as the first open water appeared and the birds made their way north. By the end of May, the Grassy Narrows families reassembled on the old reserve for the celebration of Treaty Day.

Spring on the old reserve was a time for planting; every family had an extensive vegetable garden. People planted potatoes, turnips, squash,

beans, and carrots. In mid-May, when the tourist lodges catering to sports fishermen opened, many Grassy Narrows men were employed as guides, and some of the women worked as cabin girls. Although the fishing season stretched from mid-May to the end of September, the busiest time for guides was from mid-May to mid-July and during the month of September. When the waters were too warm for sports fishing, during July and August, the berries ripened. Whole families camped alongside the picking areas, using the opportunity to socialize and make merry.[1] September was the month for the harvest of wild rice, a precious and sacred crop for the Ojibwa. When the harvest of rice was completed, a period of intense domestic activity began: families harvested their gardens, processed wild rice, and dried or smoked fish and meat for the winter. Men no longer employed as guides during the October hunting season went hunting for moose and deer. Some worked as commercial fishermen. Others fished throughout the season for domestic consumption and for commerce. Autumn was a period of preparation for the winter and the move to winter camp. In November, families began returning to their traplines.

This "snapshot" of seasonal activities introduces a discussion of changes in the traditional patterns of livelihood. At the outset, it is important to point out that the key development, the extinction of the way of life on the winter trapline, was not an experience unique to the

Grassy Narrows band. Indian people all across Canada were profoundly affected by the federal government's policy of establishing schools on reserves and, where necessary, of relocating entire bands to year-round sedentary communities. We shall have occasion to hear more about government policy later; here, we will pause for a moment to consider the context in which new patterns of livelihood emerged.

In the early 1960s, the Department of Indian Affairs adopted a policy of "community development." At the time, many officials believed that the "Indian problem" was somehow located within the Indian communities themselves. Thus, if only these communities could be upgraded by new houses, new facilities, new roads, and better infrastructure, the problem of Indian poverty would be solved. In cases where Indian bands were scattered and isolated, the solution entailed their relocation to modern town-site developments. Thus, the ideology of "development" very quickly became equated with the ideology of "modernization." Here is a description of the thinking that permeated policy making at the time: "The town-site developments would mean a massive uplift of the Indian communities, as the more 'progressive' Indians would be attracted to the well-equipped houses, work in the industries to be established adjacent to the town-site, and send their children to the new schools built within the town-site. The 'progressives' would provide an irresistible example to the more 'backward' Indians, who would then move into the town-sites as well. And so the 'Indian problem' would disappear."[2]

A critical component of the approach to solving the "Indian problem" was educational reform. Residential schools began to be closed down in the late 1950s, at the same time as a massive government effort got under way to construct federal schools on reserves. At Grassy Narrows, as elsewhere in the country, Indian people were not asked whether they wished to abandon the way of life on the trapline. Instead, they were subjected to the threat that family allowances would be cut off for parents who resisted sending their children to the reserve school. A long-time employee of the Department of Indian Affairs candidly admitted:

> At Grassy, we mixed the people all up when we started building schools. We mixed them all up because we went in there and we insisted, backed up by force and coercion, that their traplines were no good for their children, and that they had to bring their children to our schools. So, of course, a lot of the fellows fell away from the trapline because now their family had to stay on the reserve. And that's the way we disrupted their whole way of life. That was the beginning of it, of the loss of their culture. . . . I feel strongly that we moved too fast, and that we continue to move too fast. We expect more of the Indians than we do of ourselves.

At Grassy Narrows, if the threat of financial reprisals constituted the proverbial stick in the enforcement of compulsory school attendance, then the carrot was supplied in the form of promises to deliver welfare and wage jobs on the new reserve. In doing so, government officials were following national policy directives. A major shift in Indian administration policy in the mid-1960s involved a large increase in funds to be deployed directly on the reserves. Whereas previously the government's total cash input into northern Ontario communities had been limited to treaty payments, old age pensions, and monthly family allowances, in the 1960s government-funded programs quickly became the major sources of income support. As an inevitable consequence of the new circumstances, Indian people turned away from the trapline to take advantage of a mode of livelihood consistent with schools and year-round residence on the reserves.

At Grassy Narrows, evidence of a downward spiral in trapping after the move to the new reserve is reflected in two interrelated indicators: trapline registration, and the level of production, or fur harvest, from the band's traplines. In 1947, when traplines (that is, the territories within which people trapped) were first registered by the Ontario Ministry of Natural Resources (MNR), the Grassy Narrows band was allocated a total of thirty-six traplines in the Kenora and Red Lake district areas. As a condition of continued trapline use and occupancy, each trapper was obligated to report his previous year's harvest of fur to MNR district offices. Usually, this report accompanied an application for the renewal of a trapping license. The annual fur harvest, moreover, had to meet or approximate agreed-upon quotas for certain species, particularly beaver, set for the trapline in the previous year. A trapper's repeated failure to achieve his quota of fur or to file a report with MNR could result in the forfeit of his trapline and its transfer to someone else.

The records on trapline registration show that the greatest loss of traplines due to inadequate levels of production took place in the decade of the 1970s. Over the 1947–77 period, the band lost nine of its traplines: one in the 1950s, two in the 1960s, and six in the 1970s. Other traplines in the Kenora area did not pass into the hands of non-Indian users but were consolidated.[3]

The second indicator of trapping activity over time is the level of production for each of the band's traplines, aggregated to the community level. Statistics on individual traplines are kept on file cards at the MNR office in Toronto. Although there are some problems in interpreting production figures, MNR records are nevertheless an invaluable and comprehensive source of information for identifying overall trends in trapping activity. These data, as well as the band's own records of the number of furs sealed at Grassy Narrows, show that from the time of the relocation in the mid-1960s to the end of the decade, the band's trapping of furs had become very irregular; by the mid-1970s, the harvest of furs, especially mink and muskrat, had dropped sharply.

The demise of the way of life on the trapline is perhaps best illustrated by the trend in the harvest of mink. Because mink is a fall and winter fur, its harvest indicates how many trappers are on their traplines during these seasons. MNR data show that, despite fluctuations from year to year, the average annual harvest of mink was considerably higher in the years preceding relocation than following it. Furthermore, the production levels before the mid-1960s were never recovered after the move to the new reserve.

Muskrat trapping was adversely affected in the late 1950s by water-level fluctuations on the English-Wabigoon rivers. Following the damming of the rivers, the Lake of the Woods Control Board raised or lowered water levels in line with its own requirements for flood control and power generation, with little heed for the effects of these fluctuations on the supply of muskrats. Muskrats were either flooded or frozen to death as a result of sudden fluctuations in water levels. After the 1958 flooding, muskrat catches declined dramatically, and they have fluctuated around a much lower average level ever since.

The harvest of beaver was not as critically affected by the relocation as the harvest of mink. On the new reserve, most Grassy Narrows trappers substituted spring shooting of beaver for fall and winter trapping on the traplines. In April and May, trappers would leave the community for a few days at a time to shoot beaver. This adaptation to the new reserve environment, however, is a major departure from the customary migration of family groups to their winter residence on the trapline.

In addition to the corrosive effect of the establishment of schools and town-site developments on the trapping way of life, another factor may have also contributed to the decline in fur production. When one looks at the prices for mink pelts over the period 1948–78, for example, one notices that average prices began to fall in 1950–51, recovered briefly in 1955–56, and then dropped steadily for the next fifteen years. In spite of falling prices, Grassy Narrows trappers continued to trap mink at fairly stable levels, but only up to the time of the relocation. Certainly on the old reserve there were very few options for making a living other than trapping, and during the 1950s some people left the community to look for wage employment on the railroad crews near McIntosh or in the mines at Red Lake. After the move to the new reserve, however, the relatively low prices for mink pelts did influence the level of trapping activity, simply because alternative means of livelihood offered a better return for less effort. Given both the low fur prices and the uncertainty of income from trapping, it made good economic sense for individual trappers to get government-sponsored jobs, take advantage of manpower training pro-grams, or apply for welfare. Since the mid-1960s, the economic incentive to continue to trap mink, with the trapline as a base of operations, could not outweigh the pressures to remain on the reserve generated by the school and the introduction of government programs of income support.

The relatively higher average prices for beaver pelts in the 1960s and 1970s tended to support a more steady harvest of this fur. Spring shoot-ing of beaver, moreover, did not require the constancy of effort and the loneliness of residence that was called for on the trapline. As for musk-rats, the increase in average prices since the mid-1960s failed to stimulate increased catches. After the relocation, muskrat trapping at Grassy Nar-rows never again reached the levels of production recorded on the old reserve.

We can see, then, that the pressures to break with the way of life on the trapline, emanating from government policies of modernization, were not counterbalanced by forces favoring the maintenance of the trapping culture. The assurance of a reasonable financial return for trapping might have made a difference. But depressed markets and prices, in combination with the breakup of the extended family as a unit of produc-tion and the array of new government-sponsored forms of livelihood, mitigated against the viability of winter residence on the trapline. As trapping was the pivotal activity in the traditional mode of livelihood, its decline had a ripple effect on other sectors of the economy, on hunting in particular.

Hunting on the old reserve was sometimes combined with some other activity, but moose and deer were taken in special hunting trips during the late fall and early winter, and ducks and geese were hunted in the fall and spring. During the trapping season, when families were scattered in bush camps over large tracts, a trapper checking his traps might find deer or moose tracks on the trail and go hunting. In the summertime, a man might take a rifle with him on a fishing trip in the hope of catching sight of a moose feeding on the shores. Thus hunting was to some extent depen-dent upon the continuation of other traditional pursuits.

Hunting declined significantly after the relocation. Both trappers and the resident Mennonite missionaries attest to the fact that many fewer people hunt moose and deer on the new reserve. Statistics on hunting are hard to come by and not fully reliable. The Ontario Ministry of Natural Resources used to gather data on moose kills on the reserves; its records show that the average annual reported moose kill at Grassy Narrows between 1965 and 1970 was 140. However, this figure is considered to be far below the annual take of moose when people lived on the old reserve. One band member explains the decline in hunting as follows:

Here, around the new reserve, how are you going to hunt? We're too crowded here. On the old reserve, when people used to live far apart, anyone could go out hunting for moose, deer, rabbits, what have you, any time, and not disturb nobody else, and there would be enough for everybody. You can't do that any more.

Now there's too many white hunters around. There's too many people hunting right around the reserve. We're too close to the Jones Road, and everybody else uses the same road. Now there's no deer or moose around like there used to be. You have to go far into the bush to find one.

On the new reserve, hunting could no longer be easily combined with other work in the bush. It took special effort, and there was more competition from white hunters. Furthermore, the incentive to hunt for food was progressively diluted as families began to receive enough cash income from government programs to buy canned meat from the Hudson's Bay store.

As with hunting, so too with gardening. The loss of the family garden plot is perhaps the most widely and frequently lamented consequence of the relocation. On the new reserve, Indian people find it impossible to cultivate gardens. Not only is the soil too poor to support a garden ("just rock and dirt"), but the government placed the houses much too close together, leaving no space for garden plots. As one person said, "Even if someone tried to make a garden on this bad soil, it would fail . . . the kids and the dogs would destroy it soon enough." As a result, there have been virtually no family gardens at Grassy Narrows since the relocation.[4]

Guiding and commercial fishing are the two sectors of the old reserve economy that provided some continuity in the transition to a new economic order. At Grassy Narrows, guiding in the sports fishing camps and lodges came to play a significant role in the matrix of seasonal occupations. Although some band members began guiding sports fishermen as early as the mid-1930s, the extensive involvement of the people in the sports fishery did not start until after the end of World War II. In the period 1944–47, three fishing lodges opened on the English-Wabigoon river system: Delaney Lodge, Ball Lake Lodge, and Grassy Lodge. These were essentially family-run businesses. At Delaney and Ball Lake, the Grassy Narrows people helped the white owners clear the land and build the log cabins. When the lodges opened, they became guides, lodge workers, and cabin girls. It was understood that work at the lodges would be shared within family groups. Over time, as certain families came to be associated with particular lodges, special relationships developed between the owners and the Indian people who worked for them.[5]

In the postwar period, then, guiding became both an important economic activity for the people of Grassy Narrows and an integral part of their way of life. By providing wage employment for five months of the year, it fitted well into the seasonal cycle of work. It permitted families to live and work together in the camps. And it reinforced the clannish nature of their social organization as individual families carved out spheres of influence at certain lodges. Because guiding was based on acquired skills and intimate knowledge of the land, skills and knowledge passed from father to son. As in hunting and trapping, social status and respect accrued to the best guides in the community.

In other respects, however, guiding introduced new elements into the culture and range of experience of the Grassy Narrows people. According to Father Lacelle:

> The Grassy Narrows people . . . they first got used to alcohol and beer at the tourist camps. During the trapping season, they didn't drink; back on the old reserve, they used home brew, but usually only on ceremonial occasions like the naming of a child. I knew a man from Grassy who said he dreaded the tourist season because he knew that he couldn't fight liquor when he started guiding. The tourists, they would always drink heavily. I would say that the daily intake of three beers or so was a habit that the Grassy Narrows people picked up at the lodges. They got used to being able to drink every day during the summer.

In the second place, the tourist camps exposed the Indian guides to a class of wealthy people in search of "the wilderness experience." The clientele of the tourist lodges was certainly different from the outcasts and immigrants with whom the Grassy Narrows people worked on railway section gangs around McIntosh. Of the lodges on the English-Wabigoon river system, Ball Lake Lodge was the most renowned for the luxuriousness of its accommodations and the exclusivity of its clientele. Its dining room, for example, was furnished with trophies of big game and fish, splendid polar bear skins, stuffed wolves and foxes, Tiffany lamps, and handmade furniture. The Safari Room displayed magnificent zebra and leopard skins from Africa and other trophies. The entire camp, which generated its own electricity and had its own chapel, was an oasis of luxury in the wilderness. One of the top guides at Ball Lake for over twenty years, a band member from Grassy Narrows, has this to say about Ball Lake's clientele:

> Over the years, Ball Lake was a favorite place for Hollywood movie stars, oil millionaires from Texas, and top executives from large American companies. From May to June, we usually guided men who came to Ball Lake especially for fishing; from July to August, we had very rich American families; and from September to October, we guided single men who were there to fish and hunt. Ball Lake was a very famous place.
>
> It was also a favorite place for the Chicago Mafia. One day, this one big shot arrived with two bodyguards . . . he took two guides, one for himself and one for his bodyguards. I also used to guide for the Hollywood stars. It was very

interesting to meet such famous people and to guide for them. Guiding, it was a good life.

In the third place, guiding became an important source of cash income. All the lodges hired guides and camp workers at one fixed daily rate of pay that was set at the beginning of each season. The rate was consistent from camp to camp, and, because the guides had no organization of their own, they could not bargain for higher wages. Wage rates rose from $4 a day in 1947 to $12 a day in 1970 and $25 a day in 1977. Tips were often more important than wages. The best guides at Ball Lake commanded $20 a day in tips, and average guides received about $5 a day in tips. Although skill and experience were not reflected in the base scale of wages, the most experienced and knowledgeable guides were usually assigned to the most socially prominent or important guests. In addition, the top guides were not subject to layoff during slack periods or to a decrease in wages as a result of reassignment to camp work.

Lodge owners depended heavily on the experienced and professional guides to bring back business year after year. Much of the financial success of their operation was tied to satisfied sports fishermen spreading the word back home.[6] It is not without some justification, therefore, that Indian people from Grassy Narrows say they helped build the clientele of Ball Lake Lodge and the fortunes of its owner, Barney Lamm. Indeed, for the first five years of Ball Lake's operation, all the guides came from Grassy Narrows.

In addition to exploiting the available pool of low-priced Indian labor, lodge owners accumulated wealth in other ways. The Indian people, accustomed to living off whatever they took from the land, did not have enough experience with a cash economy to measure the worth of money or to save it. One of the Mennonite missionaries describes "the closed system" of earning and spending at the lodges:

> At the end of the summer, the people who worked in the camps never came back with any money to show for their labor. The Grassy Narrows families who lived at Ball Lake, for example—they had to buy their groceries at the store at the lodge. Moreover, every night the guides would drink three or four beers, but the owners never gave it to them, they sold it to them. They would take it off their wages. If one of the guides wanted to use a boat and motor to come back to the reserve, sure, the owner would let him take the boat, but the guide had to pay for it.
>
> At the end of the season, no one came back from Ball Lake with any savings. Everything was spent at Ball Lake as soon as it was earned at Ball Lake.

Yet the people at Grassy Narrows liked the way of life that guiding afforded, and interest in guiding has remained high since the lodges opened. Almost three-quarters of the male guides now over forty-five years of age started guiding in the late 1940s and early 1950s. Some have been guiding for over thirty-five years. The majority of the Grassy Narrows people involved in sports fishing were employed by Ball Lake Lodge, Delaney Lodge, and Grassy Lodge; some worked in smaller camps, at Big Canyon Lodge, Maynard Lake Lodge, South Shore Lodge, Red Indian Lodge, and Rocky Lake Camp. In the late 1960s, over three-quarters of the households on the reserve had one or more members involved in the sports fishery as guides or cabin girls.

Unlike other sectors of the old reserve economy, guiding was not adversely affected by the move to the new reserve. The attractiveness of guiding was actually enhanced by certain government programs that followed relocation. The most important of these, from the point of view of the guides, was unemployment insurance. Beginning in the mid-1960s, it became possible for the summer guiding period to be followed by a period of transition covered by government unemployment subsidies.

In 1970, when mercury was discovered in the English-Wabigoon river system, the owner decided to close Ball Lake Lodge. Pollution temporarily disrupted the entire tourist industry dedicated to sports fishing in northwestern Ontario, but the industry gradually revived, and employment in guiding continued to be a critical component of the new reserve economy. A more detailed discussion of the impact of the closing of Ball Lake Lodge on the economy of Grassy Narrows is contained in part III.

Finally, commercial fishing was the most recent activity to be added to the seasonal pattern of the old reserve economy. The Grassy Narrows people had been fishing for food for centuries, but they were able to use fish as a commodity of exchange only in the mid-1950s, when air transportation made it possible to deliver fish to the Kenora market quickly. In 1957, the band received its first license from the Ontario Department of Lands and Forests to fish commercially for pickerel, pike, bass, whitefish, and tullibee in designated lakes between April 1 and September 30.

From the beginning, commercial fishing at Grassy Narrows was closely related to guiding. According to government records for the mid-1960s and a 1977 household survey, twenty-three full-time guides were also commercial fishermen; they fished from the end of the guiding season to freeze-up. Many guides had access to fishing equipment (boats and motors, nets) because they were sons or brothers of persons engaged in the fishery full-time. There were fourteen persons, including four women, who fished year-round for the maximum amount of time possible during the open-water season. Fishing was usually a family enterprise, with fathers working with sons and wives looking after the nets while their husbands were guiding. Younger men were engaged in commercial fishing as helpers. Because commercial fishing enabled people to make fairly good money in a short time, it was an important source of income. Need-less to say, as a by-product of commercial fishing and guiding activities, fish was easily obtained for domestic consumption.

Over the period 1957–69, the total harvest of all species of fish by commercial fishermen at Grassy Narrows was 465,055 pounds.[7] The most economically important species were whitefish, northern pike, and pickerel (walleye), which together constituted 91 percent of this total, or 421,366 pounds. Other species, such as chubs, tullibees, ciscoes, ling, mooneye, suckers, perch, bullhead, rock bass, lake trout, saugers, and goldeye, made up the remaining 9 percent. The average annual catch of all species from the commercial fishery at Grassy Narrows over the thir-teen-year period was recorded as 35,774 pounds.

Norman Schantz, a Mennonite missionary at Grassy Narrows, observed that commercial fishing declined after the move to the new reserve. The available data support his observation. Compared to an average annual catch of 40,773 pounds of whitefish, walleye, and pike from 1958 to 1965, the average annual catch from 1966 to 1969 was only 22,914 pounds. Although MNR data underestimate the total production of fish in any given year, this decline is unlikely to be simply a function of difficulties in the reporting of the catch to provincial government officials. Rather, the decreased importance of commercial fishing in the economy of the new reserve is probably related to the same factor that influenced the decline of trapping, namely, the availability of other economic options that prom-ised an equal or higher return for less effort. In fact, an examination of government records for Grassy Narrows during 1965–70 reveals high participation rates by the male labor force in make-work projects and in manpower training courses.

In 1970, the discovery of mercury in the river system was followed by a ban on all commercial fishing operations. Because commercial fishing was one of the few economic activities that permitted families to work together, the ban hit hardest traditional families struggling to maintain the old way of life. In part III we will look more closely at the economic impact of mercury poisoning on Grassy Narrows.

## The Economics of Dependency

The most comprehensive record of the extent of government involve-ment with the Grassy Narrows band in the years immediately following relocation comes, somewhat surprisingly, not from the Department of Indian Affairs but from the Department of Manpower and Immigration. In the mid-1960s, in line with the emphasis of public policy on the provi-sion of the same services to Indians as to other Canadians, the Depart-ment of Manpower began a massive effort to promote training courses on

Indian reserves. From no expenditures at all on the old reserve, the department's spending at Grassy Narrows jumped to an annual average of $88,000 in the three years following the move to the new reserve. In each year, an average of forty-one band members, representing almost two-thirds of the male labor force, were paid a weekly allowance of $60–80 to attend Manpower-sponsored training courses. As an economic option providing steady, dependable income, the best course, Basic Training for Skill Development, offered twenty-four weeks of a good wage in return for classroom instruction in math, science, and English language skills. For many heads of household, attendance at these courses meant not only a steady source of cash income but also a higher-status form of employment than being on welfare. People thought of these courses as special variants of the habit of "going to work every day." Often the same people returned to Manpower courses year after year. Participation in training courses quickly became entrenched as a way of earning a good wage on the new reserve.

Over the period 1966–77, the Department of Manpower spent an average of $65,000 a year on the Grassy Narrows reserve. Since almost the entire amount was spent on training allowances to course participants, the level of expenditure in any one year had a direct and immediate effect on household incomes. The highest level of spending occurred in the years just following relocation, when the federal government provided incentives for Indians to give up winter trapping and settle into a sedentary pattern of year-round residence on the new reserve. After the initial burst of enthusiasm, manifested in an average annual expenditure of $88,000 in 1966–68, the department's spending dropped to an average of $53,000 a year in 1969–71 and $59,000 in 1975–77.

An analysis of the participants suggests that the courses provided economic opportunity primarily for male heads of household. Of the 247 band members who attended Manpower courses over a nine-year period, 88 percent were men. It is not surprising that courses were seen as more economically attractive options than the traditional occupations they displaced. The training allowances were subject to neither uncertainties of supply (of fur-bearing animals, for example) nor to unforeseen fluctuations in price; they did not depend on skill, fortune, or effort. At Grassy Narrows and elsewhere, the availability of these new forms of government-sponsored "employment" created a unique set of circumstances that accelerated the shift away from the traditional occupations of hunting, trapping, and gathering.

But the most telling change to take place at Grassy Narrows was the Indians' rapid slide into dependence on the Department of Indian Affairs and Northern Development. I will anticipate a point to be made later in the book by disclosing how remarkable it is to have found no record of

DIAND activity in the years just preceding and following relocation. Records of DIAND expenditure at Grassy Narrows prior to 1969–70 are exceedingly skimpy. An exhaustive perusal of all old files pertaining to Grassy Narrows, for example, produced only a set of 125 vouchers totalling $114,178 for wages and materials related to the construction of houses on the new reserve during 1963–65 and for the year 1967. Approximately 38 percent of this amount was spent on wages. Obviously, these statistics do not give a complete picture of DIAND's presence in the economy of transition between the old and new reserves.

Much better records of DIAND expenditure on the Grassy Narrows reserve exist for the 1970s. The data are presented in table 7.1. As striking as these figures are in showing the sharp increases in spending over the decade, they still tell only part of the story. The rest is hidden in the figures documenting welfare payments on the Grassy Narrows reserve.

On April 1, 1965, DIAND adopted for its social assistance program the same scales of payment, eligibility conditions, and types of services as were applicable to all citizens under existing provincial programs. In doing so, the department changed the form of the payment of welfare from vouchers for goods to cash; it also committed itself to much higher rates of payment and a greater diversity in the kinds of social services Indian people would be eligible to receive.[8] Expenditure data on social assistance at Grassy Narrows reflect the policy and legislative changes made at the national level. Whereas in the first four years of the 1960s, DIAND spent an

Table 7.1  DIAND Expenditures at Grassy Narrows, 1969–1977

| Fiscal Year | Amount ($) |
| --- | --- |
| 1969–70 | 37,600 |
| 1970–71 | 106,400 |
| 1971–72 | 143,100 |
| 1972–73 | 356,800 |
| 1973–74 | 413,300 |
| 1974–75 | 377,600 |
| 1975–76 | 442,135 |
| 1976–77 | 708,970 |
| 1977–78 | 950,900 |

Source: The data from 1969–70 to 1972–73 were provided by the Kenora district office of DIAND and correspond to band financial records. Data for 1973–74 on came from the band's audited financial statements.

average of only $5,634 per year on welfare payments at Grassy Narrows, in 1968–70 it spent an average of $29,660 per year. Expenditures on social assistance over the period 1968–77 are presented in table 7.2.

The data suggest a close relationship between welfare payments and the rising level of financial commitment to Grassy Narrows by DIAND. In 1970, welfare payments represented 81 percent of the total amount of money channelled into the reserve. This unprecedented allocation was a response to the discovery of mercury in the English-Wabigoon River and the ban on commercial fishing. Government officials used welfare to provide immediate relief to affected families. The people say, however, that for the next few years welfare was given out indiscriminately and in very generous amounts. One seventy-year-old man blames welfare for the people's alienation from the land and their traditional occupations. "It was on the new reserve that welfare started in a big way. . . . Now people don't want to go hunting or trapping anymore. They just sit around. People are becoming less Indian. This is all on account of welfare."

For government officials, on the other hand, welfare was easy to administer, required no new initiatives in program design, involved no changes in policy, and was unlimited in terms of a ceiling on expenditures. In spite of the band council's repeated requests to the federal government to provide employment programs as an alternative to welfare, social assistance continued to be a predominant source of disposable income until 1976.

Finally, DIAND appointed a special coordinator for the Kenora district office to encourage and provide funding for band work programs on

**Table 7.2   Social Assistance Payments at Grassy Narrows, 1968–1977**

| Fiscal Year | Amount ($) | Percentage of Total DIAND Expenditures |
|---|---|---|
| 1968–69 | 25,149 | |
| 1969–70 | 34,171 | |
| 1970–71 | 90,656 | 81 |
| 1971–72 | 81,794 | 54 |
| 1972–73 | 85,263 | 23 |
| 1973–74 | 132,455 | 33 |
| 1974–75 | 128,475 | 33 |
| 1975–76 | 140,738 | 30 |
| 1976–77 | 124,949 | 17 |

*Source:* Same as table 7.1.

the two mercury-affected reserves of Islington (Whitedog) and Grassy
Narrows. In 1976–77, it spent almost a quarter of a million dollars at
Grassy Narrows on work-opportunity programs. Welfare costs, as a proportion of total expenditures, declined to half their former level, or 17
percent. Even though "work opportunity" usually meant make-work
projects such as clearing bush, building walkways, or constructing a skat-
ing rink, the band council insisted that any kind of work program was
preferable to welfare. As a result, DIAND district officials allocated ever
greater amounts of money to job-creation programs: in 1974–75, for
example, employment projects constituted only 7 percent of total DIAND
expenditures at Grassy Narrows; in 1975–76, they rose to 21 percent,
and in 1976–77, to 26 percent.

Whatever the balance that eventually emerges between expenditures
on welfare as opposed to work-opportunity programs at Grassy Narrows,
there is no longer any doubt that the federal government has become the
community's main employer and most critical economic resource. In just
fifteen years, it has made a quantum leap in the extent of its intervention
in the reserve economy, to the point where DIAND alone now spends well
over a million dollars at Grassy Narrows each year. Other departments
(National Health and Welfare, Secretary of State) followed DIAND's and
Manpower's lead in providing health and community development programs. During the 1970s, moreover, provincial government ministries
(Culture and Recreation, Natural Resources) also made funds available
for programs of social and economic development.

In sum, in the economy of the new reserve the great majority of the
adults are directly and immediately affected by any change in the amount
of money made available by government for various forms of subsidy and
income support. If dependence on continued government grants has
thus been created, it is because the very magnitude of government subsidies for welfare, training, or make-work has eliminated any incentive to
look for employment off the reserve or to produce commodities for exchange in the context of traditional occupations.

So far, our analysis of the changes in the traditional economy after the
move to the new reserve has focused on only one side of the coin, the side
of government expenditures. The other side of the coin is a profile of how
individual households in the community provide for their material needs.
For the purposes of a study of household incomes that I carried out at
Grassy Narrows in 1977, a household was defined as the number of
people who regularly ate together as a group.

Table 7.3 documents the extent to which Grassy Narrows is beholden to
the government for continued support. Of the total of $962,446 that
flowed into the community in 1977 as income to households, 82 percent
came directly from government. Government was responsible for all the

**Table 7.3  Household Income at Grassy Narrows, 1977**

|  | Amount ($) | Percentage of Total Income |
|---|---|---|
| *Earned income* | | |
| Government-sponsored programs | 431,615[a] | 44.9 |
| Nongovernment sources: | | |
|   Summer guiding | 88,935 | 9.2 |
|   Trapping | 21,290 | 2.2 |
|   Wild rice | 38,743 | 4.0 |
|   Private sector wages | 24,286 | 2.5 |
| Total earned income | 604,869 | 62.8 |
| *Unearned income from transfer payments* | | |
| Welfare and foster child allowances | 93,619 | 9.8 |
| Family allowances | 72,024 | 7.5 |
| Old age pensions | 70,557 | 7.3 |
| Family benefits (provincial) | 51,036 | 5.3 |
| Unemployment insurance | 50,421 | 5.2 |
| Disability allowances | 19,920 | 2.1 |
| Total unearned income | 357,577 | 37.2 |
| *Total household income* | 962,446 | 100.0 |
| *Government share of total income:* 82%[b] | | |

*Source:* Tables 7.3 to 7.7 are based on data originating in a 1977 survey of eighty-eight households on the Grassy Narrows reserve. This number represents 95 percent of the total number of households on the reserve (93) during that year. The data were obtained from a questionnaire that probed patterns of employment, household income, and expenditures. The data obtained were cross-checked and validated by an exhaustive and separate study of band and government documents. Additional information on payments made to individuals, aggregated to the unit of the household, was obtained from the following sources: the payroll for band office employees; the payrolls for all band work programs and all construction projects; the pay lists for welfare and family benefit programs; computerized printouts of unemployment insurance payments; and pay lists of training allowances and other honoraria. Information on the amounts of money coming into individual households from such diverse sources as old age pensions, disability allowances, and family allowances was also sought from the manager of the Hudson's Bay Company, who cashed almost all government checks coming into the reserve.

The result of this study is as accurate and verifiable a statistical profile of household incomes as the evidence would permit. Because of the rigorous criteria applied to the calculation of household income, however, money recorded as having been received by the band for certain income supplement programs, but not recorded as having been received by certain individuals, was not included as household income. Thus the margin of error is on the side of underestimating total household income rather than the other way around.

[a]The $431,615 includes wage payments for band office staff, band work programs, subsidized band enterprises, construction projects, and training allowances.

[b]This includes all unearned income ($357,577) and 71.4% ($431,615) of earned income.

income originating in transfer payments, of course, but it was also responsible for 71.4 percent of the total income earned on the reserve from all
economic activities. This table also shows the distribution of earned versus
nonearned income on the reserve.

In the light of the government's dominant role in the community's
economy over the last decade, it is not surprising that the people of Grassy
Narrows have developed boundless expectations that this new way of life
will continue indefinitely. Having been displaced from their former occupations by relocation and mercury pollution, many people feel that the
government owes them a living and that it is the responsibility of the band
council to negotiate ever greater amounts of money for job creation. On
the old reserve, a question like "Who is responsible for getting people
jobs?" would have been greeted with incomprehension. It was understood that each family group was supposed to be self-sufficient in providing for its needs. In contrast, 90 percent of all the heads of household who
replied to this question in the 1977 survey stated that the Chief and
Council, with money provided by the government, are responsible for full
employment on the reserve. Others (7 percent) said Indian Affairs is
obligated to take care of the people. Only a few (3 percent) hinted at the
idea of individual responsibility. In short, the political leadership of
Grassy Narrows has been placed in the untenable position of carrying the
burden of the people's expectations without having the authority or resources to meet their demands. Yet, aside from the statutory provision of
transfer payments, the government can withdraw or substantially decrease its funding of band work programs at any time for reasons of
"fiscal restraint," without prior consultation with the band council.

Any withdrawal of government support would pose grave difficulties
for Grassy Narrows. Almost three-quarters (71 percent) of the community's population is under the age of twenty-four. This group has neither
the knowledge of the bush nor the skills and experience that would enable
it to survive independently of government grants. Furthermore, its expectations of the good life revolve around steady and well-paid white-
collar jobs, cars, frequent trips to town, color television, video recorders,
and stereo equipment.[9] Although most people recognize the dangers
inherent in their dependence on government, they can conceive of no
alternative to the present system because of the extent of the rupture of
the old way of life.

Included in the survey of households was the following question: "Only
fifteen years ago, people at Grassy Narrows used to be independent. Now
almost everyone needs money from the government to live. Is this good
for the community?" Aside from a few people who said that the question
was irrelevant because "the government is paying us for taking away our
land," 86 percent of all heads of households made the following observations on the issue of dependence:

> People at Grassy Narrows can't be independent anymore . . . the old way of life
> began to disappear when the government came in to force our children to go to
> the reserve school, when we were forced to move from the old reserve. . . .
> Today, we need jobs. We need money from the government to survive.
>
>   It is not good for the community to be so reliant on government . . . people
> lose pride when they cannot provide for themselves by trapping, hunting, or
> fishing. But we cannot fish because of mercury; we can't hunt like we used to
> because there are fewer animals. So we really can't go back to the old way of life.
> We can only go forward.

At the same time, most people are convinced that if government funds
were to be cut off or sharply reduced, Indians would somehow survive by
returning to intensive trapping or by finding work outside the reserve.
Others are more pessimistic, arguing that only chaos, hunger, and helplessness could result from such an event. They point out that even though
band members have more disposable income today than ever before,
"people are already depressed, lost, and unhappy." Still others think they
will always be able to go on welfare. The old people are particularly
concerned that in accepting government programs, Indian people are
losing their identity and forsaking their special relationship to the land.
They decry their dependence on institutions they cannot control but feel
powerless to turn back the tide.

It is important to emphasize that similar changes in the traditional
patterns of livelihood took place on Indian reserves all across Canada.
Whether or not they were physically relocated, very few communities
escaped the pressures to turn away from land-based occupations and
embrace "modern" ways of making a living. The big push for modernization gained momentum in the 1970s, after the government's White Paper
on Indian Policy articulated a commitment to the "full, free and nondiscriminatory participation of the Indian people in Canadian society"
and recommended, among other things, a massive infusion of public
funds for Indian economic development.[10] Within a few years, DIAND
and other government departments began to supply Indian bands with
large amounts of money for job creation. New programs were delivered
under such names as Local Employment Assistance Program (LEAP), Canada Works, Work Opportunities Projects (WOP) and Federal Labour Intensive Projects (FLIP). The material provisioning of many reserves began
to depend almost entirely on government funds. In more isolated northern communities in Ontario and Manitoba, between 50 and 90 percent of
all disposable income often came directly from the federal government.[11]

Paul Driben and Robert Trudeau studied the effect of DIAND economic
development programs on the Fort Hope band in northern Ontario.
Their analysis of "the dark side of the relationship" between Fort Hope
and the government points to the generally perfidious outcomes of government Indian policy:

From a political standpoint these measures may have been undertaken to show the people in the band that they could acquire the same government benefits as other Canadians. But when [government] agencies started to pay band members educational and training allowances and hire them on a part-time and full-time basis, they did not make them economically independent. . . .

Nor was the Fort Hope experience an isolated event. Elsewhere in the country Indian people were being bombarded with White Paper programs with the same unhappy results. During the 1970s federal expenditures for adult education increased from $84 million to $242 million; expenditures on economic development programs went up from $40 million to $86 million, and expenditures on job creation increased from $1.4 million to almost $30 million. Despite all of this spending, the economic prospects of Canada's Indians remain abysmal. . . . The inescapable conclusion which one must reach is that as matters now stand, Indian people face a future which promises little aside from wider impoverishment and greater dependency.[12]

## Social Inequality and Ethics

The economic order of the new reserve of Grassy Narrows ushered in other transformations in the Ojibwa way of life. An extremely important change has been the emergence of social inequality. We started to speak of the "new class" in the chapter on communal order, where we discussed the political and power relationships among clan groups that influenced access to work opportunity. At this point, we will shift the emphasis to the economic system itself and the nature and extent of social segregation inherent in it.

One of the structural consequences of the new reserve economy has been the creation of a bureaucracy at the band level. Until 1970, the band's administration consisted only of the chief, his council, and one band administrator. By 1976, in addition to these original members, the band's administration included a social councillor, a welfare administrator, an economic development worker, a projects' coordinator, an outreach worker, a construction supervisor, a recreation director, a truant officer, a mercury worker, and two projects' bookkeepers. Administrative costs mushroomed as more and more people were hired as band office staff. In 1973–74, administrative salaries totalled $27,540, or 7 percent of total DIAND expenditure; in 1976–77, they rose to $90,480, or 14 percent of the total expenditure. The development of this elite of relatively privileged bureaucrats has added to the tensions of transition, because the people at the band office are perceived by many in the community to be essentially nonproductive.

Furthermore, according to the best intentions of government officials, DIAND economic development programs were to upgrade the community as a whole. But in little over a decade, these programs resulted in an unprecedented level of inequality in earning opportunity. As people became dependent on government programs, in a very real way they also became dependent on the people at the band office. Indian bureaucrats decided who should get work, for how long, and at what rate of pay; they determined who should get welfare and who needed a new house. Decisions on these most basic human needs became subject to political maneuvering. Those families not represented in the band administration by a close relative found themselves at a disadvantage in this competitive environment. At the same time, other pressures and constraints made it difficult for them to continue to live off the land in the traditional way. Caught between the old and the new ways of life, such families became almost totally dependent upon the statutory provision of social assistance. They came to constitute the underclass of Grassy Narrows society.

If "class" becomes real as people experience it, then this forty-year-old woman knows her place in the new order. "The chief talks about 'my people,' and 'our people.' Hell, on this new reserve, there are those who work steady, and those who are on welfare and drunk most of the time. We're the ones on the bottom of the heap. Why doesn't somebody give us a chance?"

It is not coincidental that this speaker makes a connection between being on welfare, at the bottom of the social order, and being "drunk most of the time." One of the correlates of social stratification at Grassy Narrows is drinking behavior; almost all the families belonging to the underclass are hard-core, very heavy-drinking families. By way of comparison, a study of alcoholism among the Inupiat people in Barrow, on the Alaskan North Slope, concluded that a surge in alcohol abuse there was intimately related to the rapid social and economic changes brought about by energy development activities. The findings of the Barrow study are most pertinent to the Grassy Narrows situation:

> Drinking is a way of dealing with stress. A main source of stress for people derives from . . . changing social organization as a traditional [Inupiat] society gives way to a bureaucratized "urban" society. Relatively permanent and fixed social differences appear in a society that was nearly unstratified. . . . A new elite class coming into power consists of individuals able to manage . . . new bureaucratic organizations. The new stratification is, basically, political.
>
> The emerging conflicts of social stratification, resulting from increasing cash and bureaucratic power being concentrated in the hands of a few, have resulted in social stresses for the many which are associated with the drinking.[13]

It is important to emphasize that the kind of social inequality we are talking about at Grassy Narrows is not exclusively a function of the level and distribution of income in the community. The data (table 7.4) speak for themselves. In 1977, the average household income was almost $11,000. The median household income (the income of the forty-fourth household in the survey of eighty-eight households) was $11,540. These

**Table 7.4   Distribution of Household Income at Grassy Narrows, 1977**

| Range of Income ($) | Number of Households | Percentage of Households | Percentage of Population | Average Income ($) |
|---|---|---|---|---|
| 20,000 and over | 6 | 7 | 11 | 21,600 |
| 17,500–19,999 | 4 | 5 | 6 | 18,900 |
| 15,000–17,499 | 8 | 9 | 14 | 16,330 |
| 12,500–14,999 | 13 | 15 | 18 | 13,815 |
| 10,000–12,499 | 12 | 14 | 15 | 11,250 |
| 7,500–9,999 | 19 | 21 | 21 | 8,560 |
| 5,000–7,499 | 18 | 20 | 12 | 6,400 |
| 4,999 or less | 8 | 9 | 3 | 4,300 |

figures represent after-tax income, however, since Indian people pay no federal or provincial taxes on income earned on the reserve and they are also exempt from property tax, excise tax, and sales tax on goods purchased for use on the reserve. Although household size is an important factor (table 7.5), income inequality is not nearly as pronounced at Grassy Narrows as it is in Canadian society as a whole.

In spite of the relative affluence of the Grassy Narrows people today, many families feel much poorer than they did on the old reserve. Their feeling of deprivation, however, is related not to the level of their income but rather to its source. The 1977 survey produced an interesting finding: those heads of household who felt they were on "the bottom of the heap" had one thing in common. At least 40 percent or more of their total annual income came from welfare and other transfer payments. Actually a substantial portion of households at Grassy Narrows depend heavily on nonearned income for subsistence (table 7.6).

Of the thirty-three heads of household who derive less than 24 percent of their total annual income from transfer payments, half are between twenty and twenty-four years of age and two-thirds are less than thirty-four years of age. All are employed full-time; eighteen work in the band administration, twelve have steady jobs in various band work projects, and three work in the private sector. In contrast, of the nineteen heads of household who derive between 40 and 74 percent of their total income from transfer payments, sixteen are over thirty-five years of age. All members of this latter group have to rely to a much greater extent on income from trapping and guiding, and they depend heavily on welfare and/or unemployment insurance between periods of occasional work and participation in traditional activities. Many people in this group face major barriers to occupational mobility. Finally, the group that is most de-

**Table 7.5   Household Income and Household Size, 1977**

| Household Size | Number of Households | Average Income ($)[a] |
|---|---|---|
| Single individual[b] | 10 | 5,040 |
| Two persons[c] | 9 | 6,040 |
| Three persons | 15 | 8,975 |
| Four persons | 13 | 11,535 |
| Five persons | 8 | 15,730 |
| Six persons | 7 | 10,370 |
| Seven persons | 11 | 12,855 |
| Eight persons[d] | 5 | 11,960 |
| Nine persons | 6 | 17,535 |
| Ten persons | 2 | 12,850 |
| Eleven persons | 1 | 18,190 |
| Thirteen persons | 1 | 24,400 |
| | 88 | |

[a]Average income figures have been rounded to the nearest 0 or 5.

[b]Single individuals usually live in a house with other people, but they may not share their food and/or income with them. In this group, three people receive their entire income from social assistance, the remainder depend on a mix of social assistance and occasional wage labor.

[c]Of these two-person households, five couples are pensioners, and the rest depend heavily on welfare. In general, households of three or more persons earn an increasing portion of income from wages.

[d]The heaviest dependence on welfare as a source of income is shown by larger households. For example, of the five households consisting of eight persons, only one does not depend on welfare as a primary source of income. Of the six nine-person households, five are completely dependent on welfare. The thirteen-person household receives more than half of its income from social assistance.

pendent upon transfer payments as a source of income includes old age pensioners, single parents, disabled persons, and female heads of household.

In sum, the economic system of the new reserve is inherently discriminatory. For the limited number of year-round jobs available, two-thirds of which are in band administration, the system favors younger people who speak English, who can deal with the outside society on its own terms, and who can service the needs of the government agencies that fuel the economy in the first place. No wonder that the older and more traditional families of Grassy Narrows feel excluded from the benefits of the new economic order. Given the traditional values of personal autonomy, self-reliance, and hard work, their dependence on welfare has a stigmatizing social effect.

Table 7.6   Dependence on Transfer Payments, 1977

| Percentage of Total Annual Household Income Derived from Transfer Payments | Number of Heads of Household | Percentage of Total Households |
|:---:|:---:|:---:|
| 75–100 | 17 | 20 |
| 50–74 | 9 | 10 |
| 40–49 | 10 | 11 |
| 25–39 | 19 | 22 |
| 0–24 | 33 | 37 |
|  | 88 | 100 |

But that's not all. The new economic system provides its own ethic, which, like acid on metal, slowly dissolves other cherished values of the Ojibwa way of life. Anthropologist Michael Asch defines the problem as follows:

> An aspect of the traditional economy is the value placed on collective organization of the work, on the sharing of results, on the notion of a group sustaining itself or reproducing itself. In general, this is not the view that we take as westerners . . . and this is reflected in the way in which we organize our economy as a whole . . . in particular the wage economy. There is one thing for sure, and that is that wages are paid to individuals. That emphasizes that it's the individual rather than the group that has been responsible for whatever the labor component was that provided this wage.
>
> [Furthermore] the social relationships that one enters into in a wage economy, and particularly as a worker, are the kinds of institutions that are very different from the institutions that exist in the bush. In the bush there is perhaps a boss, a leader of some sort, but he is selected by the group to be that leader by some traditional means . . . and no one truly bosses someone else around. The fact is that the structure of our economy is very much one of a chain of command; there is a boss, there is a worker. . . . For a native person to move into this kind of orientation . . . is to submit to two different ways of dealing with the world.[14]

Moreover, the new economic order undermined customary Indian values of sharing and mutual aid. On the old reserve, bush resources such as moose meat and wild rice were always shared within the kin group. Cash income, on the other hand, was treated as private property and was not shared except perhaps to purchase certain tools that were needed by the kin group. It is not surprising, therefore, that the form in which payments of wages or welfare were given on the new reserve—that is, to individual households—contributed to a fundamental shift in communal ethics, away from the Indian values of mutual sharing and toward the values of individual accumulation characteristic of our own society.

Just like wages which are paid to the individual, so welfare is paid to the individual household on the basis of the needs of that household. If we talk about the needs of households in a traditional way of life . . . [they] are met by the collective responsibility of all of the households in the local group. Now with welfare, what happens is that the responsibility that is held collectively, by the extended family to each of the individual households within it, is cancelled. And what you get then is the beginning of the individualization of poverty, the beginning of the marking of who's making it and who isn't making it, the beginning of rich and poor. That is a very important negative consequence of using welfare payments.[15]

Some Grassy Narrows people are conscious of the effect of welfare on the values of collective responsibility and mutual help. "Welfare is a real problem for us. We don't support each other any more. On the old reserve, if a man had a broken leg and couldn't get his own food or couldn't chop his own wood, the neighbors or somebody would chip in and help him with his wood, or with food, or whatever. Today, as soon as a family runs out of groceries because they spent all their money on booze, the people go and see the welfare administrator. This dependency on welfare is bad for the community."

The speakers, a young husband and wife, make a subtle distinction by using the word *food* when speaking of the old reserve and *groceries* when referring to the new reserve. This choice of words embodies crucial differences in meaning. It leads us to consider the effect of the new economics on the diet and health of the Grassy Narrows people.

## The New Economics and Diet

It would not be an exaggeration to suggest that the economy created by government cash subsidies contributed to a sudden and radical shift in traditional patterns of food production, preparation, and diet. In a span of only one generation, the Grassy Narrows people changed from being active producers of most of their own food to passive consumers of store-bought groceries. Their eating habits changed from a protein-rich diet of game and fish to a nutritionally inferior diet of imported food staples heavy in starch and sugar.

On the old reserve, people relied predominantly on "country food" like moose, deer, beaver, muskrat, and rabbit; on fish like pickerel, whitefish, trout, and northern pike; on fowl like ducks, wild geese, and partridge. Both meat and fish were smoked or dried for winter use. Berries like strawberries, blueberries, and raspberries were gathered and dried. Much of the Indians' vitamin A and C came from berries, and dried raspberries were used to reduce fever. People also gathered other vegetable food, such as roots and leaf greens, to supplement meat and fish. Thus the diet was rich in protein but not completely devoid of carbohydrates. Bannock made from flour was an important staple after the advent of trading and trapping, and wild rice always had a very special place in the culture of the northwestern Ontario Ojibwa. Certain vegetables such as potatoes, onions, turnips, and squash were cultivated in family garden plots and kept in root cellars for winter use. Imported food was limited to flour, lard, baking powder, salt, sugar, raisins, tea, and canned evaporated milk, purchased from the Hudson's Bay store. The quest for food was not only an integral part of the mode of livelihood on the old reserve; it was also closely linked to other aspects of the culture, to moral values, spiritual beliefs, ceremonial practices, and social customs.

After the relocation, the quest for food lost its central place in the way of life of the Grassy Narrows people. As male heads of household went to work for wages from eight to four, or for training allowances from nine to five, women went shopping for groceries at the Hudson's Bay store. The Bay, of course, expanded its stock to take advantage of the influx of cash income into the new reserve. Its new location on the Jones Road also made it easier to obtain a greater variety of foodstuffs from Kenora. By the early 1970s, the Grassy Narrows people were buying over 75 percent of their food supplies from the Bay.[16] They were buying primarily white bread, prepared macaroni dinners, canned beef stew, pork sausage and hamburger, cans of spaghetti and pork and beans, white rice, and large quantities of "junk food" and carbonated beverages.

The shift from "country food" to store-bought groceries has had at least three major nutritional effects. First, there has been a marked decrease in protein intake and an increase in fat consumption. It is well known that game meat and fish are much richer in nutritionally important protein and less potentially harmful in fat than the meat of domesticated animals. The protein content of moose, for example, is 26 mg/100 g edible portion; that of hamburger is 16 mg/100 g. The fat content of moose is 1.1 g/100 g; that of hamburger is 28 g/100 g.[17] Second, there has been a significant increase in the intake of carbohydrates. In the traditional Indian diet, carbohydrates were available in limited amounts and in a slowly digestible and complex form. The new reserve diet has become much heavier in those forms of carbohydrate (pasta and sugar in particular) that are rapidly absorbable and lead to sudden blood sugar peaks. In fact, there has been a phenomenal rise in the consumption of sugar, especially by children, in the form of soft drinks (which can contain up to 10 percent sugar), candies, and cookies. Finally, on the new reserve there has been a marked change from breast-feeding to bottle-feeding of infants. While baby formula may be as nutritionally adequate as mother's milk, people are replacing the formula with tea made with stagnant lake water, a little condensed milk, and several spoons of white sugar. The day-care supervisor at Grassy Narrows has observed "all the children here eat a lot of potato chips, candy, and chocolate, and their teeth are often rotten-black. Some in grade one don't have teeth except rotten stumps, and this is also true of about half of my children in day-care. A lot of that is due to babies left sleeping with a bottle in their mouth which contains tea with lots of sugar; the sugar just sits in the baby's mouth. . . . You've got to remember that the women here use bottles for feeding until the child is about four years old."

There is now ample evidence from studies of similar situations that government policies of modernization, and the changes in dietary patterns that followed, have led to new health problems for both Indian adults and children. We have mentioned the disastrous effect of increased sugar consumption on dental health. Excess caloric intake, from alcohol as well as from fats and other carbohydrates, has also led to diseases that were either absent or very rare among Indian people in the past, like gallbladder disease and diabetes that sets in during adult years. Indians now have problems with obesity, acne, vitamin deficiencies, anemia linked to iron deficiency, and excess fat and cholesterol levels in the blood and in tissues. In addition, they are now prone to certain cancers, particularly of the colon and lower gut.[18] These are all problems typical of more affluent societies.

Related to the change in diet and the transition to store-bought food is yet another change of far-reaching social importance—namely, the displacement of women from their role as food producers and providers.

## Transformation in the Role of Women

The effects of government policies on Indian women have not been adequately documented either in government reports or in the academic literature. Yet from what is easily observable at Grassy Narrows, it is the women who have borne the brunt of the shock of being ripped out of a meaningful cultural setting. They are the silent victims of modernization.

On the old reserve of Grassy Narrows, the woman was an equal partner with the man in the activities necessary for subsistence and survival. On the trapline, she skinned the animals while the man checked the traps. Aided by her children, she set snares for rabbits, fetched water, and cut wood. In the wild-rice fields, she shared the onerous task of harvesting and later processing the green rice. In those families involved in commercial fishing, she was often the mainstay of the enterprise. In the summer garden, she was responsible for planting, caring, and harvesting. She gathered berries and dried them; she gathered roots and other medicinal herbs. She tanned hides and made clothing and moccasins. She created artwork. She alone was responsible for food preparation and food storage by drying or smoking.

After the move to the new reserve, the woman lost her function as a producer and partner in making a living; she became a consumer. This happened suddenly. She did not have time to adjust, to redefine her role, to find a substitute for certain vital activities that no longer belonged to her. Two areas of her work were swept out from under her immediately: trapping ceased to be a way of life for the family when the children were brought to the reserve school; and gardening was impossible given the soil conditions and space limitations of the new reserve. As if that were not enough, wage employment was not an option open to women. The jobs initially available in construction went to men; the opportunities to earn an income from participation in training courses went to men; and men took most of the jobs in the band office. In addition, with the shift to a cash economy and store-bought groceries, the woman could buy packaged and ready-made food. This eliminated the effort required to cook meals or to prepare food for storage. The woman could now purchase everything that she had once produced. To be without work was to be idle, and yet the daily bread appeared whether one was idle or not. There was always welfare. In this way, the connection between the obligation to work and the necessities of life was dissolved. If the work of woman was not needed for survival it followed that the woman was a person not needed. Life and work, once knotted together, were rent apart.

This general description applies to the majority of women at Grassy Narrows, who do not work and remain at home with nothing to do. There are very few job opportunities for women on the new reserve. The day-care center offers employment to three or four women. The only other positions open to women are janitorial jobs, nurse's aide, secretary in the band office, alcohol worker, and possibly one or two other positions in the band administration. Of the total female labor force (age 16–64) on the reserve in 1977, only twelve (13 percent) were employed full-time.

This transformation in the role of women on the new reserve did not affect all generations of women equally. Today, women under the age of twenty-five know nothing of traditional Ojibwa culture. They have experienced no other way of life than that represented by packaged, convenience foods, Pampers, and bottle-feeding for their infants. Their perceptions of the world are derived from television and advertising, and their values are constantly being influenced in the direction of consumerism and cultural uniformity with the mainstream society. In contrast, the generation of women over fifty years of age are now grandmothers and matriarchs of large family groups. They occupy themselves with the care of grandchildren, thus performing a traditional role. Moreover, these women have lived on the traplines, tanned hides for clothing, used moss for diapers, and fed their families from the abundant resources of the land. These women are very secure: they know who they are, they have the traditional skills, and they have not lost the culture.

They may lament passionately the changes that have taken place in their world. But as individuals and as a group, they have not lost their ability to relate their lives meaningfully to an entity larger than themselves.

The impact of modernization policies on women was felt most acutely by women between the ages of thirty and fifty, who were caught between two ways of life. These women are the daughters of the matriarchs and the mothers of the modern generation that lives by the beat of rock and the pulse of the TV screen. The women in this group in particular have been reduced to the state of passive consumers; they are the ones who have lost the connection between traditional skills and the opportunity to use them in an effective or useful way. Their experience of a loss of capacity, of marginalization in terms of meaningful activity, has resulted not in an adaptation to the new environment but in a capitulation to it. One can go so far as to describe their response to the change in society, and to their role within it, as "catastrophic."

Since the term *catastrophic response* has a specific meaning in psychology, a word should be said about the context in which it is applied. Andrew Mikita, a clinical psychologist, explains:

> The situation at Grassy Narrows reminds me of the work I did with patients that had, as one of the effects of brain damage, a loss of a sense of capacity over previous functions which they can no longer account for. For example, you ask a person to do a certain task. The patient can sense that she had the capacity to do this task before, but cannot cope with it now. She has a definite sense of loss, a feeling of helplessness, impotence. . . . The first reaction is to give in, to capitulate to the loss of capacity. Or there is an attempt to rationalize, to compensate. The entire process is very subtle, and also very profound, and that's why psychologists didn't know what to call it except "a catastrophic response."
>
> How does this analogy apply to Grassy Narrows? Well, we know that the women were especially hurt by the uprooting. We also know that when their basic nurturing, productive, and life-supporting role is eroded over one generation, then after a while the next generation doesn't even know what it has lost. Yet there is a sense of loss. . . .
>
> One kind of reaction to this is to develop completely inappropriate responses. Another is simply to be passive, to capitulate to the new state, and accept the forces beyond one's control. But this is a state of nothingness, and the human organism cannot tolerate such a state for a prolonged period. Therefore, the response to a loss of capacity on a collective level, by women for example, may well take the form of alcoholism, social pathology, and self-destructive behavior.[19]

At Grassy Narrows, the "catastrophic response" of women to the social and economic order of the new reserve is manifest in various ways. More than three-quarters of the women between the ages of thirty and fifty are very heavy drinkers. Only four of the thirty-three women in this age-group are employed. The greatest incidence of child abandonment, neglect, and child abuse is found among the families of women in their middle years. These women have stopped "caring for tomorrow." More important, in not caring for their own offspring, they have produced another generation of women who have no role models to follow in caring for their offspring. Thus, the economic system that has rendered irrelevant the productive capacities of one generation of women by redefining their role in terms of its own requirements for consumption continues to affect succeeding generations. I would venture to suggest that government modernization policies have had a much more devastating impact on the women of Grassy Narrows than on the men. In the absence of opportunities on the productive side of the economy, the women have been sentenced to lead marginal lives.

To government planners who wished to upgrade the material standards of Indian community life, it was probably not obvious that a biweekly wage, allowance, or subsidy could never replace the multiple and complex rewards of the traditional patterns of livelihood on the old reserve. In programming the new reserve to take advantage of the benefits of modern life, government officials no doubt had the best of intentions. Only in retrospect has it become clear that the two modes of organizing the material base of existence cannot coexist, and that it is impossible to substitute wage labor and an industrial mode of production for aspects of the traditional economy without tearing down a great deal besides.

## Net Benefits of Modernization

The Grassy Narrows people are not entirely unaware of the contradictions imposed upon them. They recognize certain material benefits arising from the new reserve way of life, yet they are also conscious of the price they have paid in terms of their dependence, the social costs of alcoholism, and their loss of freedom. In the words of a former chief and elder in the community:

> When the people moved to the new reserve, they became better-off in some ways. They got better houses, more cash, they were nearer to a road, they got better care by doctors. Life on the old reserve was much harder. People worked hard to eat; they were skinnier. Today, life is much easier, but why are so many people dying from alcohol?
> Life is more easy now. But before . . . you could depend on your own people, and now you have to depend on the white man. The white man has taken over in all the basic things. Now the government people tell you what to do. We had a lot more freedom in the old days. We gave up the freedom to use the land in exchange for getting things from the white man. I say that freedom was not a good thing to trade.

It is a poignant commentary on the modern way of life that whereas 80 percent of all the heads of household surveyed in 1977 believe that life on the new reserve is easier and more prosperous in material terms than it was in their father's time, 78 percent say that they are "not happy spiritually." The majority of the people feel lost, disturbed, ill, and cut off from their roots. They feel terribly insecure in the economic system because jobs are limited and government funding of make-work projects is unpredictable. They also know that they have no control over what the government does or how its programs impinge upon and interact with their social structure, values, and everyday lives. So it's easy to understand why the old people speak with nostalgia about the security of seasonal work, the independence and self-sufficiency of family groups, that characterized the Indian way of life. At the same time, Indian people now face a formidable dilemma. Once they have become used to, and dependent upon, the material benefits of "economic development," it is hard for them even to imagine what life might be like without them. The ever increasing materialism of contemporary life poses grave impediments to the attainment of the moral principles and aspirations embedded in their traditional culture. Thus, their identity as Indians and their future become more and more difficult.

To conclude this chapter on economic change, I would like to pose two general questions. First, who really benefits from the kind of development set in motion in Indian communities by the federal government? Second, has this development led to the stated policy goal, namely, "the full, free, and nondiscriminatory participation of Indian people in Canadian society?"

The first question is answered, in part, by statistics on household expenditures at Grassy Narrows (table 7.7). The data show, first, that an immense proportion of the money that comes into the reserve in the form of transfer payments and wages flows out immediately in the form of payments to outside suppliers of goods and services. About 97.4 percent ($886,000 in 1977) of the total amount of income received by households leaves the community. The lion's share of this amount (47 percent) is absorbed by the Hudson's Bay Company, but a significant percentage (21 percent) returns to the Ontario Liquor Control Board. Only a tiny proportion (2.6 percent) is spent in the community. One can see that there are few linkages among sectors; very little income is generated in the local economy through spending; and the multiplier effect is almost nonexistent. Secondly, an overwhelming proportion of total income is spent on consumption rather than investment in productive assets or equipment. Further, much of this consumption is oriented to the purchase of goods and services that people used to produce themselves on the old reserve.

The only reasonable conclusion one can reach from the evidence is that the real beneficiaries of the kind of "development" practiced on Indian reserves are the companies and individuals who profit from the increased

**Table 7.7   Household Expenditures, 1977**

| Category of Expenditure | Amount ($)[a] | Percentage |
|---|---|---|
| Food, clothing, hardware, tools, supplies and deposits on account for major purchases in the Hudson's Bay Company store | 448,000 | 46.6 |
| Food, clothing, tools, supplies purchased from Kenora stores other than the Bay | 34,000 | 3.5 |
| Children's allowance[b] | 29,500 | 3.1 |
| Energy costs: fuel oil, payments for wood and electricity, gasoline for vehicles, skidoos, boats | 83,100 | 8.6 |
| Deposits or partial payments on houses and vehicles | 6,000 | 0.6 |
| Savings | 7,000 | 0.7 |
| Entertainment[c] | 12,000 | 1.2 |
| Indebtedness[d] | 40,250 | 4.2 |
| Expenditure related to alcohol use | | |
| Alcohol purchase | 201,000 | 28.5 |
| Transportation to town, taxi costs | 60,250 | |
| Payment of fines related to alcohol offenses | 13,000 | |
| Subtotal | 934,100 | |
| Expenditure unaccounted for by above items | 28,346 | 3.0 |
| | 962,446 | 100.0 |

[a]The amounts have been estimated on the basis of household survey data, financial accounts at the Bay Company and interviews with suppliers to the reserve.
[b]This is a significant item of expenditure, because people give children large amounts of money for junk food [(candy, potato chips, carbonated beverages).]
[c]Entertainment includes such things as trips to Winnipeg and bingo games on the reserve.
[d]This category includes the money owed to various businesses in Kenora—for example, Mel and Ruth's taxi service and Walstein's air service. It does not include indebtedness to the Bay Company.

demand of the Indians for the goods and services they have to offer. In this sense, Indian development policy is remarkably similar to Canada's aid policy to the Third World, whereby people of a different culture have to be educated to want the goods and services that the Canadian society has to sell. Fueled by government cash subsidies, Indians are made to become more efficient consumers. Certainly at Grassy Narrows, given the relationship between production and consumption, the relatively high levels of disposable income on the new reserve cannot be interpreted as proof of the flow of "benefits" to Indian people. Whatever the income earned from wage labor or received from transfer payments, the final calculus of benefit has to take into account the staggering economic and social costs of separating the Indian people from the means of production and reducing earnings or goods in lieu of earnings from land-based and traditional activities.[20]

This brings us to the final point. However the net benefits of development, interpreted as modernization, are calculated, the Grassy Narrows people perceive that there has been an improvement in the material conditions of their existence. The fact that this is not a consequence of their participation on the productive side of an expanding economy, however, has important implications with respect to the question of whether or not the kind of development promoted by the federal government has brought the Indian people any closer to the goal of free and equal participation in Canadian society. The answer has been implicit in our discussion all along. What government policy has accomplished is to push the Indian people further away from participation in the productive activities of the nation than they have ever been, to separate them from the means of production embodied essentially in land and in the resources of the land, and to turn them into men and women who have neither land nor capital nor even a secure place among those Canadians who exchange only their labor for a subsistence wage. The increase in the material standard of living on Indian reserves, therefore, must be seen not as a result of free and equal participation in Canadian society but as compensation, paid by the society, for the continued exclusion of Indian people from the productive processes of the nation. The ultimate hallmark of this kind of development is not participation but marginality.

# 8 • GOVERNMENT POLICY AND DECISION MAKING

The previous chapters in this part have described what happened to the people of Grassy Narrows after they were moved from the old to the new reserve. We tried to imagine what the culture of the old reserve looked like from the inside, from the perspective of how ideas, symbols, and rituals helped shape human personality and behavior, how institutions gave form to core values, and how relationships were structured within and among family groups. Then we watched in dismay as the glue that held the society together came unstuck and signs of disorder, confusion, and alienation appeared alongside fundamental changes in community life. It was hard to believe that the relocation alone was responsible for such radical transformation. One could not help wondering whether the seeds of disintegration had not been planted earlier. Perhaps the changes had been evolving over a longer period of time, and the relocation had simply brought things to a head by "focusing" the troubles. Still, the physical uprooting seems to be a symbol, a clear point of departure for a new alignment with the white society and the inevitable collision with the modern world. Whatever our own predisposition regarding the issue of causality, it is significant that the people of Grassy Narrows perceive the relocation as a watershed in their lives. They see it as the beginning of the end of their Indian way of life.

How did this relocation come about? Who made the decisions? What was the ideological and policy context for the decision to relocate? What was the nature of the planning process at the time? These questions form the framework of this chapter.

## The Policy Context

In the early 1960s, the "Indian problem" was perceived by the top political and bureaucratic leadership within the Indian Affairs Branch of the Department of Citizenship and Immigration as a problem of poverty: "Among many of Canada's Indians, all the classical signs and symptoms of poverty are to be found: underemployment and unemployment, large families, poor health, substandard housing, low levels of education, idleness, an attitude of despair and defeat. To many Indians in northern settlements, these conditions are the only way of life that exists. They have known no other. They accept poverty as they accept the weather."[1] This analysis, articulated by one of the highest ranking bureaucrats in the Indian Branch, was followed by a statement that "poverty on Indian reserves can be ended by a [government] program," and therefore the government must "wage war on Indian poverty."

The assumptions underlying the entire approach to the "Indian problem" are easily discernible from public pronouncements: first, Indians are on a path from a traditional, backward society to a modern and dynamic one; second, movement along this path is inevitable, irreversible, and of course beneficial to Indians; third, the appropriate government strategy is to assist the transition to modernization primarily by providing physical improvements and social services to Indians on the basis of equality with other Canadians; and fourth, the main barriers along the path to modernization are the attitudes and culture of the Indian people; therefore, it is incumbent upon government officials to change these attitudes if the war on poverty is to be won. The specifics of the approach are stated as follows:

> What can we do? We can improve the employability of the individual Indian . . . have a placement and a relocation service . . . more industrial development to make jobs for Indians . . . make a physical and social environment to develop self-respect . . . provide more social services [welfare, child care] of the sort we naturally assume to be in operation among our own communities . . . .
>
> Programs and policies vital to the elimination of poverty from Indian communities are undergoing review. The first attention is being given to the development of the physical community . . . housing, planning . . . . Directly this is completed, we shall turn to industrial development and relocation programs, each of which requires expansion.[2]

According to government officials, the attitudes that had to be overcome in the war on poverty were the Indians' feelings that "the government owes them a living," their attitudes toward time, their absence of discipline in showing up for work every day, the tendency to accuse the Indian Branch of paternalism, and their attitude toward property.

Although the specifics of implementing all these elements of the new approach to Indian poverty varied locally, in due course the policy changes conceived at the national level affected Indian bands across Canada. The Indian Affairs Branch began new housing programs, built new schools, encouraged adult education and occupational training courses, and greatly increased other capital expenditures on the reserves. In the mid-1960s, community development became an important feature of Indian administration policy. At the same time, Indian Affairs began to extend the concept of local government, already in existence for southern Ontario reserves, to northern communities. This meant that under regulations provided by headquarters, Indian bands could now administer certain programs such as social assistance, recreation, and work opportunity programs. In the late 1960s, both federal and provincial government agencies began to hire community workers as teachers' aides, welfare administrators, and community development officers. By the mid-1970s, government became, directly and indirectly, the major employer on Indian reserves across northern Ontario, making Indian people more dependent on government support during this decade than at any other time in history.

It is in the context of the evolution of national policy that the decision to relocate Grassy Narrows must be understood. Obviously the new site provided much easier access to the reserve from Kenora by road, and it gave government planners a free hand to rearrange people, houses, and community facilities in line with their own concepts of what was modern and economically efficient. According to the Indian Agent in Kenora, the new reserve was destined to be "a model community." In the end, Grassy Narrows did become a model community beyond anyone's expectations. But it now epitomizes the disaster created by good intentions on the part of those who had little respect for Canada's indigenous people.

## The Decision to Relocate

The story of the relocation decision is not an easy one to reconstruct. An extensive search of government documents and sources turned up only a handful of references to this event.[3] The single most pertinent document is a letter dated July 8, 1964, from the then superintendent of the Kenora Indian Agency, Eric Law, to the Minister of Mines and Technical Surveys in Ottawa, the Honorable W. Benedickson. This letter contains the only known exposition of the government's attitude and stance on the issue of relocating the Grassy Narrows community. Law writes as follows:

> About five years ago the Grassy Narrows Band Council requested a Day School be constructed on their Reserve. They also wanted a road into their reserve from the Jones Road so that they could go to Kenora and the new Hudson Bay Store which was planned for construction on the Jones Road . . . .
>
> The Band Council had several meetings with me and they decided where they wanted their road and the new school. Finding it impossible to get a road into the old settlement, and their location of the road and the new school five miles away, the Band decided on a long range plan of developing a new community around the area they set aside for the new school and sports ground.

The memory of the Grassy Narrows people is at odds with Law's contention that the band council made the relocation decision. An elder who over a period of thirty years held either the position of chief or band councillor remembers things differently: "When we were moved, nobody asked us anything. They told us what we had to do. First they built five houses, at least two years before anyone moved to the new site. I was still on the old reserve when John Kennedy died, and that was in November 1963. They, the government, just gave the Indians orders. They also told us that if we didn't move to the new reserve, all the people would have their family allowances cut off. That's the way it was."

A similar perspective is voiced by another band member: "One day the Indian Agent asked the chief if the government could move the reserve without gathering the band council for a meeting, without talking to anybody. The chief and the Indian Agent only talked to themselves, in private. They never told anybody anything. Indian Affairs people just came into the reserve one day and said, "We're going to move you people. You'll be close to the Hudson's Bay store. We'll give you a school, and houses, and hydro. We'll give you welfare and jobs on the new reserve."

Recollections of the personality of the Indian Agent in Kenora by persons who had worked with him, combined with the prevailing policy of the Indian Affairs Department to "manage and control Indians," tend to confirm the people's assertions that the relocation was imposed on them. One long-time Indian Affairs employee, who arrived in Kenora shortly after the Grassy Narrows relocation, remembers Eric Law as an authoritarian type who had little contact with or understanding of Indian people. It is now recognized that in this period of departmental administration of Indian affairs,

> There was a certain coercion or lack of involvement of Indian people in decisions. In terms of relocating communities in those days, leadership at the community level in some cases was either weak or nonexistent. I am sure arbitrary decisions were made by government bureaucrats, partly well-intentioned, under the impression that because the Indians could not articulate their own needs, "we know what's best for them, and the best thing for them is to move them." In the case of Grassy Narrows, people in the district probably thought that they were bringing the Indians closer to civilization . . . "what the hell, the Indians can buy a car and drive to work in Kenora" – kind of attitude. It was wrong, very wrong, and we live with the results of this attitude today.[4]

The relocation took three years to implement at Grassy Narrows. The first houses were constructed in 1961, yet by late 1963 only four families had moved to the new site. Despite the carrot and stick approach, the promises of jobs and welfare and the threat of family allowance withdrawals, the people moved to the new reserve slowly; the last family left the old reserve only in 1972. Father Lacelle described the people's attitude to the relocation this way: "The people hated to move to the new reserve, but most of them moved because they had no choice. The houses had been built and that was it. Some told me that at least they were happy that they would have a new house, because the houses on the old reserve were quite poor. The question that still troubles many people at Grassy is why they were moved in the first place."

In his letter, moreover, Law stated that it was "impossible to get a road into the old settlement," presumably because the old reserve was composed of islands and peninsulas accessible only by water or air. But the people do not believe that the technical difficulties of constructing a road to the old reserve constituted the real reason for resettlement. There was already an old logging path connecting the main territory of the old reserve with the Jones Road. The people believe they were relocated in order to further the interests of the Hudson's Bay Company. The Bay had moved from the old reserve to a new location on the Jones Road in 1959 in order to take advantage of lower transportation costs and profit from the tourist trade, but it still needed the Indians' business. Conversations with old-timers bring out the hidden agenda in the relocation decision:

> I say, look here . . . you white people built a highway right across Canada, a big highway from the Atlantic to the Pacific. You built a railroad too, coast to coast. Now you tell me, why couldn't Indian Affairs build a road, go just a few miles to the old reserve from the Jones Road? Why? No, they moved the whole reserve instead.
>
> They moved us to be closer to the Bay. And there were never any meetings with the band council. Nobody ever asked the people whether they wanted to move. They ordered us. And the move was very bad for us. There was no reason at all for us to move.
>
> We could have been on the old reserve today, but the Bay wanted us to move and live closer to the road. They told us that prices for our food and supplies would be lower if we did that. But when we moved, we found out that prices were not lower; they were higher. And now, on the new reserve, we can't have vegetable gardens like we used to . . . . Soil here is no good for planting, just dirt and rock. And we're too crowded here. Now we can't grow our own food. Now we have to buy everything at the Bay at higher prices.

One of the consequences of the relocation, then, intended or unintended, was to transform the Grassy Narrows people from independent producers of most of their own food to consumers heavily dependent upon the Bay.

This perception of the relocation decision as a product of conspiratorial planning and cozy relations between two dominant white institutions in Indian life is no doubt rooted in people's memory of past colonial practice. Although such accommodation by Indian Affairs to the commercial interests of the Hudson's Bay Company cannot be ruled out,[5] it would not be correct to base the entire rationale for the decision to relocate on this presumption of motive. An alternative explanation would have to take into account the government's policy, in the late 1950s and early 1960s, to extend education, housing, and community infrastructure services to remote Indian communities. Given the mandate to upgrade Indian reserves, district officials of DIAND were probably primarily interested in efficient housing construction and in certain economies of scale in the extension of water, electricity, and sewage networks to the exclusion of all other considerations. Relocation thus became a by-product or derivative of technical and engineering concerns. In the case of Grassy Narrows, the chief engineer of the Kenora Indian Agency might well have thought that the most efficient way to provide houses and services to Indians was to move them all closer to a road, cluster them in what looked like a suburban subdivision, and establish a town-site similar in layout to any white town. Indeed, this line of reasoning seems to have been operative in DIAND district offices all across northern Manitoba and Ontario, because a number of Indian reserves there were relocated at about the same time and in the same manner as Grassy Narrows.[6]

Although comparative information on other relocations points in the direction of good intentions on the part of government officials in implementing community development, the truth about the decision to relocate Grassy Narrows cannot be known. In this case, not only are the facts hard to pin down from the records, but the little information that can be harvested from government sources mysteriously tends to disguise the fact that the resettlement took place. Paradoxically, the absence of evidence leads one to speculate that DIAND officials conducted the relocation for their own reasons and interests, without even considering it to be of any consequence or importance to the Indian people. They probably assumed that the benefits arising from closer contact with "civilization" would be good for Indians, since these "children of nature" did not really know what is best for them. The arrogance of officials with the legislative mandate to control and administer the lives of Indians and their lack of understanding and respect for Indian culture were reflected not only in the decision to relocate but also in the layout of the new community.

## Planning the New Community

The paramount issue in planning the new community revolved around the location of houses. According to Eric Law, the physical plan prepared by his district officials had the full support of the band council. He writes: "The plans for this community development have been going nicely. We have two new wells, and our housing has been planned so that if power becomes available it wouldn't be too costly to supply the people. We have had the full cooperation of the Branch and the band council . . . ." In the same letter, Law refers to only two dissenting opinions on the government's plan for the layout of the new reserve: "I had a meeting with the people who were to get the new homes, and after explaining the reasons for wanting them to build within the development area, they all agreed but Richard Ashopenace and Pierre Taypaywaykejick.[7]

Fortunately, a rather extraordinary exchange of correspondence between band members and government agencies has survived to shed light on exactly how locational decisions were made. From this correspondence, we learn that there was widespread opposition to the government's town-site plan, that the people were very much aware of the adverse consequences that would flow from the implementation of such a plan, and that the plan was implemented by coercion and threat. By way of evidence, one of these letters will be quoted in its entirety. This handwritten letter from Richard Ashopenace, undated, and addressed to Indian Affairs, reads like a manifesto on the right to choose where one lives.[8]

> We have rights to live where ever we choose to live or to build a house in the reserve or outside the reserve. The white man said that when they signed Treaty with the Indians long ago.
>
> Now they won't make the houses where we choose the land, to make the houses in our reserve. Some of the Indian Boys did some cutting brush and trees to clear the places where we choose to make the houses, and they got paid by the Indian Affairs to do that work.
>
> Now they don't want to make the houses on those places. They want to make the houses about a mile away, from the places we choosed. They want to make the houses on one spot close together.
>
> We don't like to live so close together for some reasons, toilets and too much drinking and disturbance. The kids see somebody drunk and they want to do the same thing. And we can't do any work around the house like making a garden, too many kids together.
>
> And it will be a long ways to walk to the store too, from the houses. And its no good for health to live close together too.
>
> The Indian Agent Mr. Eric Law, told us if we don't like to live close together with the others, he said we won't get a house, we need the new houses very bad.
>
> So we would like to have our houses built where we want them. We want to live in peace. This is all for now.

A second set of letters makes fascinating reading because it records one man's determination to challenge the authority of the Indian Agent to impose locational decisions without regard for the expressed concerns of the Indian people. This correspondence involves two government agencies and three levels of the Indian Affairs bureaucracy.[9] Pierre Taypaywaykejick, a fifty-six-year-old Indian, asked Norman Schantz, the Mennonite missionary, to write to the National Parole Board and explain why there was a problem with the layout of the new reserve. Apparently in 1964, there was already some drinking at the new site. In the words of Schantz:

There are eight houses close together that the government built. This year they are going to build eight more, close to the others, but all the people who paid for the houses wanted them scattered within 1½ miles from the school because of the heavy drinking at the present site.

Also outside toilets all being so close will be a health problem. The Indian Agent said they are going to build them there and "if you don't want them, we will give the money back, and give [the houses] to someone else."

Now Pierre would like to know if you could help him to get his house built here close to the mission . . . . Thank you for any help you can give him.

After letters back and forth between the National Parole Board and Indian Affairs, the "official" position of headquarters on the layout of the houses was stated by A. G. Leslie, Chief, Agencies Division of DIAND in Ottawa: "It is desired that housing on Indian reserves be on a community-planned basis so that all services such as stores, schools, etc. will form part of the housing community. Many times in the past houses have been constructed for the convenience of the individual and when we try to provide roads, water and sewage systems it is a most difficult problem."[10]

Obviously the phrase "on a community-planned basis" had a different meaning in the context of DIAND decision making in the early 1960s than the idea of community involvement in planning might connote today. It is also very clear that the entire conception of community planning revolved exclusively around physical plant (stores, schools, houses) and infrastructure (roads, water, and sewage) considerations. It seems that no one at Indian Affairs even bothered to check out the terrain of the new site for Grassy Narrows. For all the emphasis on the efficiency and economy of providing water and sewage to every house, it is ironic that the rock upon which the new reserve is situated makes it impossible to build a community-wide water and sewage system except at astronomical expense. In the meantime, for the past twenty years, there have been major health problems caused by the proximity of outhouses, exactly as the people had predicted in their letters to government officials.

The case of Pierre Taypaywaykejick was finally decided by Eric Law. Law apparently decided that he had to "punish" Pierre, not only for wanting to build his house outside the development area, but also because he thought Pierre was organizing resistance to the government's community plan. Law believed that because most families were opposed to the plan, Pierre was inciting others to follow his lead, stirring up dissent, and mobilizing protest. In a letter to the regional supervisor of DIAND in North Bay, however, he stated that it was "the chief . . . [who] does not want all the other band members building outside of the planned community." In the end, he decided that Pierre would have to construct his own house, at no cost to Indian Affairs, near the mission where he wanted it. In his view, the fact that Pierre would have to pay for his house when everybody else was being given a house free by Indian Affairs would serve as a deterrent and "help discourage others from wanting to build outside the planned area."

These letters are important because they provide insight into the conflicting perspectives on the issues of location and ordering in space. The Grassy Narrows people tried to tell the district officials of DIAND that the government's community plan violated fundamental precepts of their society. A seventy-year-old elder and former chief put the matter perfectly:

> If only we could have made the government people listen. We tried to tell them why space was important to us.
>
> The most important thing is that it's from the culture—that's the way our people have always lived. We don't live like the white man, that's not our way. The white man lives close together, but we don't. We like to live far apart, in families. On the old reserve, you knew your place. Everybody respected your place. Nobody didn't build right next to your place . . . . It wasn't private property, but it was a sense of place, your place, your force around you.
>
> And another thing. When you have the space, you have a better chance to look after yourself, to be independent.
>
> As soon as they started to bunch us up, the problems started, the drinking, the violence. This has a lot to do with being all bunched up.

The other major problem was access to water. In the old settlement, the customary law of equality of access to life-supporting resources was reflected in the spatial arrangement of houses along the shoreline of the river. The elder comments on this as well: "On the old reserve, every family could get to the water without crossing anybody else's path. This was good. On the new reserve, we wanted our houses to be close to the lake. But the Indian Agent wanted the houses further away from the shoreline and much closer together. He said that we would not need to walk to get water. We would have water and sewage." DIAND officials paid little attention to the Indians' concerns over water. They designed the layout of the new community on the assumption that water and sewage would be provided to every household. Twenty years later, however, only a handful of families in the core area of the new reserve have piped-in water. The rest still have to obtain their water from the lake. Many families have been completely cut off from the lake by other houses standing in the way; women and children often have to walk a fair distance to obtain water and bring it into their homes. So for reasons not hard to understand, the Grassy Narrows people feel bitter and betrayed that "all this bunching up . . . has been for nothing."

Even more painful to some than the unnecessary concentration in space was their physical and spiritual separation from the English-Wabigoon River. The new site was not on the magnificent, wide, open river but on a stagnant, small, and lifeless lake. To quote Norman Schantz, "The people . . . they just hated to move to the new reserve. They wanted to be near fresh, flowing water, near their river. Garden Lake, where the government put the new reserve, was just a small lake. It was not The River. It was not A Living Thing. . . . Even after they moved to the new reserve, some people kept going back to their houses on the old reserve. They just couldn't stand it on the new reserve."

The consequences of the kind of community planning that was done by the Department of Indian Affairs at the time of the Grassy Narrows relocation are now reflected in the words that people use to describe their community. One woman says bluntly, "It's just like you get out of a cage when you go from here to the old reserve." Others call the new reserve "a concentration camp." They feel crowded, impounded, imprisoned, reduced to the status of animals herded into a corral: "When you have a bunch of cattle, it's better to have a corral to feed them . . . the government built this corral which is the new reserve. Now, you might as well throw in the food, so that they can get it. This food is the welfare that the government is giving us. But I say, if you're corraled like that, well, you might as well live and act like cattle."

It is difficult not to conclude that the Department of Indian Affairs is morally responsible for the desperate situation in the contemporary community. The physical layout of houses, the sense of order in space dictated by the standards and values of the dominant society, has had a profoundly negative influence on community life. Sociologist Kai Erikson visited Grassy Narrows in January 1979 and observed:

> Village compounds of the type supplied by the government have traditionally been suited to the needs and values of an agricultural people, and they violate the sense of space customary not only to the Ojibwa people in particular, but to hunting and gathering people everywhere.
>
> For one thing, [the village compound] disrupts old ways of relating to the land, to nature, and to the idea of communal ownership of natural resources. For another, it compresses space in such a manner that traditional ways of relating to other people no longer work.
>
> Every people, every culture, has its own sense of how much distance should be maintained between neighbors, how wide a margin of privacy is necessary to protect individuality; and when that sense of spacing is changed by circumstance, the almost ironical result is that neighborliness breaks down. When people are pressed together too closely, they can become more distant emotionally and spiritually: hostilities and aggressions, once insulated by a cushion of space, now fill the narrow gaps like a kind of electricity . . . .
>
> Grassy Narrows has become not only a tight concentration of people but a tight concentration of troubles.[11]

Certainly the ideological framework of government Indian policy, the overriding emphasis on modernization, and the prevailing views of community planning, militated against an alternative path to development, the outcomes of which might have been less devastating to the indigenous people. At that time, because Indian Agents also had sweeping powers over the lives of Indians, it was impossible to challenge "the system." In the end, the system proved its extraordinary effectiveness in pursuing the objective of assimilation. In the span of only one generation after the relocation of Grassy Narrows, the central institutions of the Ojibwa culture, the people's moral values and beliefs, customary social relationships, political organization, and mode of production—all were rendered impotent, useless, even superflous under the imposed conditions of the new reserve.

It's hard to say whether the consequences of government policy were harsher, more traumatic, more deeply felt at Grassy Narrows than elsewhere. In the 1960s, many bands were similarly wrenched out of a way of life, but even those that were not relocated did not escape the relentless pressures to change from traditional ways to more modern ones. In the process, indigenous communities experienced massive social and cultural disintegration, a state of injury only partially reflected in the mounting national statistics on Indian suicide and other forms of self-destructive behavior. What makes Grassy Narrows unique is that only seven years after the relocation, the people were confronted with the poisoning of their English-Wabigoon River by methyl mercury. They hardly had time to work their way out of one calamity, one bereavement, before they had to face another crisis, another loss. In part three we will try to understand how an environmental disaster contributed to the etiology of social breakdown at Grassy Narrows.

## PART III
## RIVER OF POISON

The mercury sank in the mouth of the dying day.
　　　　　—W. H. Auden, "In Memory of W. B. Yeats"

*Pijibowin* is the Ojibwa word for poison. It is used by the people of Grassy Narrows to describe the mercury that now contaminates their sacred English-Wabigoon River. Between 1962 and 1970, Dryden Chemicals Limited, a pulp and paper mill located about eighty miles upstream from Grassy Narrows, dumped over 20,000 pounds of mercury into the river system as effluent from its chlor-alkali plant. By March 1970, when the Ontario Minister of Energy and Resource Management ordered the company to stop discharging mercury into the environment, the damage was complete and irreversible. Over three hundred miles of the English-Wabigoon river system, with all its biological life, would probably remain poisoned for half a century or more.

An environmental disaster can be assessed in many ways. One can measure the sheer force of the impact, the extent of the damage, the effects on human health, the economic losses sustained, or the length of recovery time. Any major disruptive event, however, should also be judged by looking at the vulnerability of the people who are exposed to it. It seems logical that a community that has just suffered a traumatic upheaval in its way of life will experience the effects of yet another crisis much more acutely. In such a situation, environmental contamination can no longer be measured in isolation, for its impact interacts with previous events in a complex manner to form a pattern of cumulative injury.

Coming only a few years after the relocation, the discovery of mercury dealt a devastating blow to the community of Grassy Narrows. Having just been wrenched from their moorings on the old reserve, the people were ill prepared to cope with yet another misfortune. They had but a precarious hold on the conditions of their existence on the new reserve. They could no longer draw strength either from their relationship to the land or from the well of their faith, which had once given meaning and coherence to their lives. In the context of their traditional religious beliefs, the contamination of the river could only be interpreted as punishment by the Great Spirit for some serious violation of the laws governing man's relationship to nature. People had great difficulty comprehending this "unseen poison" of mercury, whose presence in the water and in the fish they could not see or taste or smell. They could not understand how something that happened so far away from them could hurt them. Many could not believe that the natural environment, which had nurtured them both spiritually and materially could suddenly betray them. To accept the fact that their "River of Life" had turned into a river of poison meant to lose forever their faith in nature and in the source of life itself.

In the community, the suspicion of pijibowin and the feeling of loss of control over the environment ran like a strong undercurrent beneath the tangible and measurable effects of the contamination. The tangible effects—the disruption in guiding, the loss of commercial fishing, the warnings against taking fish for food—struck a further blow to the people's already weakened ability to produce their own food and make an inde-

pendent living from the resources of the land. Just as important were the intangible effects—the massive intrusion of outsiders, the confusion and misunderstanding about the effects on human health, the political manipulation of the mercury issue, and the acceleration of government intervention in community life. Far from being just a medical and an economic problem, the pollution of the river became a serious psychological problem. The way in which the governments of Canada and Ontario handled the mercury issue and the exploitation of the Grassy Narrows people by self-seeking groups and individuals were in the end as severely demoralizing as the fact of the poison itself. Any analysis of the impact of this environmental disaster, therefore, has to take into account the relationship of Indian people to the Canadian society as a whole. Indeed, the way in which the mercury issue was defined, managed, and politicized mirrors much of what is so wrong with our own mainstream society.

While there is no way to measure with any precision how much of the current crisis at Grassy Narrows is attributable to mercury and how much to the collapse of a way of life, the people's own perception of the importance of mercury is significant. They speak of mercury poisoning as the event that pushed them over the edge of their ability to feel secure in nature, to relate to each other and to the world around them, and to be self-reliant in providing for their material needs. They call mercury "the last nail in the coffin."

# 9 • MERCURY IN
   THE ENVIRONMENT

Mercury is one of the oldest metals known to us. Aristotle described it as "liquid silver" in the fourth century B.C. Its ore cinnabar was used to make the red dye found in prehistoric cave paintings in Europe. During Roman times, it was used to purify gold and silver. In the first century A.D., Greek physicians used it to heal open sores and burns. Centuries later, mercury ointment became a treatment for syphilis. But the hazards of mercury, as well as its uses, were also well known from early times. The miners of this metal, for example, developed violent tremors, muscular spasms, and character disorders. The Romans therefore chose convicts and slaves to mine the metal, and this precedent of using forced labor was followed by the Spaniards in the mercury mines they developed in the New World.

Miners, however, were not the only ones susceptible to the toxic effects of exposure to mercury. In the eighteenth century, a physician called Ramazzini wrote that goldsmiths using mercury in their craft "very soon become subject to vertigo, asthma, and paralysis. Very few of them reach old age, and even when they do not die young, their health is so terribly undermined that they pray for death."[1] Of artisans who used mercury to coat the backs of mirrors, he wrote: "You can see these workmen scowling and gazing reluctantly into their mirrors at the reflection of their own suffering and cursing the trade they have adopted."[2]

The popular expression "mad as a hatter" grew out of the observation of tremors, manic-depressive behavior, and temperamental instability among hatmakers who used mercuric nitrate to improve the felting quality of wool and fur. The toxic and potentially fatal effects of working with metallic or inorganic mercury, therefore, have been well established in recorded history.

Today, mercury and its compounds are used in about three thousand industrial processes by over eighty industries. Mercury is a valuable element because it is the only metal that is liquid at room temperature, and it also has special electrical properties that make it almost irreplaceable. It is used in making dental fillings, paints, electronic controls, thermometers, disinfectants, preservatives, and lotions. It is a catalyst in many metallurgical processes, and it is used in the production of vinyl chloride, a component in the manufacture of plastics. The single most important use of mercury (prior to 1970) was in chlor-alkali plants that served the huge pulp and paper industry. Here, mercury was used in the electrolytic production of caustic soda and chlorine, and it was this industry that "lost" mercury in great volume both in wastewater and through exhaust gases.[3] While individual cases of industrial mercury poisoning have been fairly well documented,[4] it took the massive epidemic of poisoning in Minamata, Japan, in the late 1950s and 1960s to shake the world out of its complacency about the dangers of discharging mercury as industrial waste.

## An Insidious Poison

Minamata is a village of about forty thousand persons, located on the southernmost island of Japan, Kyushu, on a bay of the Shiranui Sea. Its inhabitants make their living by commercial fishing, tourism, and working in the giant petrochemical complex owned by the Chisso Corporation. The town is associated with Minamata disease, which is known to have taken 107 lives and by 1970 had left over a thousand people with irreversible neurological damage, crippled limbs, blindness, paralysis, internal disorders, and loss of bodily functions. The disease fell most heavily on the poorest people of the area, who were most dependent on a steady diet of fish and shellfish.

Signs of the poison appeared in 1950, when fish in the bay began to float to the surface, swim erratically, and thrash about wildly before dying. Two years later, cats began to leap up in the air and turn in feverish circles, like whirling dervishes, before dying. People called it "the cat-dancing disease." In April 1956, two victims of what was at first diagnosed as cerebral palsy were admitted to the Chisso Factory Hospital. By mid-summer, so many similar cases had been reported that the director of the hospital, Dr. Hosokawa, declared that "an unclarified disease of the central nervous system had broken out." By the autumn of that year, a research team of the Kumamoto University Medical School suspected that the mass poisoning was traceable to a heavy metal concentrated in the flesh of fish and shellfish taken from Minamata Bay. It took years of research to identify organic mercury as the cause of the disaster and to provide conclusive evidence that the source of the poison was the effluent from the chemical plant of the Chisso Corporation. Indeed, a full decade passed before enough evidence could be accumulated to establish Chisso's legal liability for the damages caused by industrial pollution. Meanwhile, the company's executives refused to cooperate with the scientists, continued to dump mercury as effluent until 1968, and used their considerable economic and political influence to stifle criticism and frustrate the research effort.[5] In the end, the Chisso Corporation was forced to pay compensation to the victims of mercury poisoning, but the cost in human life was staggering. It is estimated that, aside from the actual and potential cases of congenital mercury poisoning, the number of Minamata disease victims may ultimately exceed ten thousand because of the long-term effects of past exposure.

Although outbreaks of mercury poisoning have occurred elsewhere,[6] the disease is always associated with the Minamata experience. This tragedy was followed by an extensive investigation of the causal links between inorganic mercury dumped as industrial waste, the contamination of the marine food chain by methyl mercury, and the onset of clinical symptoms of poisoning in humans. Scientists discovered a rather extraordinary natural phenomenon whereby inorganic (or metallic) mercury, which settles into the sediment of a body of water, is transformed into the much more toxic form of organic (or methyl) mercury in a process known as biomethylation.[7] What happens is that microorganisms living in the sediment, in order to protect themselves, convert the inorganic mercury into methyl mercury, which is much less toxic to them. The transformed mercury is then absorbed by microscopic underwater life such as plankton or algae, which serve as food for insect larvae. The insects are consumed by little fish; the little fish are consumed by bigger fish; and in this manner, the burden of methyl mercury in fish increases in concentration and toxicity as it passes up the food chain. Once inorganic mercury has been added to a water system, it takes a very long time for the mercury to clear the marine biosystem. Scientists estimate that only about 1 percent of the sediment's burden of inorganic mercury is converted into methyl mercury each year. Further, the biological half-life of methyl mercury in fish is very long. As a result, the process of contamination of marine life is continuous, persistent, and irreparable.

Of the two kinds of mercury, methyl mercury is more dangerous to human beings. Structurally, it differs from inorganic mercury simply through the addition of one or more carbon atoms to the mercury atom. Although both types are toxic, inorganic mercury does not do as much damage when taken by mouth. It is not as readily absorbed by the body; it is much more easily expelled from the body; and it does not accumulate in the body's vital organs and brain. Methyl mercury, on the other hand, is quickly carried by the blood through body tissues, concentrating in the heart, intestine, liver, and kidneys. But its greatest damage is reserved for the brain, and most of the clinical symptoms of mercury poisoning are related to brain and nerve lesions.[8] Methyl mercury destroys cells in the cerebellum, which regulates balance, and the cortex, which influences vision. It finds its way to other regions of the brain like the frontal lobe, where it may cause disturbances in personality. The toxin is singularly difficult to trace as a cause of illness because the symptoms of poisoning are not very specific and may be simulated by alcoholism, diabetes, severe nutritional deficiencies, old age, and many other disorders of the central nervous system. Therefore, a complete assessment of mercury poisoning can be made only at autopsy. Postmortem studies of the brains of Japanese victims, for example, revealed a marked atrophy or shrinkage of the brain caused by the destruction of nerve cells; the remaining nerve-cell tissue was characterized by a spongelike quality.

Neurologists have identified the clinical symptoms of Minamata disease as follows: numbness of the mouth, lips, tongue, hands, and feet; tunnel vision, sometimes accompanied by abnormal blind spots and disturbances in eye movement; impairment of hearing; speech disorders; difficulty in swallowing; loss of balance; a stumbling, awkward gait; clumsiness in handling familiar objects; disturbances in coordination; loss of memory, inability to recall basic things like the alphabet; loss of the ability to concentrate; apathy; feelings of extreme fatigue; mental depression; emotional instability; and a tendency to fits of anxiety and rage. These initial symptoms of mercury poisoning may eventually lead to severe disability, uncontrollable tremors and convulsions, deformity, paralysis, coma, and death. There are no remedies or therapy for the victims of mercury poisoning; the disease is considered to be irreversible.

Aside from these dreadful symptoms, methyl mercury has other characteristics that make it a particularly insidious poison. In the first place, it has a special affinity for unborn children. In the body of a pregnant woman, not only is the mercury immediately passed from the placenta to the fetus, but the fetus actually concentrates the lethal toxin. In Japan, blood concentrations of methyl mercury in infants at birth averaged about 30 percent higher than in the mother. There were many cases of infants born with what seemed like cerebral palsy; some had deformed limbs, showed uncontrollable muscle spasms, and were seriously mentally retarded. These were the congenital vicitms of Minamata disease who had acquired the poison prenatally. Postmortem studies of such children showed massive atrophy in brain size and underdeveloped and malformed tissues in the central nervous system. To illustrate: the normal brain weight for a two-year-old child is about 960 g; for a three-year-old child, about 1,125. Minamata disease victims aged two and three registered brain weights of only 650 and 630 g, respectively.

Second, mercury continues to affect brain cells even after a person has stopped eating contaminated food. It has a half-life of at least seventy days in human blood and perhaps longer in the brain. This means that after seventy days, half of the burden of methyl mercury still exists in the body; it takes another seventy days to eliminate half of the remaining burden, and the balance is halved again every seventy days. Yet brain damage can be caused by minute amounts of mercury.

Third, individuals have different tolerances for the toxin; some are so sensitive to methyl mercury that even very brief exposure to contaminated food can cause significant damage to the brain. Some people also retain the poison in the body for a much longer time than others. So there are no guarantees that an individual who is exposed to small amounts of mercury over a long period of time will escape the pitiless and progressive degeneration of the nervous system.

Fourth, methyl mercury is a poison that follows no specific timetable between the time of exposure and the onset of symptoms of neurological injury. The damage done to the brain may not be manifest for several years.[9] In Japan, some patients diagnosed initially as chronic cases of low-level mercury intoxication developed symptoms of acute poisoning three or four years later. Thus there are no assurances that cases of low-grade or subacute poisoning will not worsen later on.

Finally, since many of the first symptoms of mercury poisoning (a "pins and needles" sensation in the arms and legs, tunnel vision, tremors) are also characteristic of other illnesses and nervous afflictions, it is very difficult to make a positive and early diagnosis of Minamata disease. No wonder, then, that the correlation between levels of exposure to methyl mercury and neurological symptoms of mercury poisoning has presented scientists with a formidable analytical challenge. It does not help matters when different laboratories use different units to measure the burden of mercury in the body or when significant differences appear in the interpretation of symptomatic evidence. But all scientists agree on one point: the amount of mercury in the blood is positively correlated with the potential health risk a person bears. Blood levels of mercury are indicated by the ratio of mercury to whole blood calibrated in parts per billion (ppb). In Canada, the norm for the level of mercury in the blood of persons who are not fish-eaters is considered to be about 5 ppb; this rises to about 20 ppb for people who eat a lot of fish. Some countries recognize 200 ppb of mercury in blood as a "safe" level. Others (for example, Canada, the United States, Sweden, Finland, and Japan) accept 100 ppb as a "safe" level; anyone with more than 100 ppb is considered to be at risk.

The body burden of mercury can also be measured by the analysis of mercury values in human hair. It so happens that as hair is being formed on the head, mercury is being incorporated from the bloodstream. Thus there is a constant concentration ratio between the amount of mercury in the hair and in the blood. Once in the hair, methyl mercury remains there unchanged. Since hair grows at the rate of about one centimeter per month, scientists have an inbuilt and permanent record of previous levels of exposure to the toxin.[10]

Because of individual variations in tolerance and in the length of the

retention period, it has been very difficult to establish the precise relationship between blood concentrations of mercury and the incidence of
symptoms of Minamata disease. The available data, gathered from an
outbreak of mercury poisoning in Iraq, are shown in table 9.1.[11]

Symptoms of poisoning, then, begin to appear when levels of mercury
in blood fall in the range of 500–1,000 ppb. Studies published by the
World Health Organization confirm that lower levels of exposure are
associated with a significantly decreased degree of risk; at mercury blood
levels in the 200–500-ppb range, there is presumed to be a 5 percent
chance that adults will show the initial symptoms of Minamata disease.[12]
It is worth repeating that very little is known about the long-term effects
of even very modest concentrations of mercury in the human brain. In
Japan, a few particularly sensitive individuals developed initial symptoms
of mercury intoxication at blood levels close to 200 ppb; in Sweden, some
chromosome breakage was observed at the 400-ppb level. Autopsies have
also shown brain damage in individuals whose exposure to methyl mercury was considered insufficient to provoke actual symptoms. In general,
however, fully developed methyl mercury poisoning will occur only when
the concentration of mercury in the blood is in the range of 1,230–1,840
ppb.[13] With prenatal exposure to the toxin, the risks of poisoning are
considerably higher, perhaps three or four times.

## An Environmental Disaster

Following the dreadful experiences of Minamata and Iraq, a series of
international conferences on heavy metals took place in the late 1960s to
publicize the link between the industrial uses of mercury and the potential
dangers of mercury contamination. At about the same time, Swedish
scientists described the process of biomethylation and established that
abnormally high levels of mercury found in fish and wildlife were related
to upstream chlor-alkali and pulp and paper plants. In Canada, early
warnings to government health officials about the hazards of mercury
spills seem to have gone unheeded.[14] Then, in 1967–68, Norvald Fimreite, a Norwegian graduate student at the University of Western Ontario, studied the effects of industrial mercury losses on birds and fish. He
found very high levels of mercury in the fish of the southern part of the
Saskatchewan River, downstream from a pulp and paper mill and chlor-
alkali plant. In 1969, he alerted the officials of the Ontario Water Resources Commission that the fish of Lake St. Clair had unacceptably high
concentrations of methyl mercury. It did not take long to confirm that
fish taken downstream from all the chlor-alkali plants in Ontario carried
body burdens of mercury that were sometimes more than forty times the
standard of 0.5 ppm set for export and human consumption by the

**Table 9.1  Relation of Clinical Symptoms of Methyl Mercury Poisoning in Iraq to Blood Levels of Mercury**

| Whole Blood Methyl Mercury Concentration Levels (ppb) | Percentage of Patients Showing Symptoms | | | | | |
|---|---|---|---|---|---|---|
| | Paresthesia | Ataxia | Visual Changes | Dysarthria | Hearing Defects | Death |
| 0–100[a] | 9.5 | 5 | 0 | 5 | 0 | 0 |
| 101–500 | 5 | 0 | 0 | 5 | 0 | 0 |
| 501–1,000 | 42 | 11 | 21 | 5 | 5 | 0 |
| 1,001–2,000 | 60 | 47 | 53 | 24 | 0 | 0 |
| 2,001–3,000 | 79 | 60 | 56 | 25 | 12.5 | 0 |
| 3,001–4,000 | 82 | 100 | 58 | 75 | 36 | 17 |
| 4,001–5,000 | 100 | 100 | 83 | 85 | 66 | 28 |

Source: From F. Bakir, S. F. Damluji, L. Amin-Zaki et al. "Methylmercury poisoning in Iraq: An Inter-University Report," *Science* 181 (1973), as reproduced in David Shephard, "Methyl Mercury Poisoning in Canada," *Canadian Medical Association Journal* 114 (March 1976): 463–72.
[a]The data from Iraq suggest that the range of 0–100 ppb of mercury in whole blood is associated with a 9.5 percent incidence of paresthesia (numbness in the extremities) and a 5 percent incidence of ataxia (stumbling gait) and dysarthria (slurred speech). Medical authorities concluded, however, that at this concentration, the symptoms were probably caused by factors other than methyl mercury.

federal government. The Lake St. Clair fishery was closed. In March 1970, the Ontario Minister of Energy and Resource Management ordered all the companies in the province with substantial industrial mercury losses to stop discharging mercury into the environment. One of these companies was Dryden Chemicals Limited, a subsidiary of Reed Paper Limited. In May 1970, the Ontario government banned commercial fishing on all lakes and tributaries of the English-Wabigoon river system.

There was cause for concern. Fish in the 300-mile river system, from Dryden to the Manitoba border, were found to contain mercury burdens comparable to those found in the fish of Minamata Bay. Levels of methyl mercury in the aquatic food chain of the system, including plankton, bottom-dwelling organisms, fish, wildfowl, and fish-eating mammals, were found to be ten to fifty times higher than those in surrounding waterways off the system. The greatest concentration of mercury was found among the organisms dwelling on the sediment bottom, particularly crayfish. In 1970, the average value of mercury in crayfish was 10 ppm, a value about twenty times greater than that in crayfish from unpolluted adjacent lakes and rivers.[15] Comprehensive studies of the mercury burden in fish in the early 1970s revealed levels of contamination so high that no species of fish from any lake on the river system was fit for human consumption. The range of mean mercury concentration (measured in parts per million, ppm) in the three most commercially viable species of fish found in the English-Wabigoon river system was as follows (1975 data): pike, 2.31–5.18 ppm; walleye, 1.58–5.98 ppm; whitefish, 0.47–2.01 ppm. The mean level of mercury in the same species and size of fish taken from off-system lakes was, by contrast, several times lower: pike, 0.47–1.39 ppm; walleye, 0.38–1.08 ppm; whitefish, 0.04–0.24 ppm.[16]

Since these peak values were recorded, in the early 1970s, there has been a decline in the amount of mercury in fish, but it has not been of sufficient magnitude to inspire confidence that the river system will heal itself quickly.[17] Not only is the process of biomethylation singularly unenergetic, but there is also a great deal of inorganic mercury sitting on the bottom of the riverbed. It may therefore take anywhere from fifty to seventy years for the poison to clear the system. The pressing question is: Who is responsible for an environmental disaster of such proportions?

Between March 1962 and October 1975, Dryden Chemicals operated a mercury cathode chlor-alkali plant that produced chlorine and other chemicals for use as bleach in the adjacent pulp and paper mill of Reed Paper Limited (Dryden Division). During that period, scientists estimated that about 40,000 pounds of inorganic mercury were "lost" to the environment via aquatic and aerial discharges, of which about 20,000 pounds entered the English-Wabigoon river system.[18] Prior to the promulgation of the 1970 government control order to stop all mercury discharges into water systems, all the waste from the mercury cells was going into the air and the Wabigoon River. In 1970–71, treatment systems were installed to isolate the heavy metal in the effluent. Although this resulted in a significant decline in the amount of mercury going into the river, aerial emissions continued. The loss of mercury to the environment was finally halted in 1975, when the company changed the technology in its chlor-alkali plant.

Executives of Dryden Chemicals and Reed Paper Limited have repeatedly insisted that mercury occurs naturally in the environment of the Canadian Shield and that therefore the effluent from the mill was not the only source of mercury in the river. But the sheer volume of mercury discharged as waste and the fact that fish taken from the polluted waters show much higher mercury levels than fish caught in adjacent lakes and rivers undermine this argument. After studying the problem, scientists of the Ontario government came to the conclusion that "factors such as mineralization, mining activities, and aerial fallout cannot account for the elevated mercury levels found in fish from the Wabigoon-English system of lakes. The major source of mercury pollution in the area is the chlor-alkali plánt/pulp and paper complex in Dryden, Ontario."[19]

Throughout the 1970s, corporate executives continued to deny any culpability for the contamination. They pleaded ignorance of the process of biomethylation. They argued that the mercury in the Wabigoon system was less harmful than the mercury discharged in Minamata Bay. And they insisted that they had no records of how much mercury was purchased, used, or discharged into the environment. The litany of rationalizations in their public pronouncements sometimes bordered on the absurd.[20] But the strongest line of defense was marshalled around the idea that the company had "a license to pollute" from the Ontario government. It had, after all, respected existing environmental regulations and standards; therefore, it could not be held exclusively liable for the disaster.

Robert Billingsley, president of Reed Paper Limited, succinctly asserted the company's position in an interview filmed in September 1975. "I think there are many instances in our society where people are harmed in one way or another through no fault of their own, and it's particularly difficult where blame is not exclusive, where there is [sic] complicating factors; and since we operate on a principle of law in this country, then you almost have to define [blame] in the courts, split up where is the responsibility, do it on a legal basis and assign . . . the consequences. . . . I don't know exactly what we've done. Nobody has told us what the consequences of our actions were." The company's defense, then as now, rested on the premise that mercury pollution was a societal responsibility and that any claims for damages would have to be fought out in the courts. But as we come to understand the kind of injury and loss sustained by the Indian people, we will recognize the immense hurdles of definition, proof, and lack of precedent that would have to be overcome to obtain justice through the Canadian courts.

# 10 • "THE LAST NAIL IN THE COFFIN"

## On Being "At Risk"

Throughout the last pages of the preceding chapter, the following question may well have haunted the reader: Have the people of Grassy Narrows been spared the grim and infinitely cruel effects of mercury's assault on the tissues of the brain? There is no simple answer. There are people in the community who have come to feel that their bodies are not working properly, whose arms and legs and joints are hurting, and whose reflexes are not what they used to be. One hears complaints of malaise, listlessness, and "bad nerves" all over the village, as if everybody had been drained of energy and depleted of psychic resources. But former guides and fishermen speak of more specific, more localized disturbances:

> Sometimes I can't sleep at night. My legs from the knees down feel numb . . . I have a tingling sensation, like a thousand needles. My hands and tongue feel that way too. There's a tightness around my forehead, as if someone had tied twine around my head real tight. I take pills to sleep. The doctor tells me it's 'cause of what I was eating . . . the fish. But I don't know what it is. I worry about my family. I used to guide for twenty years in the summer. Every day I used to bring home fish.
>
> One day I got a letter from the government saying that I had a high mercury level. I think it was over 200. The letter said I was "at risk." But what does that mean? What does 200 mean for me, when everybody else is supposed to have 20? I sometimes get angry at this here mercury . . . but I don't know what to do about it.

We already know that the early bodily sensations of mercury intoxication are indistinguishable from the symptoms provoked by a variety of other disorders. Equally difficult to pin down are the psychosomatic effects of fear, apprehension, and a sense of abandonment and powerlessness. As a result, neurologists who have examined Indian people for mercury-related illness have come up against an unyielding problem of definition and diagnosis. Yet it is important to get the story straight, to order the evidence in such a way as to understand why there are gnawing doubts that the specter of Minamata has not been eliminated completely. We begin by looking at data on the levels of exposure to methyl mercury at Grassy Narrows. Tables 10.1 and 10.2 show the aggregate results of a

**Table 10.1  Levels of Exposure to Methyl Mercury at Grassy Narrows**

| Year | Total Number of Tests[a] | Blood Levels of Mercury (ppb)[b] | | | | | | |
|---|---|---|---|---|---|---|---|---|
| | | 0–19 | 20–99 | 100–199 | 200–299 | 300–399 | 400–499 | 500–699 |
| 1971 | 70 | 12 | 45 | 11 | 1 | 1 | | |
| 1973 | 72 | 18 | 46 | 6 | 2 | | | |
| 1974 | 75 | 49 | 17 | 7 | 1 | | 1 | |
| 1975 | 131 | 29 | 44 | 42 | 11 | 2 | 2 | 1 |
| 1976 | 487 | 377 | 94 | 13 | 2 | 1 | | |
| 1977 | 519 | 413 | 94 | 7 | 3 | 1 | 1 | |
| 1978 | 253 | 204 | 40 | 5 | 3 | | 1 | |

*Source:* From *Methylmercury in Canada* (Ottawa: Health and Welfare Canada, Dec. 1979), pp. 126–69.
[a]These figures are the total number of tests on the hair and the blood over the period 1971–78. They include follow-up or repeat tests on individuals.
[b]The levels of mercury in hair have been converted to blood equivalents. In all cases, the highest segmental level of mercury in any hair sample has been chosen for conversion to a blood equivalent and inclusion in this table. These figures, then, represent the peak levels of mercury found in any given test on any one individual.

**Table 10.2   Individuals at Risk at Grassy Narrows: Blood Levels of Mercury Above 100 ppb**

| Year | Total Number of Persons | Blood Levels (ppb) | | | | |
|------|------|------|------|------|------|------|
| | | 100–199 | 200–299 | 300–399 | 400–499 | 500–699 |
| 1971 | 10 | 8 | 1 | 1 | | |
| 1973 | 7 | 6 | 1 | | | |
| 1974 | 6 | 4 | 1 | | 1 | |
| 1975 | 39 | 27 | 8 | 1 | 2 | 1 |
| 1976 | 10 | 8 | 2 | | | |
| 1977 | 6 | 3 | 1 | 1 | 1 | |
| 1978 | 9 | 5 | 3 | | 1 | |
| | 87 | 61 | 17 | 3 | 5 | 1 |

*Source:* As in Table 10.1.

testing program carried out by the Medical Services Branch of the Department of National Health and Welfare over the period 1971–78. table 10.2 identifies the number of individuals whose blood levels of mercury have, at any point in time, exceeded the "safe" limit of 100 ppb. This is the population considered to be at risk.[1]

The data show that over seven years, mercury levels of 100 ppb or more were recorded for eighty-seven persons from Grassy Narrows, sixty-one of whom registered in the 100–199-ppb range, and twenty-six in the over 200-ppb range. At these relatively low levels, the history of attempts to correlate individual neurological disturbances with exposure to mercury has left a legacy of inconclusive results, contradictory opinions, and unanswered questions. Let us examine the medical record.

In May 1973, eighteen persons at risk from the two Indian communities on the river system, Whitedog and Grassy Narrows, were invited to undergo extensive clinical examinations at the Winnipeg General Hospital. Tests on the six individuals who agreed to these examinations revealed no evidence of mercury intoxication.

In 1974–75, Peter Newberry became the first resident physician at Grassy Narrows. In the course of a year, he performed tests on seventeen volunteers and found a very high incidence of tunnel vision and at least one symptom of mercury poisoning in fifteen individuals. He left the community convinced that as many as ten persons had been affected by methyl mercury.

In March 1975, one of the world's leading diagnosticians of mercury poisoning, Masazumi Harada, visited Grassy Narrows and Whitedog. He observed that some of the fish, aquatic birds, and fish-eating mammals (such as otter and mink) in the polluted area had levels of mercury in tissue as high as those recorded in Minamata. He confirmed that the behavior of cats near Whitedog that had been fed mercury-contaminated fish was identical to the behavior of cats observed in Minamata, where many had died from mercury poisoning. But he could not make a positive diagnosis of Minamata disease among the Indian people. After examining eighty-nine residents of Grassy Narrows and Whitedog, he described his findings as follows:

Health surveys were conducted . . . on the two reservations by the same methods applied in our mass examination for Minamata disease in Japan . . . . Many neurological symptoms were found. It cannot be concluded that all of these symptoms resulted from methyl mercury. However, symptoms observed frequently in Minamata disease . . . were immediately recognized.

We conducted health surveys of eighty-nine inhabitants and found the following: disturbance of eye movement (twelve cases); impaired hearing (forty cases); sensory disturbance (thirty-seven cases); contraction of the visual field (sixteen cases); tremor (twenty-one cases); hyporeflexia (diminution of reflexes) (twenty cases); ataxia (eight cases); dysarthria (five cases). The neurological symptoms are characteristic of mercury poisoning. However, the symptoms are relatively mild, and many of them were thought to be caused by other factors.

Epidemiological studies comparing polluted groups with nonpolluted groups are necessary for the detection of illness. Even though typical cases [at Grassy Narrows and Whitedog] may be absent, methyl mercury poisoning must be suspected whenever there is a high incidence of contraction of the visual fields and sensory disturbance, especially when the same symptoms are prevalent in families.[2]

Harada acknowledged that there were substantial differences between Minamata and northwestern Ontario in density of population, mode of life, diet, and source of pollution. He admitted that sensory disturbance of the "glove and stocking type" (numbness in the extremities), a characteristic early symptom of Minamata disease, is also observable in alcoholism and many other diseases. The influence of methyl mercury in causing the various neurological symptoms was therefore declared as "possible" but not certain.

In the same year, the Medical Services Branch of the Department of Health and Welfare obtained the consulting services of an internationally known expert on mercury poisoning, T. W. Clarkson, of the University of Rochester. After an extensive program of testing for levels of exposure to methyl mercury, Clarkson concluded:

Several individuals in both reserves still have unacceptably high blood levels of methyl mercury. [This] continues to be a serious problem with guides working at fishing camps. The highest concentrations of mercury ever reported from White Dog and Grassy Narrows reserves, approximately 150 ppm in hair, equivalent to 500 ppb in blood, occurred in the summer of 1975, despite the fact that warnings against eating contaminated fish have been in effect for several years and that an intensive health education campaign has been in effect during the past year.

Wives of guides have a higher exposure to methyl mercury than other females. A matter of most serious concern is the exposure to methyl mercury of pregnant females.[3]

Working from a longitudinal analysis of hair samples, Clarkson found that the highest blood levels of mercury corresponded to periods of heavy fish consumption, during the summer and early fall; at other times, mercury levels were considerably lower. The cyclical pattern of exposure to methyl mercury was particularly evident for guides working in sports fishing camps, because they prepared shore lunches and ate fish with the tourists during the guiding season. Clarkson became particularly concerned about exposure to mercury by pregnant women when he tested a newborn infant and found a level of mercury equivalent to 100 ppb in the blood. In his report to the federal government, he therefore recommended priority attention to the expansion of neurological examinations of Indian people, increased emphasis on the surveillance of pregnant women for exposure to mercury, a program to reduce the fish intake of guides, and a continuing program of health education about the hazards of eating mercury-contaminated fish.

In 1976, another well-known neurologist with experience in methyl mercury poisoning, J. S. Prichard, of the University of Toronto, visited Grassy Narrows and Whitedog. After testing residents in 1976 and again in 1977 and 1979, he concluded that clinical examinations alone were inadequate for a definitive diagnosis of mercury poisoning:

> I found a number of people [at Grassy Narrows] with tremors . . . . I found a number of people who were not very skillful with their hand movements. There was minor pathology, minor neurological abnormality. The trouble is that with the small amounts of mercury [in blood], the kinds of symptoms and signs that they have are very nonspecific. The first thing is tingling in the fingers or very slight tremor. Alcohol will lead to a tremor, and it'll lead to staggering and so on, which is the same kind of thing that mercury can do . . . . Whether the pins and needles or the tremor has been caused by mercury, or one of the numerous other things that can cause it, is a very difficult decision indeed. And in fact in an individual case, I don't believe you can tell. I think you need an epidemiological study to really decide whether mercury's involved or not.[4]

By the end of 1978, Dr. Prichard had clinically examined forty persons at risk from Grassy Narrows and Whitedog. His findings with respect to neurological abnormalities caused by methyl mercury were negative for twenty-five cases; positive and not related to mercury in five cases; and positive but only possibly related to mercury in ten cases.[5]

In sum, a definitive diagnosis of Minamata disease in northwestern Ontario continues to elude the medical establishment. So far, the association of peak mercury levels in individuals with positive clinical findings has been random; so far, postmortem studies of the brain have proved inconclusive. What we do know is that the very high levels of mercury in the blood associated with this disease in Japan and Iraq have not been encountered among the Indian people. Over the period 1971–78, the highest levels of exposure to mercury recorded at Grassy Narrows have fallen in the range of 200–500 ppb, with most findings clustered at the lower end of the scale. Yet, the very difficulties of diagnosis in this situation are a cause of concern.

In the first place, there are differences of opinion between Japanese and Canadian neurologists, as well as among Canadian neurologists, with respect to the specific symptoms that are required for a positive diagnosis of mercury poisoning. One of the problems hampering agreement has already been identified: namely, the nonspecific nature of the initial symptoms and the difficulty of attributing them to methyl mercury rather than to some other condition. Some Canadian doctors argue, however, that this diagnostic quandary does not constitute a sufficient basis for presuming that mercury's effects on health have been negligible:

> In view of this lack of specificity, which may lead one neurologist to attribute a sign such as tremor or constriction of the visual field to mercury poisoning, yet another to be less definite, one must to some extent rely on circumstantial evidence if one is to give a definite answer to the question of whether mercury poisoning exists in Canada.
>
> A close look at the available evidence suggests that mercury poisoning is a possibility, if not a probability. The evidence for mercury poisoning is credible, whereas there is no evidence that mercury poisoning does *not* exist.[6]

In the second place, the relevance of data on Minamata disease from Japan and Iraq to the situation in northwestern Ontario is not entirely clear. The pattern of exposure to methyl mercury among the Indian people is different. The Indians eat fish seasonally; their diet is not totally dependent upon fish, even in summer; and while the consumption of fish is heaviest among guides and their families, fish is relatively unimportant in the diet of wage-earners, who prefer to buy food from the store. This pattern of intermittent exposure to a wide range of daily intakes of fish repeats itself every year. Clearly it differs markedly from the Iraqi experience where the eating of mercury-contaminated grain led to intensive exposure to large doses of methyl mercury over a very short period of time. It also differs from the Japanese pattern of exposure to significantly higher levels of mercury and greater reliance on fish in the diet, sustained over a longer period of time. Indeed, in Iraq the effects of methyl mercury poisoning were not identical to those in Japan.[7]

This variability in effects, which is linked to the pattern of exposure, may mean that the dose-response relationships documented in other contexts are of limited applicability to northwestern Ontario. The fact is that scientists and doctors know a lot more about the consequences of large concentrations of mercury in the human body than about the effects of chronic, low-level, and seasonal exposure. Thus, we may not be noticing organic effects that are subclinical and possibly cumulative. There may be subtle neurological and behavioral changes in the Indian people that are not detectable at the present time. Canadian medical officials have alluded to this: "Milder forms of mercury poisoning, though difficult to prove conclusively, quite possibly are occurring. Certainly, given the levels found in some individuals, cause for concern and caution exists."[8]

A third problem is that methyl mercury's damage to the tissues of the brain may not be limited to the poison's "organic" effects. To have a gnawing fear that there is a poison in one's body, not to know the difference between being at risk and being poisoned, is to live in a state of constant apprehension. It is a well-known phenomenon that the human mind will sometimes respond to a specific fear by actually precipitating the dreaded event. Something like this may be happening at Grassy Narrows. The hidden corrosive effects on the psyche of fear and anxiety, as well as the apparent symptoms of possible organic damage, were recognized by Clarkson at the time he tested the Indian people for levels of mercury in blood:

> For a normal person, who may not indeed have had a very extensive education, to be told, "You have a poison in your body," and then, "Well, there's only a 5 percent risk," is almost incomprehensible . . . . I think even pretty well-educated people . . . become alarmed [when] correlations are made with Minamata, and pictures of people are shown who are grossly poisoned and deformed.
>
> Such things would never, as far as I could tell, happen at Whitedog or Grassy Narrows because the amount of mercury they're exposed to isn't that high. But I believe that there is a possibility that some people may have adverse health effects due to methyl mercury.[9]

Finally, there are much broader considerations. The effect of an illness on any organism depends upon its existing state of health. It can be argued that a community is somewhat like an organism, that it can be damaged in ways that are not reflected in the damage experienced by each of its individual members. Testimony to this comes in the form of a statement by Prichard. Even though he could not prove (or disprove) that methyl mercury caused neurological disturbance in the individual cases he examined, he nevertheless became convinced that mercury had wreaked tremendous damage on the community as a whole:

The people of Grassy Narrows have had a rough time for the last few years. They have had to change the location of their reserve, they have been regimented into these hideous little houses. They've loved fishing, it's been their life. And someone has said, "You can't fish." They've had all kinds of problems with alcohol and drugs. And on this background, they've had this horrible thing of someone saying, "You can't eat the fish, they'll poison you. And not only that, but the fish you have eaten probably have poisoned you, and you probably are dying." It's an appalling thing. And they see these pictures of people from Japan with these extraordinary movement disorders.

And I think the fear of this, and the consequent effect on their whole lifestyle, way of living, society—I think these people have been affected by mercury. I think their lives have been severely affected by mercury—but not by the organic effects.[10]

Later in this chapter, we will see how the images of human wreckage left in the wake of Minamata, as well as the facts and the physical evidence of mercury, were used to control and manipulate the Grassy Narrows people. I will argue that the politics of mercury left an imprint on the community every bit as cruel and demoralizing as the poison in the river. But in the chronicle of this disaster, there is more to be said about the tangible effects, for mercury delivered a major blow to the Indian way of life when the fishery was closed by government decree.

## Damages to Livelihood

One day [in May 1970] government people just came and told us to stop fishing. Nobody explained what mercury is or how people get sick from it. All they told us was not to eat the fish any more. Next thing that happened was that Barney Lamm closed down Ball Lake Lodge, and suddenly, everybody who guided for Barney was out of a job.

The abrupt collapse of the commercial fishery and the disruption of guiding sent shock waves through the community. In the absence of information about mercury, the people could not understand how something that happened far away in Dryden could affect them; they could not taste or see the mercury in fish; and they could not believe that the river that had always sustained them was now doing them harm. Some turned to the only explanation that made sense to them: mercury "was something the white people made up . . . to take away our fishing rights and our right to live in the Indian way."

The loss of a sense of confidence in nature as a bountiful provider and the loss of an economic base from which people could be relatively self-reliant cannot be measured by conventional means. Similarly, it is not possible to put a value on the loss of one of the few remaining occupations, after the relocation, that permitted families to work together. Because sons worked alongside fathers and wives tended nets while husbands were guiding, commercial fishing had provided some continuity with the traditional ways of organizing work within a family group. Moreover, the loss of the trapline way of life just seven years earlier made commercial fishing even more important as a link with customary ways of living from the land. Although it was not a traditional occupation as such at Grassy Narrows (since it began only in the mid-1950s), seven out of the nine families that worked in the fishery in the late 1960s were families who struggled to maintain the Indian way of life.

Commercial fishing offered other advantages. It fit very well into the seasonal cycle of work, and it allowed people to be flexible in allocating their time. Men who guided during the week could fish during the weekend; those who guided every day for the full season (mid-May to mid-October) could take up fishing for the last three or four weeks in the fall or until freeze-up. This was in fact the preferred strategy. "I did pretty good at commercial fishing. I had my own boat, I bought new nets . . . just before this mercury started. My wife and I used to work together. She tended nets while I was out guiding. Every day when I came home from guiding, I took over, and I fished from the end of the guiding season to freeze-up. Fishing was good 'cause we could make good money in a short time. And we also took fish from the river for food. I would say many guides used to commercial fish after the tourist season was over. But some Grassy Narrows families fished year-round in open water."

In the late 1960s, about twenty-three full-time guides took up commercial fishing after guiding was over, while about fourteen band members (men and women) fished full-time during the entire open-water season. A handful of younger people also worked in the fishery as helpers when they needed extra income. In short, commercial fishing provided a very important economic option at Grassy Narrows, although it never achieved the same prominence in the community economy as it did at Whitedog.[11]

For twelve years, the fishermen of Grassy Narrows delivered thousands of pounds of fish to the Kenora fish market. They were proud of their ability to supply fresh pickerel, whitefish, and pike. Because their income from fishing was good, their economic losses as a result of the closure of the fishery were substantial. A reasonable method of calculating these losses to the community is to take the average annual catch of fish (by species and weight over the number of years that the fishery was in operation) multiplied by the average price per pound in the late 1960s, then project this over the number of years that the fish will remain poisoned and unfit for human consumption and export. This assumes that the levels of production from the commercial fishery at Grassy Narrows during the period 1957–69 would have continued into the 1970s and beyond, an assumption that is itself dependent on a number of factors.

First, from a biological viewpoint, we do not know whether the maximum sustainable yield per species in the English-Wabigoon river system during the 1960s could have been sustained on a long-term basis. This is a question that only fisheries biologists can answer.[12] Second, from a policy perspective, in recent years sports fishing has not only been given priority over commercial fishing, but the Ontario government has been trying to enforce ever increasing restrictions and quotas on commercial fishing by Indian bands in the Lake of the Woods area. It is not out of the question that the fishing effort of the Grassy Narrows band would have been curtailed in the 1980s, or at least not allowed to expand. These considerations have a bearing on the assumption that the band's average annual harvest of fish in the 1957–69 period would have continued indefinitely.

On the other side of the ledger, however, is the very high probability that the recorded levels of production from the Grassy Narrows fishery underestimate the true harvest of fish in any one year. For one thing, the system of reporting the total fish catch to the Ontario Ministry of Natural Resources was based on a collective responsibility; but the band had to depend on individual fishermen to report their daily catches faithfully. Many of the casual fishermen did not report their catches, and private sales to noncommercial buyers also went unrecorded. Moreover, ministry officials readily admit that those bands that had weight quotas on certain species of fish written into their commercial fishing licenses had little incentive to report their total catches accurately. For these reasons, available data on the levels of production from the Grassy Narrows fishery before 1970 should be considered as the minimum estimate of the total fishing harvest.

Our estimate of the total economic loss to the Grassy Narrows band resulting from the closure of the commercial fishery has been developed subject to the following assumptions: first, that the band's fishing effort, measured in terms of the average annual harvest of fish in the period 1957–69, would have remained more or less the same; second, that the limitations on the total catch and the season specified in the band's license since 1957 would have continued to prevail; and third, that average prices per pound of the three most commercially valuable species of fish would have increased by a 6 percent average annual inflation rate after 1970.[13] Finally, since scientists cannot estimate with precision how long the fish will remain poisoned with unacceptable levels of methyl mercury, the analysis has to take into account different assumptions with respect to time. The most optimistic estimate of the period of recovery, based on the pattern demonstrated in the St. Clair system, is twenty years; however, sedimentation, flushing, and methylation rates in the English-Wabigoon river system may be different enough to warrant an estimate of fifty to seventy years for recovery.

Based on an average annual production level of 15,382 pounds of whitefish, 9,249 pounds of walleye, and 7,782 pounds of pike over a thirteen-year period (1957–69), and an average annual value of $5,076 for whitefish, $4,625 for walleye, and $1,323 for pike, the projected economic losses resulting from the closure of the fishery for twenty-, fifty-, and seventy-year periods are estimated in table 10.3.

It cannot be overemphasized that this calculation of economic loss does not take into account interest on this money; it should be considered as a minimum approximation to the total real value of the commercial fishery lost to the Grassy Narrows band.[14] Furthermore, at the time commercial fishing ceased, some families had a considerable investment in gear and equipment, such as a boat and motor, nets, twine, and other miscellaneous items. Aside from boats and motors, which could be used for other purposes, the capital invested in commercial fishing gear was effectively lost. In sum, even by the most conservative and cautious estimates, the economic loss of the fishery was significant.

Between 1970 and 1973, the Ontario government attempted to make compensatory payments to nineteen Grassy Narrows commercial fishermen. These "forgivable loans" averaged only $311.08 per person. The total compensation paid out to the community amounted to a mere $5,910.[15] It is easy to understand why the people feel cheated: "About our commercial fishing at Grassy Narrows . . . I feel very strongly that up to now we should have been compensated. Most of the people who were fishing are now getting old. They haven't benefited anything from the government. Reed Paper that polluted the river didn't pay any compensation—nothing at all. This is very unfair. Many people lost something that was precious to them."

Needless to say, the Indian people also lost the river as a source of food. In the summer months, all species of fish were readily available as a by-product of commercial fishing and guiding and they had become a staple

Table 10.3   Estimated Economic Losses from the Closure of the Fishery

|                                                      | 1970–90    | 1970–2020   | 1970–2040    |
| ---------------------------------------------------- | ---------- | ----------- | ------------ |
| Whitefish                                            | $101,520   | $253,800    | $355,320     |
| Walleye                                              | 92,500     | 231,250     | 323,750      |
| Pike                                                 | 26,460     | 66,150      | 92,610       |
|                                                      | $220,480   | $551,200    | $771,680     |
| Total value, assuming 6 percent price inflation per year | $405,500   | $3,193,700  | $10,670,129  |

in the diet of the families engaged in these activities. A 1973 report on dietary problems at Grassy Narrows and Whitedog confirmed this:

> Fish consumption was not important in the winter months [and] aside from one or two individuals in each community, there was no exclusive fishing for subsistence. Almost all the fish consumed were by-products of either the commercial fishery or the fish guiding industry . . . . The guide would frequently bring some of the day's catch home to his family in the evening . . . . Among the commercial fishermen, unsalable small fish were used for food.
>
> The total community could be divided into three groups from the point of view of diet. First there were those who worked for wages and purchased all their food from the store. Second, those who guided ate fish while guiding, augmented by store food during winter. Thirdly, there were the very few trappers who would eat store food in the summer (with considerable fish) and who would live almost exclusively on bush food in the winter.[16]

This study found that after 1970 the consumption of fish by people in both communities was drastically reduced. The diet had become heavily dependent on starches, and "most people were not eating fish if there was something else to eat." Historically, the Ojibwa have always concentrated on large game in the diet, using fish as a backup food staple only when moose and deer were scarce. There was always the security of knowing that the river would be a bountiful provider, however, if the hunt failed. The loss of fish as a backup option in the diet eliminated a valuable source of protein and placed a heavy burden on those families that could not afford to purchase food. Recognizing this problem, the Ontario government in 1975 began delivering uncontaminated fish to Grassy Narrows and Whitedog. Stored in freezers on both reserves, this fish was available to all band members. But the people did not like the frozen fish; they found it mushy and tasteless when cooked. In any case, this Fish for Food Program provided only a partial solution to the need for an alternative protein source. The much greater loss that could not be replaced was the ability of the people to provide for themselves without being dependent upon external sources of supply. The net effect of this as well as of other government programs was to move the Indian people further from being producers to being consumers, subject to the mercy of an impersonal bureaucracy.

The other important sector of the Grassy Narrows economy affected by the contamination of the river was guiding. Early in the summer of 1970, Barney Lamm decided to close down his lodge at Ball Lake, presumably because he felt that he could not expose either the guests or the guides to the risks of eating contaminated fish. The closing of Ball Lake, the most exclusive and luxurious lodge in the area, was a blow to many Grassy Narrows people who had worked there since 1947.

Before the mercury came, we were still pretty good at making our own living. The fishing camps opened in May and closed in September. And after that, some of our people guided hunters for moose. That means we had work for maybe five, six months of the year. And some of us old-timers, we've been guiding for a long time—ever since the first camps opened after the Second World War.

Our people built Ball Lake Lodge . . . I'd say we helped make the lodge famous. The guests kept coming back for the fishing. But it's the guides who had the skills, who knew the best fishing holes, and we made sure nobody ever went home disappointed. Guiding . . . it was a good life for many, many years.

Certainly the Grassy Narrows people had a stake in the enterprise of Ball Lake Lodge. They built the first cabins and saw the lodge grow from humble beginnings to a resort of considerable renown, especially among wealthy Americans. They felt they had helped Barney Lamm make a personal fortune from the lodge, since satisfied sports fishermen were Ball Lake's best publicity agents. But above all, the people liked to guide, liked the way of life it made possible. Barney Lamm was the "patron," the "seigneur," who ran his estate with just the right mixture of controlled benevolence, familiarity, and discipline to allow him to capitalize on the supply of cheap and unorganized Indian labor. And Indian people considered him a good employer. Even though almost no one came back to the reserve with any savings to show for the season's labor, "guiding . . . it was a good life."

No wonder, then, that the closing of Ball Lake Lodge meant much more to the Indian people than the loss of just a job or wages. Yet the economic impact of the closing on Grassy Narrows was not insignificant. Although journalists have tended to exaggerate the absolute figures for the loss of income and employment,[17] nevertheless, Ball Lake Lodge probably contributed at least half of the total income from guiding (sports fishing and hunting) that came into the community each year. If we estimate gross income from guiding to have been in the range of $90,000–$110,000 per year prior to 1970,[18] then the closing of Ball Lake Lodge could have effectively removed $50,000–$60,000 from the community economy.

Ball Lake Lodge was unquestionably the most desirable place to work as a guide. Barney Lamm hired both Indian and non-Indian guides, and a sizable proportion of his full-time Indian guides always came from Grassy Narrows. In 1968, for example, seventeen men from Grassy Narrows (of a total of twenty-seven Indian guides) were employed either full-time or part-time by Ball Lake Lodge. In 1969, the last year the lodge was open for fishing, fourteen of the twenty-three Indian guides employed for the full season came from Grassy, as did five of the seven part-time guides.

After the lodge closed, a number of old-timers, who had been guiding at Ball Lake for twenty years or more, stopped guiding altogether. The rest eventually found guiding jobs elsewhere. In the immediate vicinity of the reserve, Delaney Lodge and Grassy Lodge remained open, and their owners continued to rely almost exclusively on people from Grassy Narrows to provide guiding and other services. It is fair to say, however, that the entire sports fishing industry on the English-Wabigoon river system suffered from the uncertainty surrounding the hazards to human health posed by the mercury pollution of the river. A tremendous amount of negative publicity led many tourists to stay away from northwestern Ontario. As a result, guiding employment dropped sharply, particularly during the first three seasons after 1970. This general disruption in the tourist industry was very much a function of the politics of the mercury issue, a subject to be discussed in a moment.

There are two points to be emphasized, however. First, the net effect of the economic impacts directly attributable to mercury pollution—the end of guiding at Ball Lake, the loss of commercial fishing, the loss of fish for food—was to further undermine the conditions for self-sufficiency, to intensify dependence on government support, and ultimately to accelerate the breakdown in community life. Moreover, the mercury-related damages were more devastating at Grassy Narrows than they might have been in the absence of other massive societal changes taking place at the same time. The trauma of resettlement was harsh enough, but the people might have been able to adapt. At a minimum, they could have continued to be producers, thus preserving a measure of self-respect; as fishermen, they could have maintained a degree of continuity with customary skills, sensibilities, and ways of organizing work. But the mercury poisoning came along and stopped this alternative cold.

Second, the measurable economic impacts tell only part of the story. For people who had traditionally lived off the land, its products, and its waters, it must have been a horror to confront the fact that the land had somehow turned against them and become poisonous. It is hard for us to comprehend how desolate and painful such a realization must have been. But as one woman said, "People have been trusting the fish for many years, and suddenly you don't know whether to trust them any more . . . . It's not so much a fear, it's a suspicion." Mercury thus presented a haunting psychological problem, because the world of nature, not only the world of men, could no longer be trusted.

## The Politics of Mercury

Mercury triggered a political process whose rhetoric and posturing left an imprint on the people's values and hopes every bit as ruthless and destructive as the poison in the river. After more than a decade of meetings, briefs, submissions, pleadings, and formal and informal negotiations for just compensation for damages to life and livelihood, the Grassy Narrows people have gained little more than platitudinous programs designed to placate. The fundamental inability of government to deal holistically with a shattered society has remained as constant as the Indians' powerlessness to effect social justice. Throughout the decade of the 1970s and to this day, the political process has been directed by the perceived imperative on the part of both government and industry that any responsibility for contemporary conditions in the Indian community must be denied and that any course of action that might imply acceptance of legal, moral, or social liability must be avoided. In the context of such principles of political conduct, it is not surprising that the decade-long struggle has only reinforced the Indians' feeling of helplessness, apathy, and alienation.

It would be easy to devote an entire book to the politics of the mercury issue. The story is both complex and fascinating, for each actor on the political stage feels a need to create the illusion of righteousness and virtue to justify self-serving conduct. In relating the events and situations as they happened, our purpose is not to unmask the villains in the play but rather to draw aside the curtain of illusions in order to reveal the nature of the society in which the political drama takes place. We begin at the beginning, in May 1970.

Some ministers of the Ontario government believed sincerely that the mercury problem was a temporary one. George Kerr, Minister of the Environment, said in a radio interview in Kenora (August 13, 1970) that it would take about twelve weeks "for the fish to lower their mercury count." As a precaution, however, the Ministry of Natural Resources, which regulates sports fishing, sent letters to tourist camp operators on the English-Wabigoon river system recommending that guests and guides "fish for fun" only and not eat their catches. Fish for Fun signs were posted along the shore warning people against eating fish. Later that year, the Premier of Ontario, John Robarts, met with tourist camp owners in Kenora to discuss the possibility of governmental assistance to those who might want to relocate their fishing camps or convert them to multi-activity tourist operations.

Early in 1971, the Ontario government became aware of the economic implications of mercury pollution: "If the problem [of mercury] is not resolved . . . as many as 400 people could be out of work in northwestern Ontario . . . with a probable loss of at least one-third of the tourist trade for this year, which would translate into several million dollars of lost tourist revenue."[19] When, in March of 1971, William Davis succeeded John Robarts as Premier of the province, and Leo Bernier (former member of the provincial parliament for Kenora) was appointed Minister of Natural Resources, the internal politics of the conservative cabinet became even more sharply focused on the delicate problem of balancing the risks to health posed by mercury against the potential loss of tourist revenue in the region. Ministers of different portfolios, representing different interests, contradicted each other publicly. Whereas the Minister of Health, Richard T. Potter, wrote strongly worded letters to camp operators advising them not to eat fish from contaminated waterways, Bernier announced on the Kenora radio that "the tourist could come up here for three weeks, eat the fish two or three times a week, and be fine." Other cabinet ministers agreed with Bernier that the pollution problem had been overstated and exaggerated. René Brunelle, Minister of Resources Development, said on April 26, 1971, that the mercury problem was getting far too much emphasis because "most of our lakes in the Precambrian Shield . . . have a high natural background of mercury."

The interests of the tourist industry seemed to be very well represented in the deliberations of the Ontario cabinet on the mercury problem. The Fish for Fun posters came down in 1971 and never reappeared. Booklets for sports fishermen with information about mercury were quietly withdrawn from circulation. And to offset damaging publicity about the existence of mercury in provincial waters, the Ministry of Tourism and Information was directed to spend an additional $70,000 advertising Ontario's superb sports fishing country. While offering no assurances that risks to health did not exist, the ministers of the Crown decided that the public interest would best be served by a concerted effort to downplay the seriousness of the mercury situation. Such a strategy was no doubt meant, among other things, to dampen public criticism of the Ontario government for allowing the industry to pollute the waterway in the first place. After 1971, perhaps to deflect any possible implication of liability, there was also no more talk of compensation or relocation assistance to camp owners.

Individual tourist camp operators were left to make their own decisions about subjecting their guests and guides to the health risks associated with mercury. Most of the camps were small family-run operations that could ill afford any major disruption to business. Assured by the government that the problem of mercury was not a long-term one, they elected to stay in business. There were two exceptions: Barney Lamm, as we have seen, closed Ball Lake Lodge in 1970; and in 1971, Colin Myles closed his Separation Lake Camp. Since Barney Lamm became a key player in the politics of mercury, no description of events would be complete without reference to his role.

With unremitting determination, backed by considerable financial resources, Barney Lamm pursued the objective of achieving compensation for the loss of his lodge. To this end, he paid for a study of the levels of mercury in fish, and he gathered an impressive library of information on mercury and its effects. In 1971, he launched a lawsuit against Dryden Chemicals Limited, claiming $3.7 million in compensation for his losses in land, fixed assets, and foregone profits. He became a thorn in the side of government ministers, especially Leo Bernier, because he openly and effectively protested the continued operation of the tourist camps. He skillfully used the national media to publicize his cause, providing pilots and aircraft to anyone who wanted to visit Ball Lake Lodge, Grassy Narrows, or Whitedog. Certainly the publicity he generated presented a formidable counterweight to the government's attempt to tread more softly on the issue of mercury pollution.

In Kenora and Dryden, however, people felt victimized by the relentless, sensationalist, and overwhelmingly negative treatment of the mercury issue in the national media. They did not appreciate the unqualified adulation in the press of Barney and Marion Lamm, who were portrayed as champions of justice, protectors of the environment, and soulmates to the Indians who had been poisoned by mercury. They knew that prominent Toronto journalists and national media personalities enjoyed the Lamms' hospitality. And there was wide speculation that Lamm financed much of the unpleasant publicity, including the Troyer and Hutchison books on mercury (*No Safe Place* and *Grassy Narrows*). The rumors around Kenora that Lamm had financed the publication of *Grassy Narrows* may have been the reason for Hutchison's denial of them in the acknowledgment section of his book. Meanwhile, Lamm left no doubt that he was a rich American with a cause; doubts surfaced only about whether his interests were moral as well as financial.

The key players in the political game in 1970–73, then, were the government of Ontario and Barney Lamm. While the government tried to minimize the gravity of the pollution problem, Lamm tried to maximize it. Each accused the other of misleading the public, distorting the truth, and hiding narrow political or pecuniary personal goals behind the veneer of public interest. The people of Grassy Narrows and Whitedog did not know what to believe. In the first of many formal presentations to the Ontario government in March of 1973, the Grassy Narrows band stated: "We have undergone many tests on the effects of mercury on our health and we are still in the dark as to what to do about the mercury problem."[20]

Indian people were tested for mercury levels in the blood and the hair by officials of the Ontario Ministry of Health in 1970, 1972, and January 1973. But no one bothered to communicate the results of the tests to the people who were supposedly at risk from mercury poisoning. On November 22, 1972, the Grassy Narrows band council wrote a letter to federal and provincial officials stating that the people were tired of being "used as specimens" and demanding to know the test results. Anxiety over the effects of mercury on health heightened in the community when forty-two-year-old Tom Strong died, presumably from a heart attack, in August 1972. He was known to be a heavy fish-eater. An inquest was held on January 26, 1973. According to various newspaper reports, G. James Stopps, the head of the Environmental Health Services Branch of the Ontario Ministry of Health, suggested that the coroner's jury ignore testimony that a postmortem blood sample from Tom Strong showed a level of mercury of 224 ppb; in his opinion, the sample had probably been contaminated by mercury in the pathology laboratory. This explanation did not rest well with the Indian people, who had little faith in the Ontario government to begin with, and the incident reinforced their suspicions that the provincial government was engaged in a cover-up of medical data.

In 1973, the provincial government continued to send out contradictory and confusing information about the hazards of mercury. Stopps wrote one kind of letter to the camp owners and another to the band councils. He advised the camp owners in no uncertain terms that "fish from the English-Wabigoon River should *not* be eaten"; but he told the band councils: "From the measurements we made and our conversations with your people, we did not find any effect of mercury upon the people's health; however, it would be wise to tell those people with particularly high mercury levels to *reduce* the amount of fish they eat and we are making this recommendation in the letters sent to those few people who do have such levels."[21]

Ironically, at the time that Stopps wrote this letter to the band councils, the people with high mercury levels had not yet been informed of the test results. When the information was finally produced, on March 8, 1973, it was not only contained in a form that the people could not understand but was also delivered in a very irresponsible and insensitive manner. Just as visiting government officials were about to board a plane to depart from Grassy Narrows, they handed out sealed envelopes containing individually addressed form letters that listed the levels of mercury in blood. The Indian people, left on the ground reading their mercury levels, had no idea what these levels meant, nothing had been explained to them, and those who might have been able to explain had literally flown away. Those at risk read a letter that said: "From this measurement, and our conversation with you, there is no suggestion that mercury is affecting your health, but experts in the effect of mercury would agree that your level is somewhat too high and that, as a safety precaution, it would be wise to lower it."

Such a letter, with its gratuitous advice, did not illuminate the problem for people still in the dark about the medical and technical aspects of mercury contamination. And the incident reinforced what Indian people had always suspected: that government officials really didn't care about them because they were Indians. In interviews with people at risk, I was astonished to discover how poorly informed they were. Here is a representative sample of responses:

> The doctors never told us anything, just not to eat fish. One day I got a letter that told me that my mercury count was 236 ppb. They took many samples of my blood and hair. I can read and write, but I don't understand what these letters say.
>
> I have been on the Wabigoon all my life . . . I've been guiding for over twenty years . . . nobody told me about mercury either.
>
> My mercury count was over 200 ppb. Nobody ever explained mercury to me.
>
> One day I received a letter from Health and Welfare with some numbers on it; I was told I was at risk. I didn't understand the letter, and nobody told me what the numbers mean. I guide every summer and eat fish.

At the same time, reports in the press were carrying articles describing mercury as a slow killer that was already crippling the people of Grassy Narrows and Whitedog and causing social violence. Mercury was held responsible for "character and personality changes . . . and behavioral problems resulting in violent death." A typical article on mercury was headlined "Mercury—The Indians' Deadliest Enemy." A typical story painted a portrait of an imminent catastrophe: "Indians [have been] kept in the dark for three years about a health hazard that scientists and doctors say should have killed many of them. Tests . . . revealed dangerously high mercury levels, in many cases 40 to 150 times that of the average Canadian and well above the level at which neurological damage begins . . . . The mercury levels found in Indians are as high or higher than those found in thirty-six fishermen killed by mercury poisoning in Japan."[22]

By this time, moreover, well-meaning white people had visited the reserves to explain Minamata disease. They showed pictures and films of horribly disfigured Minamata victims, writhing in pain, waiting for death. For the sake of impact, they emphasized the hideous and the grotesque. And they warned of the treachery of the government. On this last point, there was evidence enough to suggest that "someone" was not telling the Indian people the truth about mercury.

The fear of mercury and the uncertainty and confusion about its effects on health were compounded when the federal government became involved in the mercury issue. In what is now considered to be a classic example of government obfuscation on the subject of mercury as a health hazard, Peter Connop, director of the Thunder Bay Zone for the Medical Services Branch, wrote to individual Grassy Narrows band members on March 17, 1975, as follows:

> Your level of mercury was found to be _____ parts per billion . . . . Most of the band members have mercury levels that are higher than the people living in

southern Ontario who do not eat very much fish, but this is to be expected, and the mercury level does vary from person to person without necessarily having any effect on their health. We consider your mercury level to be in the range of measurements which would not affect your health.

We realize that the matter of mercury in the fish is a difficult one to understand and the experts are still learning more about mercury and its effects, but it is also important to remember that to keep healthy, it is necessary to eat balanced meals which contain some meat or fish as well as starch foods such as bread, and fats such as margarine or butter.

Connop then advised the people not to eat more fish than they usually did from the English River and to eat small fish rather than large fish. In short, the message was that the people could eat as much fish from the contaminated river as they had done in the past!

It may be hard to believe that the contradictory messages sent to Indian people by both the national and provincial governments were deliberate attempts to conceal information in order to deflect, or at least delay, the issue of liability for damages. But the fact is that any kind of information on mercury was extremely difficult to obtain, particularly from the Ontario government. The practice of keeping the lid on information was publicly recognized in the 1973 report of the Federal Task Force on Organic Mercury in the Environment, which stated: "The free flow of information and data on mercury in the environment within the Province of Ontario is impeded for reasons that are not clearly understood."[23]

But there is also evidence that some federal government officials were aware of and sensitive to the issue of liability and possible demands for compensation. On March 15, 1973, for example, Connop wrote to the regional director of Medical Services with the following interesting admonition: "If the Provincial Government does provide any financial compensation to these communities [Whitedog and Grassy Narrows] it would be setting an extremely expensive precedent which will undoubtedly be brought out at regular intervals for every bit of smoke, bad weather or any other adverse factors which may affect the communities in the future."

The system of secrecy and suppression of documents relevant to the mercury issue prevailed until about 1974, when public pressure, media attention, and Indian political organizations finally forced the release of certain key government reports. Among these was an Ontario government study of the levels of mercury in fish and the Report of the Provincial Interdepartmental Task Force on Mercury.

The Provincial Task Force had been set up in November 1972. Composed of representatives from the ministries of Health, Natural Resources, and Environment, it had a mandate to make recommendations to the Ontario cabinet on steps to deal with the mercury problem. When members of the task force visited the Grassy Narrows reserve on March 8,

1973, the chief presented them with a brief from the band council that clearly identified the nature of the problem facing the Indian people:

> Our people have been relocated within the past decade and we are still suffering the effects of this social upheaval. Our housing is extremely inadequate; there have been ten house fires in the past year and on the average they have burnt to the ground within one-half hour. The dislocation in our lives has resulted in an excessive number of tragic deaths, violence, alcohol abuse, broken families, school dropouts. All these are symptoms of a way of life now which is very much disrupted. In addition to the above situations, we also lost our commercial fishing and nearby guiding livelihoods owing to the mercury pollution.

Recognizing that the problem was complex and that the solution had to be a comprehensive one, the band council decided not to bring to the task force any specific proposals that might be misunderstood as requests for compensation. Instead, the council asked for "experts . . . not civil servants" in all walks of life who could help the community do research and plan a strategy for "coping with social upheaval."

The response of the provincial task force to the call for comprehensive assistance in rebuilding a broken community was to attempt to separate the consequences of the relocation, for which the federal government was clearly responsible, from the specific claims directly related to mercury pollution. Its final report stated: "It was evident that the Indian problems were complicated and that these were not just the result of mercury pollution, but the latter had created quite a disruption of their way of life, their employment habits and their livelihood; that some action was required to assist the Indians to replace the position guiding and commercial fishing had in their way of life before the two bands could hope to have anything approaching a stable community life."[24]

Although the task force proposed close cooperation between the federal and provincial governments, the provincial government was not to be held responsible for deteriorating social conditions beyond those directly caused by mercury. The task force therefore recommended that provincial assistance to the bands be limited to the replacement of contaminated fish with an alternative food source, the search for nonpolluted lakes where the bands could resume commercial fishing, compensation to commercial fishermen, more in-depth health examinations, and an information program designed to warn band members against eating contaminated fish. It recognized that the taking of fish for food should be prohibited and that "complete closing of the river system may be necessary for control purposes."

Following the submission of the task force report, Leo Bernier proudly announced to the Ontario legislature on April 27, 1973, that his Ministry of Natural Resources would assist the communities in dealing with the mercury problem. He promised that the bands would receive supplies of uncontaminated fish, that they would have access to uncontaminated lakes for commercial fishing, and that a special committee of officials would be set up to plan a better future for Whitedog and Grassy Narrows. Three years later, however, only the first promise had been implemented. In 1975, as has been noted, the province placed large commercial freezers on both reserves and stocked them with a supply of uncontaminated fish. The Grassy Narrows band also proposed that the government purchase privately held commercial fishing licenses on Maynard Lake and Oak Lake, which were not on the river system, and transfer them to the band so that commercial fishing could resume. Nothing came of this, and no alternative noncontaminated lakes were identified for commercial fishing. In January 1976, a special coordinator, Jeff Perkins, was appointed with "special powers" to organize provincial assistance to Grassy Narrows and Whitedog. Perkins resigned two months later because his efforts were frustrated by entrenched bureaucratic procedures.

The initial response of the Ontario government to the extraordinary difficulties created for the Indian people by mercury pollution clearly indicated the direction in which the government was headed. For the rest of the decade, its actions would be limited to purely remedial measures of no long-term significance. On the one hand, the provincial position was that "Indians are a federal government responsibility." On the other hand, the political response was directed by the need to avoid any action that might be interpreted as, and thus set a precedent for, compensation for the damages of industrial pollution.[25] But by 1975, it had already become clear that neither the government of Ontario nor the government of Canada was prepared to acknowledge responsibility for the social upheaval on the two reserves, let alone undertake coordinated and comprehensive measures toward social and economic reconstruction. The stage was set for confrontation. As background to the political drama of the mid-1970s, we have to catch up on the role of the federal government in the period 1970–75.

As a way of indicating his interest in the mercury issue, the Minister of Health and Welfare, Marc Lalonde, appointed a federal task force on April 3, 1973. This group reviewed past efforts to test mercury levels in individuals and observed that "previous mercury testing programs have missed a vital subgroup of the Indian population, namely the hunters and guides and their families who are frequently absent from their communities. Future mercury-testing programs must take this high-risk group into account."[26]

The task force identified the most serious consequences of mercury pollution to be not medical but economic, social and cultural. It described the federal government's approach to the problem as "fragmented and lacking cohesion." In response, the government established the Federal Standing Committee on Mercury in the Environment. Composed of representatives from Health and Welfare, DIAND, and the Ministry of the Environment, its mandate was to facilitate the exchange of information, coordinate the federal response to the problem, and advise deputy ministers as to the appropriate actions to be taken. A liaison person from the National Indian Brotherhood (NIB), the political body representing Indian associations across Canada, was to be included in all the Committee's deliberations.

The Standing Committee met only twice in 1973, once in 1974, and three times in 1975. According to its chairman, its function was neither to investigate specific problems nor to solve them; the committee was only supposed "to coordinate" and "analyze the [scientific] information received."[27] Beset by internal squabbles among its members as to which federal government department was mandated to deal with the problems caused by mercury, the committee accomplished nothing of value. Not only were interdepartmental communications at an impasse, but communication between levels of administration within the same department, and between government and the Indian people, was either garbled or nonexistent.[28] Nevertheless, the committee would have continued as the showpiece of token federal government effort to deal with the mercury problem had it not been for two developments that galvanized the departments of Health and Welfare and Indian Affairs into action.

The first was the organization of a mercury team within NIB in August 1974. With a grant from Health and Welfare, this group was to coordinate research on mercury pollution in Canada. By this time, it was strongly suspected that methyl mercury was affecting the Cree Indians of northwestern Quebec as well as the Ojibwa of northwestern Ontario. NIB hired Alan Roy as research coordinator. With the political weight of NIB behind him, Roy pursued government bureaucrats for information on their programs. He found that there had been minimal communication with the Indian people, that both Health and Welfare and DIAND were creating "misleading impressions as to the seriousness of [their] activities in dealing with mercury contamination," and that no programs of a realistic nature had been put in place to deal with the key problems of health education, an alternative food supply, compensation for loss of employment, and long-term economic development.[29] In response to a request for information, for example, DIAND had stated that its officials had intensified their efforts to find employment for the people of Grassy Narrows, and Health and Welfare had written that its officials were doing follow-up on medical tests, hiring more staff, running a pregnant female and neonatal sampling program, and studying the effect of mercury on cats. On closer investigation, however, it turned out that DIAND was not doing anything out of the ordinary to assist the band and that the programs of Health and Welfare still did not meet the requirements for health education at the community level.

On February 21, 1975, therefore, Roy wrote to the Assistant Deputy Minister of DIAND that the entire approach of the federal government had been "painfully inadequate in relation to the various recommendations made by various task forces." The political pressure on the federal government from NIB in 1974–75 was reinforced by a wave of media attention to the mercury issue and the enormous political impact of the visit of the Japanese (Minamata) doctors to Grassy Narrows and Whitedog in March 1975.

The second development, then, was the publicity given by the national media to the mercury issue. A November 1974 radio broadcast on CBC's "As It Happens," which was sharply critical of both governments and of industry, sparked a wave of letters from angry citizens to the Prime Minister's office and to the office of Judd Buchanan, the Minister of Indian Affairs. People demanded to know why the politicians had suppressed information and why so little had been done over the past four years to deal with the problem. Media attention continued unabated during 1975, helping send politicians scurrying to formulate appropriate responses to the allegations of misconduct or indifference leveled against them in the press. The invitation extended by NIB to the Japanese doctors of Kumamoto University to come to the reserves and undertake clinical examinations was widely interpreted by the press as a thinly veiled vote of no confidence in the government-run medical testing program. The wide publicity given to Harada and his colleagues also angered provincial politicians.[30] Yet it was not long after their visit that Health and Welfare approached Clarkson and asked him to mount a comprehensive and continuing program of testing for exposure to mercury on the two reserves. Obviously, the visit of Harada and his colleagues had more than a symbolic effect.

In May 1975, the first signs of activity began to appear from DIAND. Under pressure to make a report to the Standing Committee, ideas of what to do about mercury were hastily conceived and implemented on paper by all levels of the DIAND bureaucracy.[31] In letters to concerned citizens, the office of the Minister of Indian Affairs misrepresented the situation by portraying loosely formed ideas, conceived a month earlier, as ongoing programs.[32] The sense of urgency accompanying protestations of concern on the part of DIAND officials for the situation at Grassy Narrows and Whitedog was undoubtedly inspired by a series of events in 1975, all very well covered by the mass media.

After the visit of the Japanese doctors in March, the Minamata Disease Patients' Alliance invited representatives from the two reserves to come to

Minamata "and see what the dread of mercury is." On July 16, with the organizational assistance of NIB, seven Indian people left for Japan.[33] In August, Japanese doctors and scientists returned to Grassy Narrows and Whitedog to perform more medical tests. Then they took part in a cross-Canada tour to familiarize the Canadian public with mercury pollution. In September, delegates from the alliance visited the two reserves and participated in demonstrations both in Kenora and in Toronto before the Ontario legislature. The Japanese encouraged the Indians to be much more militant in their demands for compensation; they also urged them to press the governments for an epidemiological study on the health effects of mercury.[34]

By the end of 1975, there was no question that the politics of mercury had entered a new phase. The desultory years were over; the next period would be one of tremendous polarization, politicization, and belligerence. For the Indian people, it would be an ordeal beyond imagining, for they would soon discover that they had been pawns in a game of high stakes that was supposedly being played for their benefit.

By 1976, Grassy Narrows was in a state of turbulence. The people were angry. They had had enough of journalists, photographers, do-gooders, and researchers who came to get the most sensational story on their predicament. They were tired of the glaring lights of television cameras. They resented having the horror of their community's social pathology exposed to the rest of the world. And they were still confused about the real dangers to their health presented by mercury, because the media had continued to assert that the poison was slowly crippling them and causing their social violence.

In addition, the people were weary of the inquiries of task forces, the visits of government ministers, the probes of doctors, and especially the unmet promises of assistance. Nothing had been accomplished to help them either to understand the nature of the pollution danger or to cope with the social upheaval; nothing had been done to compensate them for the loss of livelihood. The escalation of welfare payments had only made things worse. As a result, people lost faith in their leaders, and their leaders lost faith in themselves. As Simon Fobister was later to explain: "There was a crisis of leadership after mercury. People could see no solution being presented to them by the chief. This put the chiefs under too much stress, and they couldn't cope. A lot of problems were caused right at the beginning when governments were trying to cover up the mercury. People were very confused."

Grassy Narrows was ripe for intervention. It was demoralized and its leadership discredited. Intervention came in the form of lawyers who presented themselves as pro-Indian; it came with the alignment of the Ojibway Warrior Society with the American Indian Movement (AIM); it came with the increasing efforts of the Treaty No. 3 political organization to control internal band affairs; and it came in the form of money. In 1976, the two bands affected by mercury, under the aegis of Treaty No. 3, received an initial payment of $121,000 from DIAND to begin research on the feasibility of taking the parent company, Reed Paper Limited, to court. Lawyers from the Treaty No. 3 office formed the Anti-Mercury Ojibway Group (AMOG), an incorporated entity with band members from Whitedog and Grassy Narrows on the board of directors. In November 1976, at the age of nineteen and with no working or leadership experience behind him, Simon Fobister entered the political arena as the new chief of Grassy Narrows.

At the same time, significant changes were taking place in the Indian Affairs Branch of DIAND. A new assistant deputy minister, Cam Mackie, was appointed. Inside the federal system, his appointment was seen as a signal of a more activist and progressive approach by DIAND to Indian matters. A strong believer in placing Indians in positions of responsibility within DIAND, Cam Mackie appointed Fred Kelly (an Ojibwa leader and former president of Treaty No. 3) as director-general in the Ontario region. A new alignment emerged in the department, one that was to be very supportive of AMOG and its politics.

With the formation of AMOG under the controlling influence of Treaty No. 3 and its lawyers, there was now a spearhead for more narrowly focused political action. The NIB mercury team worked closely with AMOG. A regular presence in AMOG-related affairs and in AMOG meetings was Barney Lamm. Since he had already filed a lawsuit against the polluter, he had an understandable interest in the development of the Indians' court case. He therefore forged close links with all the key players on the AMOG board of directors and also at DIAND and NIB, the activities of which were critical to his case for compensation.

From the beginning of 1976 to May 1977, AMOG, Treaty No. 3, and NIB waged a concerted campaign to press the governments of Canada and Ontario to close the English-Wabigoon river system to sports fishing. Concern for the health effects of mercury and interest in compensation for economic losses were welded together in the demand for closure. On the one hand, the cessation of sports fishing and the closing of all fishing camps on the river system would protect Indian guides and their families from further consumption of contaminated fish. On the other hand, it would confirm the gravity of the pollution, immeasurably enhance the chances for a successful lawsuit against Reed Paper Limited, and also force the provincial government to compensate the owners of the fishing camps and lodges. It was assumed that as part of the settlement with lodge owners, the government would also compensate the Indian people for the loss of guiding employment.

AMOG lawyers instructed the chiefs of Grassy Narrows and Whitedog on the content and strategy of action on the political front. The chiefs were told that aside from safeguarding the health of the people, closing the river would bring many other benefits:

> When the river system is closed, the government will be forced to quickly compensate the people who made a living off the river system . . . to establish alternate sources of employment . . . set up new industries. A closed river system gives the two communities an excellent lever to pry out of the governments the programs and jobs they owe us for allowing an industry to wreck the waterway.
>
> If the river system is closed, it will be much easier to win a lawsuit against Reed International. When the river system is shut down, Reed will have a much harder time proving that their pollution is not the cause of all the unemployment and ill health we see on the reserves.[35]

Precisely because it addressed the two objectives of health and compensation, the issue of closing the river invited the attention of a formidable array of interested parties, each of which desired to be perceived as a sincere advocate of the Indians' cause. Extensive and effective coverage in the press supported the Indians' position. At the federal level, NIB successfully lobbied the ministers of DIAND, Health and Welfare, and Environment to agree to the closing. But the Minister of Fisheries refused to intervene in a matter that he considered to be a provincial responsibility. At the provincial level, Stephen Lewis and Stuart Smith, leaders of the two Opposition parties in the Ontario legislature, both demanded that the Ontario government close the river. Their vocal support of the Indians' position no doubt was influenced by the fact that the government was faced with an election in June 1977. Inside the Ontario cabinet, while Minister of the Environment George Kerr advocated closure, the ministers of Natural Resources and Resources Development, Leo Bernier and René Brunelle, argued against it.

In the final analysis, the Ontario cabinet's decision was apparently swayed by the following considerations: first, closing the river would cripple the tourist industry, one of the area's principal sources of livelihood. It had been guesstimated that closing the river would mean a loss to the industry, in 1975 dollars, of $2 million in direct annual revenue; a ripple effect in the regional economy would add a revenue loss of $40 million. Second, closing would result in a loss of about three hundred jobs, at least fifty of which would be Indian-held guiding jobs; these jobs would be very difficult to replace. Third, it would cost the Ontario government $5–10 million to buy out lodge owners forced to close their operations. It was felt that this compensation would go to the lodge owners, not to the Indian guides. Fourth, although closing the river was a positive step in reducing the health hazard of mercury, it was no guaran-

tee that Indian people would stop eating contaminated fish. Finally, closing the English-Wabigoon river system would set an undesirable precedent for government action on all waterways contaminated by industrial
poisons.

The issue came to a head at a meeting of the Canada–Ontario Mercury
Committee on April 5, 1977. The committee was set up in 1976 to coordinate federal and provincial responses to the mercury situation. It was
composed of the assistant deputy ministers of DIAND and Health and
Welfare (C. Mackie and C. E. Caron) and the assistant deputy minister of
Natural Resources of the Ontario government (A. J. Herridge). At that
meeting, Health and Welfare Canada, in conjunction with the provincial
Ministry of Health and the Donner Foundation, offered the bands
$450,000 to fund a thorough epidemiological study at Grassy Narrows
and Whitedog to answer, once and for all, the thorny questions surrounding the effect of mercury on human health. This meeting was an exceptionally stormy one. Acting on the advice of the AMOG coordinator Donald Colborne, the chiefs of the two bands took the position that they would
accept the study only on the condition that the Ontario government close
the river to sports fishing. In May, 1977, Frank Miller, the Minister of
Natural Resources, announced the cabinet decision: the river would remain open to sports fishing. In the same month, the federal government
took the epidemiological study to northwestern Quebec, where the Cree
Indians were also at risk from mercury poisoning. The loss of the epidemiological study, because it was used as a negotiating tactic to close the
river, was disastrous for the Grassy Narrows band. Chief Simon Fobister
later described his consent to tie the two together as "the greatest mistake
I ever made when I was chief."

It is not necessary at this point to review the merits of closing the river.
What is significant is that the issue, prior to late 1977, had never been
debated at the community level. In the crucial years when the issue was
being engineered through the most rarified levels of the political system
and noble positions were being taken on the Indians' behalf, no one
stopped to ask whether or not the people had been consulted. It was
assumed that the chief spoke for the people, yet all around there was
evidence that the influence of outsiders, operating under the AMOG ban-
ner, was paramount. While attention was being focused on the benefits to
health and the increased chances for successful litigation, no one stopped
to consider the negative consequences of closing the river on the people's
ability to make an independent living. Yet it was clear that after the loss of
commercial fishing, guiding in the camps that still remained open was one
of the last sectors of productive employment left to Indian people. In this
depressed region, with exceedingly limited development possibilities,
guiding jobs would have been very difficult to replace; and government-

funded, short-term, and make-work jobs would have been considered a poor substitute. Finally, alternatives that might have accomplished the desired objective of minimizing the health risks posed by mercury for guides and their families—for example, the provision of box lunches to guides—were never seriously considered. The primary focus of AMOG lawyers seems to have been to win a precedent-setting lawsuit against a corporate polluter, the chances for which would have been appreciably enhanced by the closing of the river. Because of their ideological persuasion, they may have wanted to bring the government to its knees and make it pay for allowing the industry to pollute. But to single out AMOG lawyers and associates for special attention is to lose sight of the point that every actor on this political stage had particular interests to advance and protect, interests that were not necessarily grounded in direct knowledge of the community and its situation.

In the late autumn of 1977, the issue was finally debated at the community level. After hearing all the arguments presented by the AMOG coordinator, the band membership voted overwhelmingly against closing the river. Some people were angry when they found out that the Grassy Narrows band had "officially" demanded closing the river since early 1976; they had heard nothing about it, and they wanted to know who was behind it. According to the economic projects' administrator:

> *We* never said we wanted the river to close. Indian Affairs, NIB, and AMOG wanted the river to close, they told us to say that. There are only five or six people on this reserve that are for closing the river; and they are not guides either. The guides don't want the river closed because guiding is their life. Where are they going to find jobs for six months of the year? If it is so important not to eat fish in shore lunches, then why don't the lodge owners supply them with box lunches of cold meat? That would help, but closing the river will not help the future of the reserve.

Finally, questions emerged about the influence of Barney Lamm in AMOG. Why was he pushing so hard on the issue of closing the river? Even after the Grassy Narrows people had voted against closing, Lamm flew into the reserve to try to persuade the band council to reverse its decision. At that point, people wondered about all the reasons behind his decision to close Ball Lake Lodge. Did he close it to protect the health of his Indian guides, or were there other factors related to the economic viability of his operation before mercury was discovered in the river?[36] In the end, the people did not know what to believe. They were confused even more when, in 1979, Lamm offered to sell the lodge to the band "so that the Indian people could run it."[37] Torn between old loyalties to "a pretty good employer" and a historic distrust of provincial and federal politicians and bureaucrats, the Indian people felt caught in a maelstrom of uncertainty and apprehension as to who had been fighting for them and why. As Simon Fobister was later to put it, "We were manipulated. We were taken in and used by people who wanted the river closed for their own reasons. We lost the epidemiological study. After we decided against closing the river [in January 1978], the champions of the Indians disappeared. Now we have nothing. We have to start all over."

The Indians' experience with white society on the issue of the closing of the river had not been a happy one. Not only were they overwhelmed by the public attention, but the experience also served to reinforce their distrust of outsiders, especially those who supposedly came to help. In this environment, people and programs were often defeated before they had a chance to make a contribution. Yet, paradoxically, alongside the bitter confrontation over the issue of closing the river, there appeared the very first signs of official recognition that something had to be done to help Grassy Narrows and Whitedog rebuild their shattered economies.

## The Promises of Restitution

On October 31, 1975, the chiefs of Whitedog and Grassy Narrows met with the ministers of Health, Environment, and Natural Resources (Frank Miller, George Kerr, and Leo Bernier, respectively) of the Ontario government. The Grassy Narrows band presented the ministers with a detailed, seventeen-page brief spelling out the ways in which the government could provide assistance in coping with social upheaval and loss of livelihood. Central to reconstruction was the need to create employment: "The people of our reserve are anxious to exchange welfare checks for salary checks . . . We recognize that through employment lies the key to the revitalization of a solid social fabric for our reserve and its people."

On November 21, the chiefs met with Judd Buchanan, the Minister of Indian Affairs. They emphasized again that employment was of absolute priority in reducing social chaos, and they rejected his offer to relocate the two reserves to an uncontaminated area.[38] On November 26, Buchanan invited his colleagues in the federal cabinet, the ministers of Health and Environment (Marc Lalonde and Jeanne Sauvé), to a meeting in Ottawa with the provincial ministers of Health, Natural Resources, and Environment. At that meeting, all participants agreed on the need for joint action and intergovernmental cooperation on the development of special programs for the two mercury-affected reserves. Out of this consensus at the political level emerged the Canada–Ontario Mercury Committee composed of high-ranking civil servants from both governments. The committee met for the first time in January 1976. With unprecedented swiftness, both governments agreed to a special "work for welfare" program, announced by a letter dated January 23, 1976, from Judd Buchanan to Chief Simon Fobister: "[We intend] to develop a type of program whereby work could be assigned to the employable residents of the reserve, who would then be remunerated by using welfare funds and by subsidizing any shortfall through other sources. It would be a type of 'work-for-pay' program or a flexible community development program to replace welfare for all those able to work."

For all its shortcomings, this program was an important step in the right direction. In July 1976, DIAND officials were able to inform Buchanan that "for this year, approximately $920,060, including $125,000 in supplementary funds, will be expended to provide new employment on the two reserves for approximately 125 people. At Grassy Narrows, approximately $480,060 will be expended to provide 65 man-years of employment."[39]

In 1976, two other committees were convened at the federal level, the Committee on Nutritional Alternatives to Fish and the Standing Committee on Fisheries and Forestry. Both contributed various ideas on how to deal with the mercury problem. At one point, the government even considered creating a national park in the area, but this idea was quietly shelved in late 1976 because of the Indians' opposition.

Not to be outdone in manifesting a commitment to some sort of development assistance, the province of Ontario also began to provide funds for special programs. In addition to supplying uncontaminated fish to both communities, in 1975 the government helped build a day-care center at Grassy Narrows; in 1976–77, it funded travel costs for Indians to attend mercury meetings, the purchase of a skidder and sawmill engine for the band's logging operations, and a life skills program. Over a number of years, Grassy Narrows people were also given preference in such provincial job-creation projects as tree planting, pinecone collection, and fire fighting. According to records kept in Kenora by the Indian Community Secretariat, over the period 1972–77 the province of Ontario spent a total of $448,328 on the Grassy Narrows reserve.

In short, seven years after the discovery of mercury in the river, the governments finally mobilized sufficient funds to provide employment for the majority of the male labor force at Grassy Narrows in a variety of short-term, remedial, and make-work projects, These projects, which lasted anywhere from three weeks to three months, involved various "community improvement" types of activities—for example, home repairs, brush clearing, the construction of boardwalks, garbage pickup, and so on—as well as tree planting and cone picking, a sawmill and pulp operation, and a community garden. For a year or so, the band tried manufacturing canoes, but this project did not meet with much success. DIAND appointed special staff in the Kenora district office to assist in planning and implementing these projects; in 1976, for example, a forestry advisor was hired for Grassy Narrows. The predominant concern of both Whitedog and Grassy Narrows bands, however, was long-term industrial development and comprehensive socioeconomic assistance. This was brought to the attention of Cam Mackie, assistant deputy minister of Indian Affairs. "The history of requests from the two bands is one of the bands viewing their needs from a community focus within a comprehensive framework in which all parts interrelate, and being forced to deal with specific separate projects because of the type of response received from government."[40]

Mackie raised this issue with the minister, admitting that:

> *No* comprehensive approach to developing alternate employment opportunities for members of these bands was taken [by DIAND] from 1970 to 1975. Welfare payments were increased drastically following the fishing ban in 1970, and many problems resulted from these monies without addressing the problem of employment.
>
> In 1971, 1973, 1975, 1976, briefs from these bands were presented to both levels of government. These briefs were consistent in their requests for resources and expertise to assist them in planning and implementing long-term comprehensive socioeconomic development of their reserves . . . .
>
> *Inaction of both governments since 1970 has resulted in a deterioration of the social and economic fibre of these communities beyond what would have been the case if a suitable response was given in 1970, 1971, or 1973.*[41]

Despite awareness of the need for comprehensive community planning, the machinery of government continued to churn out sporadic and short-term projects that held out no hope of replacing the loss of commercial fishing with activities that might reinforce traditional social relations. The Ontario government was reluctant to press the nonnative holders of commercial fishing licences on Oak and Maynard lakes (two nonpolluted commercial fishing sites) to sell their licenses to the Grassy Narrows band. The Fish for Fertilizer program, which permitted band members to fish the river, did not provide enough economic incentive to attract commercial fishermen. A proposal for a shoe factory never materialized; and, as noted, a new canoe factory failed after two seasons of operation. Repeated requests for comprehensive development planning, submitted formally to the Canada–Ontario Mercury Committee, continued to provoke hollow protestations of concurrence and government support.[42]

The fact is that neither government was willing to commit the level of resources required for social and economic reconstruction. Furthermore, the limited assistance that was forthcoming for remedial and short-term projects was always extended in the spirit of charity; neither government wished its actions to be interpreted as an acknowledgment of legal, moral, or social obligation to redress injustice or to compensate for inflicted adversity. In the end, the committee, despite its high-ranking representation, also failed to satisfy the promises of restitution and the expectations

for socioeconomic reconstruction that the politicians had kindled in early
1976.

In April 1977, the Ontario government by an Order-in-Council appointed Justice Patrick Hartt of the Ontario Supreme Court "to conduct
an inquiry into major developments north of the 50th parallel of north
latitude." The Royal Commission on the Northern Environment was
born. For eight months, Justice Hartt toured northern Ontario and conducted hearings on a wide range of issues and concerns to northerners.
He heard native and nonnative views on resource development and environmental assessment. On January 9, 1978, he came to the Whitedog
reserve to hear the statements of the Whitedog and Grassy Narrows
bands. Chief Fobister told Justice Hartt that "our backs are against an
unmovable wall." In an eloquent and moving testimonial, he traced the
band's history; "in summation,

- the intentional undermining of our religion and our way of life from
  the Treaty to the present day by the Roman Catholic church, the Royal
  Canadian Mounted Police, and the Government;
- the loss of income from diminished muskrat trapping due to hydro
  flooding;
- the Jones Road breaking the isolation factor which helped in the preservation of a way of life;
- the progressive addiction due to alcohol made readily available by tourist outfitters and taxi-drivers;
- the interdependency and introduction of a foreign value system;
- the loss of commercial fishing due to mercury;
- the loss of employment and income when Barney Lamm's Ball Lake
  Lodge closed due to mercury;
- the easy availability of welfare [which] discouraged men from working;
- the Chief and Council's incapability to amend the mercury situation
  and to provide alternative employment,

caused the total physical, mental, and spiritual breakdown of our people. For
seven long years we suffered. The average death rate per month was one,
and other violent criminal acts were committed. Since 1970, we have had
10 chiefs. In short, we hit rock bottom and our backs are against an
unmoveable wall and now the only way out is to go forward."[43]

Justice Hartt was impressed with what he heard and saw. In his report
to the Ontario cabinet, he stated plainly: "Most shocking to me were the
submissions that described the plight of the people on the Indian reserves
of Whitedog and Grassy Narrows . . . . Their presentations gave me an
unforgettable sense of their frustration with the inability of the federal
and provincial governments to work together to ease their desperate

situation."[44] In a direct reference to the band's perception of the origins of social upheaval in the community, he wrote:

> I recognize that not all of the problems in Whitedog and Grassy Narrows are the result of mercury. They are affected by the many problems endemic to Indian communities, in part because of the impact of development. Mercury has, however, been the added factor which has pushed the situation into the intolerable.
>
> I think the whole impasse reflects clearly the chasm of understanding between the predominant white perception and the native perception of the problem. The Indian people cannot move, change their way of life, change their diet, live on welfare, lose their self-esteem, and yet remain the same people . . . . The native people value their traditions. The land is not simply a place to live. It forms a symbiotic relationship with the people and the animals which cannot be wrenched apart without serious consequences . . . .[45]

The proceedings and recommendations of the Royal Commission are important, because out of them emerged the last major political initiative that resurrected the hope of social justice and then, just a few years later, ground it into the dust. This mediation process constitutes the final phase in the bitter history of efforts to help this shattered society get on its feet.

In his recommendations to the Ontario cabinet, Justice Hartt included a proposal for a tripartite committee, with representatives of the federal and provincial governments and the Indian people, to try to settle outstanding grievances and facilitate decision making by negotiation. In the case of Grassy Narrows and Whitedog, he was also convinced that litigation against the polluter, even if successful in achieving a monetary settlement, would not accomplish the professed objective of comprehensive socioeconomic development. Yet he acknowledged that questions of legal liability and compensation properly belonged in the courts. In his report to the government, therefore, Justice Hartt recommended that "as its first priority, the [tripartite] committee should address the plight of the Indian communities of Whitedog and Grassy Narrows. Methods to ensure access to resources and viable community economies, along with related supportive programs, should be considered jointly by the committee and the communities. To facilitate this, a mutually acceptable fact finder should be appointed to review and report on available information and options within ninety days."

By this time, the bands had reached a similar conclusion. The growing awareness that "litigation was not the way to go" was enhanced by the limited utility of what AMOG had produced. The litigation feasibility study, completed in April 1977, had cost over $156,000. But the study neither defined a course of action nor produced a draft statement of claim. Still ongoing in 1978 was yet another study of the social and economic effects of mercury. Funded by DIAND, AMOG had awarded a contract for $110,200 to Peter Usher, an Ottawa-based consultant, who attempted to prove that the social upheaval on both reserves was caused by mercury pollution and the loss of commercial fishing. . . . On March 22, 1978, however, the band councils of Whitedog and Grassy Narrows met and decided that their interests would be furthered by a negotiated out-of-court settlement with Reed Paper Limited and the governments of Canada and Ontario.

On April 10, 1978, Justice Hartt invited the two chiefs, Roy McDonald and Simon Fobister, to Toronto. He promised to approach both governments on mediation and asked that the bands appoint fact finders and prepare a statement of the issues to be included in the mediation process. On May 9, the chiefs returned to Toronto and met with the Province of Ontario Steering Committee. To the Minister of Resources Development, René Brunelle, and five deputy ministers, the chiefs submitted a memorandum outlining their aspirations for a negotiated settlement. Over the summer of 1978, government officials and band representatives worked on drafting an agreement, selecting a mediator, and preparing a budget for the mediation process. In October, all parties to the mediation agreed on Edward B. Jolliffe, who had retired from the Staff Relations Board in Ottawa, as mediator. Finally, on December 15, 1978, Hugh Faulkner, the Minister of DIAND, representing the government of Canada; René Brunelle, representing the Ontario government; and chiefs McDonald and Fobister, representing the bands, signed a formal mediation agreement at Grassy Narrows. It was a day preceded by a long night of extraordinary anticipation and excitement; Simon Fobister talked until the early hours of the morning about his dreams and hopes for his people. He said then that "for us, this mediation, it means everything. It means that we have a chance to reaffirm our basic treaty rights. It means that we can try to win back our rights to survival as a people. It means we can start to hope again."

The mediation committed the two governments to negotiate a remedy for damages caused by, among other things, relocation and mercury pollution. Part of the understanding of this agreement was that there would be a concerted effort to arrive at a negotiated out-of-court settlement with Reed. According to the agreement:

> The issues to be resolved . . . are related to adverse effects on their health and to the economic, social, cultural, and environmental well-being of the bands of the said reserves directly or indirectly attributable, inter alia, to:
> (1) the artificial raising and lowering of water levels affecting the reserves;
> (2) the flooding of reserve and nonreserve land;
> (3) the relocation of the reserves and/or the residents thereof;
> (4) the pollution of the environment affecting the reserves.[46]

In the first four months of 1979, intensive interviews with the heads of all the major family groups were recorded at Grassy Narrows in order to document the damages to community life and also to arrive at an understanding of what the community desired as a settlement. Parallel with this research effort, photojournalist Hiro Miyamatsu began work on a film so that the issues in the mediation and the proposals for settlement could be presented in an effective manner. The film was carefully crafted around a series of interviews with band members about their history and their aspirations for the future. Both the film and the tape-recorded interviews gave the people a chance to speak out, an opportunity to participate actively in the political process. An enormous amount of work went into the preparation for the first meeting of the mediation panel. This historic meeting, at which representatives of Reed Paper were present, took place at Grassy Narrows on May 29, 1979.

At this first (and last) all-party mediation meeting, the Grassy Narrows band outlined its requirements for social and economic reconstruction. To the deputy ministers of the Ontario government and the assistant deputy ministers of the federal government, Chief Fobister said: "My people understand the mediation process as the reaffirmation of treaty rights, defined not only as the rights to hunt, trap, and fish, but also as the basic human rights to survive and to compete with skills and education in the contemporary technologically advanced society . . . The issue is one of choice and the freedom to make the choice between two cultures, two lifestyles, and two paths for future development."[47]

The chief asked both governments to give top priority to helping the community develop economic self-reliance and self-government. In his presentation, he identified three critical requirements: a land and resource base, a development fund, and education and skill training. In our terms, the Grassy Narrows people simply asked for the basic building blocks of development—land, capital, and investment in human resources.

We really asked for only three things in this mediation. First, we wanted our children to have a better life. Right now, with so much drinking on the reserve, most of the kids drop out of school by about grade four. We're losing a whole generation. So the people asked for a boarding school off the reserve. We wanted it to have good teachers to teach the Indian language and to have a special curriculum. It would be an Indian-run boarding school. The parents would know their children are learning and being looked after. This would really help us with the problems we are facing in our community today.

The second thing we wanted is a special fund for economic development. We feel strongly that we should have been compensated by Reed Paper Company for polluting our river. The compensation money would go into this fund. We could use the money for all kinds of projects that we really need. And this would make us less dependent on government.

Finally, we need productive land and resources, so that people who want to live in the Indian way have a chance to do that. Without land, good land, we won't survive as Indian people.[48]

Almost all the Grassy Narrows people, when interviewed on the subject of mediation, expressed a deep concern over the lack of educational achievement among their children. After much soul-searching, they came up with the idea of an Indian-run boarding school off the reserve that would allow their children to be educated in a secure setting, away from the alcohol-related problems of reserve life. The second element, productive land, was the key to the restoration of viability: "not subsidy, not a retreat, but a regrouping of traditional and new strengths." The band asked for the exclusive use of, and control over access to, land and resources that had traditionally been used by the people for trapping, hunting, fishing, and growing wild rice. As for capital, the band asked for a socioeconomic development fund, the endowment of which would be equal to the sum total of economic losses sustained by the community from mercury pollution. Detailed planning for the development fund and educational reform was to be achieved by two government task forces that would work closely with the community.

Government officials were impressed with the form and substance of the band's presentation. In their replies, senior civil servants waxed eloquent on the subject of the government's commitment to the mediation process. And they gave their assurances that the holistic nature of the settlement proposals would be respected in all negotiations.

From that point on, the history of the mediation process was a sad and bitter tale. The mediator's personality and his perception of his role were completely out of touch with the realities of his assignment, and his tenure was short-lived. The governments, in their turn, did not present him with concrete proposals to work with. By November 1983, only the federal government had made a tentative offer to settle the damages arising from the relocation.

The Ontario government continued to rationalize its inaction by the well-worn argument that "Indians are the children of the federal government."[49] On the issue of mercury-related health damages, provincial ministers made such statements as: "We don't know if the symptoms [from which the Indians suffer] have been caused by the fish, alcoholism, or venereal disease."[50] More to the point with respect to any kind of reparations, "Ontario's policy is that there will be no compensation for industrial pollution; the courts are open to individuals to take on the polluter."[51] And again: "Any liability for damages would appear to lie with those whose actions led to the presence of mercury in the water, and not with the government of Ontario."[52] In short, the provincial government took the position that politically, legally, and morally it had no responsibility to the Indian community for mercury-related damages.

Reed Paper Limited, which had expressed an interest in being a party to the mediation, has been allowed to withdraw from the process entirely. In 1979, the Ontario government made possible the sale of Reed's subsidiary, Dryden Chemicals, to Great Lakes Forest Products by agreeing to take on any liability for proven mercury-related damages over the sum of $15 million. In this transaction, in spite of the guarantee of public funds, the government chose not to demand of Reed Paper or Great Lakes any assurances that the companies would work toward a mediated settlement of pollution-related claims. After two years of negotiations, Great Lakes made a tentative offer of settlement to the bands in March 1981 but withdrew it shortly after it was tabled. Since then, there has been no new offer of a settlement. And the provincial government has taken no measures to persuade the corporations to return to the negotiating table. Instead, over the period 1979–82, it subsidized Great Lakes Forest Products, whose operating profits in 1980 and 1981 were around $174 million per annum, with approximately $52 million of government grants.

As for the federal government, as ministers and deputy ministers and assistant deputy ministers changed portfolios, the mediation process was progressively robbed of priority status.[53] The entire set of band proposals was gradually reduced to a market basket of innocuous things that the Department of Indian Affairs could do in the old way. DIAND's response to the off-reserve boarding-school proposal, for example, took the form of utter disbelief that the Indian people could know what was best for them and their children. Endless arguments were marshalled against the idea in order to convince the people that what they specified as a real need in their community was wrong. In the end, the band's proposal for a fundamental change in the system of education was reduced to a cluster of notions about curriculum development. Today, there is no one responsible for the mediation process at the federal level who has both the authority to negotiate and an understanding of the requirements for social and economic reconstruction. Most recent indications are that the federal government will attempt to dispose of its obligations to Grassy Narrows by a simple monetary settlement of approximately four million dollars.

As for the community, in March 1980 the people of Grassy Narrows did not reelect Simon Fobister as chief. Many blamed him for the failure of the mediation process. They felt betrayed again by the promises; once more they had been fooled by rhetoric. The community slid into a deeper and darker depression as a succession of chiefs tried to cope with, or in some cases to profit from, the chaos. Finally, in the fall of 1982, new hopes were generated when Steve Fobister, a descendant of the great Sah-katch-eway, took the helm. Because of his clan strength and personal experience in dealing with government agencies, people expected him to succeed where others had failed.

At the time this book was first published, in January 1985, this chapter concluded with the observation that the mediation process had to be considered a failure of nerve and political will. Not only had nothing happened in almost six years of negotiations to achieve compensation for mercury-related damages, but the public pressure on politicians to do something for Indian people had also essentially disappeared. And the fruitless rounds of talks and consultations, the dashed hopes for social and economic reconstruction, had only reinforced the Indians' feelings of powerlessness, apathy, and alienation.

Since the first edition, however, there has been a remarkable turning point in the long, hard road toward social justice. In early 1985, David Crombie, the new Minister of Indian Affairs under the recently elected Conservative government, appointed Dr. Emmett Hall, a renowned jurist and former Justice of the Supreme Court of Canada, to serve as his representative in facilitating negotiations between the Indian communities of Grassy Narrows and Whitedog and the pulp and paper companies. In June, the long-standing Conservative government in Ontario handed over the reins of power to a progressive coalition of Liberal and New Democratic Members of the Legislature. Ian Scott, a lawyer with extensive experience in environmental law, became Ontario's Attorney General. Under the formidable leadership of Crombie, Hall, and Scott, and with the political commitment of both governments to the resolution of the issue, on November 25, 1985, Canada and Ontario announced that a $16.7 million settlement had been reached to compensate the Indian bands for damages linked to mercury pollution. Of this total, Grassy Narrows will receive $8.7 million and the Islington (Whitedog) band, the remaining $8 million. The settlement comprises a payment of $2.75 million from the Government of Canada and $2.17 million from the Government of Ontario. The two paper companies involved in the negotiations, Reed Paper Inc. and Great Lakes Forest Products Ltd., will contribute $5.75 million and $6 million, respectively. To help those who have health problems related to mercury poisoning, $2 million of the total settlement will capitalize a special health disability fund. Under the terms of the settlement, the Grassy Narrows band council will also buy Ball Lake Lodge from Barney Lamm for approximately $1.3 million.

It is very difficult to judge, at this point, what ultimate impact the millions of dollars will have on the Grassy Narrows community. Certainly money alone will not solve all the social problems. The hope is that the settlement will be a catalyst in the process of rebuilding community morale and helping individuals rediscover their own strength in repairing the damage done by years of neglect. At least now there is a chance for renewal, a foundation for a new beginning, so long delayed.

# POSTSCRIPT

This book began with a description of a human community that appears to be bent on its own destruction. Grassy Narrows seems destined for more suffering, even catastrophe, because of its past history and its present configuration of powerlessness, isolation, and rage turned inward. In seeking escape through alcohol, in searching for salvation outside themselves, the people appear to be trapped in a vicious circle whereby each generation reproduces its own pathology.

Like a crystal that reveals its hidden structure only when it is shattered, a human community discloses its structure when the glue that held it together dissolves under the impact of events and pressures, both internal and external. It reveals the extent of its disintegration when, among other things, its own members no longer care about whether or not they produce healthy offspring and when they abdicate their collective responsibilities for the physical, emotional, and spiritual survival of succeeding generations.

Social scientists who study communities in decline have pointed out that social breakdown can be defined and measured by certain conventional indicators, such as the incidence of violent death and suicide in a population, the rate of crime, and the prevalence of illness, alcoholism, and child neglect. They may conclude that a community is in crisis when such indicators become so extreme that they displace customary norms of social behavior, or when they diverge sharply from the norms prevailing in other communities of similar size and composition. But we also know that the health of any society or collectivity depends upon a series of vital processes that allow individuals to grow, discover their identity, and learn the skills and ways of knowing of their people. When these processes have been disrupted or are absent, the young people of the community not only are extremely vulnerable to negative pressures from the outside but can become so demoralized that they also commit themselves to a kind of death. "Where there is no vision, the people perish" (*Proverbs* 29:18).

From this perspective, the evidence presented in the first chapter leaves little doubt that Grassy Narrows is experiencing massive social upheaval. Certainly from the point of view of what the life of these Indian people was like before their relocation, the data show that an extraordinarily rapid deterioration has taken place in personal morale and community solidarity. While heavy spree drinking plays a pivotal role in causing the many forms of social violence, and while the resulting pathology feeds on itself and passes from one generation to the next, excessive alcohol use is not the original cause of the troubles in the community. It is both a symptom and an effect of cultural devastation, powerlessness, and marginality—and it acts to perpetuate these conditions.[1]

Since the data on social pathology were first collected in 1977–78, the Grassy Narrows people have made valiant efforts to cope with their problems. They organized an Alcoholics Anonymous group. Some families formed a small subdivision within the reserve where drinking is forbidden. Young people have set up a night patrol to look after abandoned children. And there is now a crisis intervention center, whose volunteers try to prevent attempted suicide, vandalism, and family violence. When I returned to Grassy Narrows in the summer of 1981 and again in 1983, I was impressed by the remarkable strength of a few individuals in the face of awesome pressures. Yet there were other disturbing indications that the battle against the further unraveling of the communal fabric was far from won.

In the three years following the time I collected the data presented in chapter 1, ten more people died from violence. Six of them were under the age of twenty. The other four were men and women in their childbearing years. Two of these ten deaths were suicides. These recent statistics suggest that the pressures that initially led the Grassy Narrows people to embrace alcohol have not been relieved. It also appears that these pressures have been neither understood by the Canadian society at large nor seriously addressed by those who have a trust responsibility for the survival of indigenous people.

It is very difficult to define the forces and pressures that combine to tear a people apart. What information we have from Grassy Narrows gives us a sequence of events, a catalogue of changes. But each change has destroyed some aspect of the traditional culture, some prerequisite for individual identity and security. In that sense, we have the background to understand the accumulation of effects over time. But hidden from view are the complex processes by which the changes injure the psyche and numb the human spirit. All we see, finally, are the indications of breakdown that appear collectively and externally. I propose, then, that we also consider the conditions that produce psychic trauma in human populations generally, to see if they might shed some light on the principal causes of breakdown at Grassy Narrows and, by extension, in other communities.

Kai Erikson, in his superb book on the Buffalo Creek flood, has observed that there are really two kinds of disasters, or conditions of extreme stress, that have the capacity to induce trauma on a large scale.[2]

The first is an acute and unexpected assault, such as an earthquake, a flood, or a tornado, that leaves a tremendous amount of damage in its wake. The second gathers force more slowly and insidiously and is associated with certain chronic conditions, such as extreme poverty, prolonged unemployment, or long-term incarceration. Both the acute and the chronic sources of stress produce recognizable symptoms of trauma, or injury to the human mind. These include, among other things, a susceptibility to anxiety, rage, and depression; subjective feelings of a loss of capacity; a sense of helplessness in the face of conditions over which one has no control; disorientation; apathy; a retreat into dependency; a general loss of ego functions; and a numbness of spirit. These symptoms may be accompanied by drug and alcohol abuse, a loss of motor skills, and a preoccupation with death.

One can find some of these symptoms among victims of natural disasters who suffer acute bewilderment and confusion when well-known landmarks of their lives are suddenly wiped out. They can be seen in victims of culture shock who find themselves unable to cope with an alien environment in which the familiar psychological cues that help people function in society are suddenly withdrawn and replaced with new ones that are strange and incomprehensible. And they are often manifest among refugees who have been uprooted from an altogether different life and cast adrift in a society they barely understand. If all possibility of retreat to a more familiar social, physical, or cultural landscape is cut off, the trauma can be doubly severe. But it has also long been recognized that marks of traumatization can be found among people living in conditions of chronic poverty, in institutions, in urban slums, and on skid row. And certainly thousands of North American Indians show the psychological scars left by hundreds of years of colonization.

In general, then, one can find the symptoms of psychic trauma whenever people feel abandoned, separated from the life around them, or unable to contribute anything of value to the rest of the community; when they are forced to grapple with conditions over which they have no control; when cultural orientations that they have been brought up with no longer serve to interpret reality; when habitual actions no longer have the same meaning or effect; when psychological cues no longer serve to guide experience; and when social and moral values are rendered impotent in organizing work or sustaining human relationships. All incentive to maintain cultural precepts, values, and beliefs is lost if these things no longer work to structure reality. Thus a whole world ends when its metaphors die. Under such conditions, life itself can become meaningless.

At Grassy Narrows, an entire people have lived under such conditions since the relocation. In symbolic terms, they could not locate themselves on the new reserve, for they had left a world that corresponded to their understanding of themselves and their place within it, and entered one that did not. Their tribal institutions, customs, beliefs, and values simply ceased to be relevant or useful in the new circumstances. And the crucial integration between the physical and metaphysical worlds, and among the social, economic, and political aspects of everyday life, was dissolved under the impact of an entirely different and incompatible way of life imposed by a government presumably operating under the best of intentions.

The full measure of the effects of federal government policy on Indian community life is illustrated by this case study of Grassy Narrows. Many Indian bands all across Canada were relocated at about the same time, under similar circumstances and with equally little regard for collective rights to cultural identity. But even if bands were not relocated physically, the construction of federal schools on reserves and the unprecedented expansion of government programs in the 1960s sent shock waves through every aspect of native life. And the changes took an enormous toll on communal order and personal identity. Indeed, it is one of the most compelling paradoxes of our public policy that ever increasing government expenditures on Indians find an exact parallel in ever increasing indices of social disintegration on their reserves.

A few figures will suffice to make the point. Expenditures of DIAND now represent about 75 percent of total federal government expenditures on the status Indian and Inuit people. In 1970–71, DIAND expenditures totalled \$223 million; in 1978–79, they rose to \$659 million.[3] In 1983–84, the Indian Affairs Branch alone, excluding the Northern and Inuit Program, spent over a billion dollars on the provision of goods and services to approximately 312,000 status Indians. While officials may well point to statistics showing increased quantities of physical assets on reserves, higher levels of cash income, more social services, and higher levels of school enrollment, there is also evidence that there has been no significant improvement in the social and economic conditions under which Indian people live.

Today, over half the Indian adult population of Canada is dependent on welfare for subsistence. Only 20 percent of Indian children complete secondary school, compared to 75 percent nationwide. Indian housing conditions are abysmal; fewer than 40 percent of Indian houses have running water, for example, compared to over 90 percent in the country as a whole. There are more Indian children in the care of foster homes today than at any time since the early 1960s; since 1962, there has also been a fivefold increase in the number of Indian children taken for adoption. Among those Indians who survive infancy, many will die violently; about 33 percent of all Indian deaths in Canada are due to violence. Indians in the fifteen to forty-four age-group meet with violent death at a rate that is five times the national average. And suicide rates among Indian people have been climbing steadily over the 1970s. Suicides now account for 35 percent of all Indian deaths in the fifteen to twenty age-group, and 21 percent of all deaths in the twenty-one to thirty-four age-group. Suicide rates among Canadian Indians are six times the national average and are significantly higher than among Indians in the United States.

There is a sense among a number of Indian leaders in Canada that such conditions could not possibly be tolerated in the society in the absence of an implicit acceptance of Indian genocide. Certainly such a speculation is understandable in view of the wide gulf separating the stated objective of government policy, "to lead the Indian people toward the full, free, and nondiscriminatory participation in Canadian society," from the apparently negative results of policy. But the assumption of deliberate malice on the part of bureaucrats who implement policy does not fit the history of the Grassy Narrows relocation, for example. Yet in this case we can observe clearly the workings of an implacable logic that produced an outcome contradictory to the intent. Let us return, then, to the particulars of this story.

There is evidence that the Grassy Narrows people pleaded with local DIAND officials to respect certain fundamental aspects of their culture in the plan for resettlement. For example, they objected to the site chosen by government on the ground that it was a spiritually inhospitable and barren wasteland that would not support human habitation. They also asked not to be separated from their sacred ancestral sites and from the river that had nurtured them for generations. And they wanted the layout of the new reserve to accommodate the traditional clan-based residence pattern. But no one listened to the Indians' views on how a people should live. In imposing a completely alien form of settlement, local officials acted in a manner consistent with the paternalistic attitudes, ideology, and procedures prevailing within the department at the time. In fact, they did not consider the relocation important enough to warrant documentation. It was simply a means to an end, a necessary adjunct to a broader mandate to deliver services to Indian people at minimum cost and with maximum efficiency. And it seems clear that their failure even to speculate that the Indian people might have something to lose in being wrenched out of their way of life had its deeper roots in the Western way of thinking about the world. Inasmuch as this way of thinking and the department's own philosophy of development have changed little since the 1960s, we should pause for a moment to review the premises that govern the relationship to indigenous people and the attitudes as to how they should be "helped."

In the first place, government officials were probably not even conscious of the extent to which their ideas about "nature" and "culture" are polarized. Their whole idea of development and progress rested upon the notion of culture as something Western society had created or constructed. Nature, on the other hand, was the opposite of culture; it had to be tamed, subdued, controlled, or conquered. This division between culture and nature permeated their thinking as to what was civilized and what was uncivilized. Because the indigenous people were considered to be closer to nature, they were thought to be beyond the reach of culture. In order to move toward it, they had to be subjected to the white man's schools, religion, housing, social services, and economic system, for these constituted the hallmarks of civilization. The move from nature to culture constituted progress: economic progress was made when nature was transformed into resources, while social progress was made when the primitive were drawn into civilization.[4]

This attitude demeans Indians as human beings. It assumes that they had no culture before contact with the white man. It assumes that they had no conceptions of the universe; no way of ordering social relationships; no values, ideals, or norms for human behavior; and no proper means of satisfying basic human needs. And yet if the story contained in the preceding pages tells us anything at all, it is that the Indian people not only had a culture that met all the above specifications, but that this culture had survived until it was systematically, perhaps irrevocably, undermined by government intervention.

In the second place, Western society is materially and technologically oriented. We tend to see material things, technological advance, and industrial production as an absolute good, and we cannot comprehend that other people may not perceive them in this way. This attitude is reflected in Indian policy. Since the 1960s, for example, the Department of Indian Affairs has operated on the assumption that it is necessary and desirable to hasten the inevitable movement of Indians along the path from a traditional and backward society to a modern and dynamic one. In effect, officials made no distinction between the concept of development and the idea of modernization. All efforts have been directed at providing Indian communities with more nurses and teachers, better infrastructure and facilities, and more make-work programs, welfare, and other social services. And clearly the maximization of the greatest number of goods and services delivered by the department was one of the unstated criteria by which progress was to be measured.

Needless to say, many Indian people do not accept the department's philosophy with respect to development. While they may want some of the benefits of modern life, they see the loss of their culture, the loss of control over their lives, their dependence on government, the social costs of their drinking, and the ever increasing materialism of their lives as the very opposite of development. Most important, they realize that the relative increase in their material prosperity is not a consequence of their participation on the productive side of the Canadian economy; rather, it is the price paid by society for separating them from the means of production, embodied essentially in land and resources. And indeed, the ultimate hallmark and consequence of this process is not development but stagnation and marginality.

I have placed the Indian experience in context because this constitutes the background necessary to understand the Grassy Narrows case as both a unique and a generalized tragedy. It is significant that Grassy Narrows would not have come to national attention had it not been for the discovery that the English-Wabigoon river system had been polluted with a deadly poison. But if the tragedy of Grassy Narrows is treated as unique, then its broader implications may well be misunderstood, because the circumstances that made the mercury spill so pathological are common to many Canadian Indian communities. In this sense, at least, Grassy Narrows represents a grim reminder of the inherent potentialities for exceptional injury when indigenous people are the victims of a major environmental disaster.

Those who are persuaded that mercury pollution was the most important causal factor in the etiology of human breakdown at Grassy Narrows will be disappointed by the detailed discussion of the conditions that predated the mercury spill. At this time, unfortunately, we have no way of knowing how much of the trauma can be attributed to mercury contamination and how much to other factors. What we do know for certain is that the impact of mercury poisoning was far more devastating for Grassy Narrows than it would have been in the absence of resettlement. As a people whose past experiences have bruised them and made them less able to withstand new crises, the community as a whole was unusually vulnerable to the onslaught on their River of Life. All the foundations of the culture seemed to be crumbling at the same time.

No wonder the Grassy Narrows people call mercury "the last nail in the coffin." The spike was driven into the physical ecology of their community life as well as into their system of beliefs, the mystical underpinning of their relationship to the land. It turned out to be a terrible betrayal that pushed them over the edge of their ability to feel secure in nature and to be even modestly self-reliant in providing for their needs. It eliminated one of the last occupations permitting families to work together and accelerated the wrong kind of government intervention in community life. And the organic poison of methyl mercury, or the anticipatory fear and anxiety associated with the dreaded Minamata disease, has taken its toll, superimposing a whole new set of traumatic disturbances upon the stress related to uprooting, separation, and loss.

But the reaction to the first appearance of the specter of Minamata disease in Canada and the subsequent handling of the mercury issue speak volumes about who we are as a society and how we treat indigenous peoples. The direct and measurable effects of mercury pollution were cruel enough. But possibly more ruthless were the less tangible effects arising from the way in which the mercury issue was defined, managed, and politicized to meet the interests and requirements of moral, social, and political expediency.

As a grotesque addition to all the other forms of betrayal attributed to mercury, we contributed our own poison to the environment. At different times during the sad history of the mercury issue since 1970, government officials misled the Indian people, presented contradictory evidence, distorted the significance of medical findings, and suppressed relevant information. The media eagerly exploited sensational information about the hideous and crippling effects of Minamata disease and reported that the people of Grassy Narrows were dying from the poison. The parade of "helpers" who came through the community breached the invisible barriers against unwanted visitors with a vengeance, because, as it turns out, most of the visitors came to satisfy their own curiosity and then moved on to more fashionable disasters. And all the consultants, lawyers, Indian politicians, bureaucrats, and private persons involved in exploring the possibilities of litigation participated, sometimes unwittingly, in the dance of vested interests that ultimately led to another betrayal for the community.

As for compensation for the damages caused by mercury, for years both Reed Paper Limited and the government of Ontario disclaimed all legal, social, and moral responsibility for the pollution. Each blamed the other for the disaster, and neither was prepared to take any action that might imply an acceptance of liability. In fact, the provincial government quietly helped the corporation leave the jurisdiction in which any legal action or public pressure might have been brought against it. And finally, the response of both the federal and the provincial governments to the situation of massive unemployment and social unrest added to the destabilization of Grassy Narrows. The governments' inability to develop a comprehensive plan for reconstruction and their recourse to sporadic, short-term, and remedial programs only served to reinforce dependency and accentuate the sense of helplessness. In spite of the efforts of many well-meaning officials, the machinery of government simply failed to respond in a holistic way to the restoration needs of a shattered society. In the end, the visible effects of the contamination were made worse by the poisons of mistrust, empty rhetoric, and crushed aspirations that became part of our legacy to this Indian community.

And so the circle closes. In the face of both the continuity of impacts stemming from almost a hundred years of internal colonialism and the added pressures generated by the relocation and the mercury pollution, it is a testimony to the resilience of the human spirit that the people of Grassy Narrows have managed to survive at all. For not only has their entire way of life been rendered dysfunctional, but they have consistently been led to believe that their culture is barbaric and that they are a primitive and inferior people. Further, the psychic scars left by a historic colonialism are constantly reinforced by a contemporary racism. And the internalization of oppression, in the form of a morally and culturally indefensible self-image, continues to contribute to the dynamics that lead to psychological and social breakdown.

Today, even the most casual visitor to the Grassy Narrows reserve is struck with the sense of being in a no-man's-land, a place that hangs in the balance between two worlds. Here the people have been subjected to too much change in too short a time, and the direction of this change has been sharply downward in both a spiritual and a social sense. Now they are no longer hunters, trappers, and fishermen, yet they are far from absorbed into the productive processes of the nation. They no longer live in an Ojibwa community, yet they are far from accepted into the social fabric of the larger society. They no longer follow the proud traditions of earlier generations, yet they have found no replacements in the broader culture. They are a sad people, a vulnerable people, who have been dispossessed, displaced, disinherited, and entrapped between two modes of existence. And in not mattering to anyone else, they seem not to matter even to themselves.

What is to be done? Is it worthwhile to argue about who is responsible for what aspect of the tragedy of Grassy Narrows? Why can't we accept a moral obligation to assist in rebuilding a fractured society? When, in December 1978, the chief of Grassy Narrows signed an agreement with the federal and provincial governments to negotiate a settlement for the damages to community life, he clearly defined the conditions he thought were important for the survival of his people. He said that reconstruction would depend on regaining control over the conditions of life and live-lihood, and this meant self-government and self-reliance. He emphasized that the Indian people had to become producers again; they had to break their dependence on government for the satisfaction of basic needs. And he argued that the settlement for damages, therefore, should provide his people with the three building blocks of social and economic develop-ment—namely, a land and resource base, capital for a development fund, and education and skill training. And while all these things, in and of themselves, would not have performed a miraculous cure for the social ills of the community, they might have made an enormous difference in the people's perception of what the future holds for them and their children.

In the final analysis, surely it is a change in the attitude to existence that is the beginning of the process of putting back together the pieces of a shattered life.

Now fifteen years after the discovery of mercury pollution and eight years after the signing of the mediation agreement, the task of the restoration of Grassy Narrows has hardly begun. While it is true that a settlement with Grassy Narrows for mercury-related damages in the amount of $8.7 million was finally reached in November 1985, it is also probable that no amount of money will solve the problems of the Grassy Narrows people. The key to their survival lies in breaking the deadlock of their marginality. In the absence of measures to increase their resource base significantly and extend opportunities for education and training in both traditional and modern skills, there can be no movement toward this goal. And money, by itself, cannot halt the demoralization that comes from being unable to produce anything of value to the rest of the community or influence anything that matters for the preservation of a culture. At Grassy Narrows, in fact, money may well aggravate the existing inequalities of status and wealth, as well as the endemic interclan rivalries and jealousies, as families compete for political power to determine how and when the money will be spent.

At the same time, the reconstruction of Grassy Narrows can probably not be accomplished fully without fundamental changes in attitudes and public policy. There are four facets to the challenge Canada faces in its relationship to indigenous people, four aspects of one central reality, and none can be understood or resolved without the others. First of all, the country is confronting two different civilizations, two ways of being. As long as government officials continue to impose the deification of material and technological progress on an earlier civilization, there will be conflict. The indigenous peoples will be the losers, but they will not be entirely crushed, and their spiritual crisis will continue. The second aspect is economic, the dilemma of the separation of native people from land and resources, a separation that exerts a profound influence on every dimension of personal and communal life. As long as this continues, they will be an impoverished and demoralized people who have neither land nor capital nor even a secure relationship to our economic system as wage laborers. The third aspect is social, the existence of racism and our apparent indifference to the manifestation of Indian genocide. Would the response have been any different if Grassy Narrows had been a white community? Perhaps. It is a sad commentary on our times that our courts will fight to preserve an individual life otherwise robbed of function, dignity, and meaning while we look the other way when a people choose to die rather than live under equally intolerable conditions. And the fourth aspect is political, the sheer power of the state to administer and control the lives of Indians. Canada has one of the most centralized and monolithic systems of Indian administration in the world, and there are serious problems in the Indian–government relationship. But sadly, the century-old process of colonization has also served to corrupt the Indian leadership and weaken its ability to take a unified stand in the struggle for self-government and the recognition of aboriginal rights in the new constitution. In short, these four systemic conditions underlie the symptoms of social disintegration in Indian communities and reinforce causal factors of specific importance.

A great deal more could be said about the conditions for the restoration of Grassy Narrows, but I will add only one final observation. Metaphorically speaking, if the external enabling conditions constitute the firewood for the renewal of a people, then the spark to light the fire has to come from within. This spark is the process by which a human being becomes conscious of the responsibility he bears for his own destiny. It is also the process by which he rediscovers the inner freedom to take a stand for or against life. And this involves choice and personal decision. As long as the Grassy Narrows people continue to believe that they are locked in the grip of the dark power of alcohol, as long as they sanction all alcohol-related behavior, they will externalize the cause of their misfortunes. As long as they continue to blame others for their circumstances and decide that others are responsible for their survival, very little will change in their society. In the broadest philosophical sense, they have to come to understand that a slave is also a man who waits for someone else to come and free him.

The story of Grassy Narrows is important not only because it is a recapitulation, in a sense, of the ordeal of indigenous peoples on the continent but also because it reflects certain universal dimensions of human experience. For one thing, we now know that there are communities that can become unravelled to such an extent that the people in them lose much of their sense of self-worth and well-being, sometimes even their will to survive, and begin to spin off in directions of their own and die, literally or figuratively. For another, we know that this can happen when people are subjected to fundamental change, at a rate far beyond their ability to cope, in every single aspect of their culture simultaneously. In this process of total intrusion, if they also lose the hold on their spiritual selves, their vision of the future, and their hope of regaining some measure of control over their circumstances, then life itself ceases to have meaning. In this sense, Grassy Narrows serves as a poignant example of how fragile a society can be, and how we as humans may respond to conditions of unprecedented stress by destroying ourselves.

It may well be that Grassy Narrows also represents a microcosm, greatly magnified and concentrated in time and space, of the destructive processes at work in our own society. Is it not possible that the pressures that crippled the people of Grassy Narrows are the same pressures that, much more slowly and covertly, are crippling us as well? We need not search very far for an answer. We need only reflect on current statistics on violence, illness, family breakdown, child abuse, and drug and alcohol problems among our own young to divest ourselves of any illusions about our security and well-being as a society. Less evident, of course, are the many forms of uprooting that are part of modern life and that play havoc with personal morale—the loss of our moorings in faith and tradition; the loss of a sense of connection with the earth; alienation from meaningful work; and separation from a nurturing family and communal setting. And since many of our institutions no longer function to instill a sense of social unity and interdependence, each individual struggles to make it against the odds, and many are victimized in the process. And so we face an uncertain future of accelerating technological change with reflexes weakened by a sense of cultural disorientation, isolation, and impotence.

Perhaps what happened at Grassy Narrows, then, can serve as a warning that our own survival depends upon restoring a sense of mutual responsibility for one another and ultimately for the fate of the earth. Love has to become a stronger power than the poisons of self-interest and powerlessness or else we will all perish.

# NOTES

## Chapter 1

1. *While People Sleep, Sudden Death in the Kenora Area* (Kenora: Grand Council Treaty No. 3, 1973).
2. National statistics on Indian suicide are contained in a report published by the Department of Indian Affairs and Northern Development (DIAND) called *Indian Conditions: A Survey,* Ottawa, 1980, pp. 18–19. The number of Indian deaths due to suicide per 100,000 population is given as almost three times the national rate. Suicides account for 35 percent of accidental deaths in the fifteen to twenty-four age-group and 21 percent in the twenty-five to thirty-four age-group.

   As alarming as the statistics on suicide are, however, it is almost certain that they underestimate the true number of suicides in the Indian community. For one thing, in order for a death to be certified as a suicide, the coroner has to be satisfied that the person who killed himself intended that outcome. It is difficult to infer intent in deaths caused by railway impact, drowning, or automobile collision, since alcohol is often involved. Frequently such deaths are simply classified as accidents. Further, coroners depend on clues to determine suicide. But we do not know the clues to suicide among Indians, and very few Indians leave suicide notes. For these reasons, a study in Alberta has concluded that many violent deaths among Indians may actually be suicides. In short, whereas official statistics show a rate of suicide among Indians that is three times the national rate, the true figure may be closer to twelve. See Menno Boldt et al., "Report of the Task Force on Suicides," presented to the minister of Social Services and Community Health, the Honorable Helen Huntley, Government of Alberta, May 1976.
3. The fact that data are generally available only on a regional basis limits assessment of the extent to which one community shows a particularly high level of social pathology relative to another. It also hinders evaluation of the differential impact of factors unique to any one reserve—for example, mercury poisoning at Grassy Narrows and Whitedog.
4. N. Giesbrecht, J. Brown, et al., *Alcohol Problems in Northwestern Ontario, Preliminary Report: Consumption Patterns, and Public Order and Public Health Problems,* Substudy no. 872 (Toronto: The Addiction Research Foundation, 1977).
5. Ibid., pp. 108–15.
6. The spree during the first week in April is usually a little longer and more sustained than the sprees that follow normal paydays, because people receive their vacation pay at the end of March. Another big spree follows the reception of child tax-credit checks from the federal government. Many families receive a lump-sum payment of $1,000 or more. After purchase of a limited quantity of food and payment of bills and fines, a significant proportion of such lump-sum payments finds its way into alcohol-related expenditure.
7. The children in houses where there is heavy binge drinking go hungry, because food is not an item of high priority and people tend to eat little during this time. If they cannot get food from their relatives, they will vandalize the school and take food earmarked for the school lunch program. In 1979, children started to break into the houses of teachers in order to obtain food.

8. At the local level, the personalities of those employed by a police detachment, court, or correctional agency may influence which persons and acts are processed by the justice system. The policies, organizational procedures, and resources of these institutions will also play a part in interpreting which problems and events will be considered threats to community life and safety. Furthermore, court statistics may be influenced by the responses of those charged, as well as by the presence and quality of the defense counsel and the inclination of the bench. All these factors have a bearing on the statistics that are produced on the extent of public order problems in any given area.

9. The statistics on public order offenses in the northwest region and the Kenora area are given in Giesbrecht et al., pp. 60–105.

10. Indian women in particular seem to prefer going to jail to paying fines. While there, they can at least have a shower, get a decent meal, wash their clothes, watch television, meet friends, and escape from the intense pressures of reserve life.

11. Unfortunately, there are no comparative statistics on the contribution of Grassy Narrows to public order offenses in the Kenora area. I discussed this question, however, with the following key persons in the justice system: Ted Burton, Crown prosecutor; Ken Wilson, superintendent of the Ontario Provincial Police; Mrs. Cameron, administrator of the Criminal Court; and Chuck Wingfield, the adult probation officer. They made it clear to me that people from Grassy Narrows began to make up a substantial proportion of offenses (as documented in police, court, and jail records) only in the late 1960s and the 1970s.

12. The adult probation records reveal that in the period 1969–77, persons between sixteen and nineteen years of age made up 35 percent of all offenders; those in the twenty to twenty-nine age-group made up 42 percent; and the remainder fell in the thirty to forty age-group.

13. The records of the Probation and After-Care Branch, Children's Services Division of the Provincial Ministry of Community and Social Services, show that a total of ninety-nine children, seventy-three boys and twenty-six girls, were placed on probation during the period 1972–77. Children eight and nine years old accounted for 7 percent of all probationers; children aged ten and eleven made up 29 percent; and the remainder were twelve and thirteen years old (40 percent) and fourteen and fifteen years old (24 percent).

   The majority of offenses for which children were put on probation were "break, enter, and theft" (62.6 percent), willful damage (16 percent), and alcohol intoxication in a public place (13 percent). The remainder (8.4 percent) consisted of assault, criminal negligence, use of firearms, and mischief.

14. This percentage is derived from the number of children who dropped out of school (56) plus the number who were not registered during the 1977–78 academic year (18), over the total number of children of school age (161). These data are based on school attendance and registration records and on the 1977 household survey.

15. The overall pattern of enrollment in school for the fifteen to nineteen age-group is discernible in the following summary for 1977–78. Of seventeen persons on reserve aged fifteen, eleven were still in school on the reserve; of fifteen persons aged sixteen, only six were in school; of twenty persons aged seventeen, only five were in school; of nine persons aged eighteen, none were in school; and of eight persons aged nineteen, only two were in school.

16. Johanna Veldstra, "Education Cohort Analysis 1971–1979 for the Grassy Narrows Federal Elementary School" (Unpublished report commissioned by the chief and the band council and completed in 1979).

17. Letter from G. E. Norris, director of the Kenora Children's Aid Society, to Chief Fobister, March 25, 1978.

18. Many children at Grassy Narrows have impetigo, a bacterial infection that starts when a tiny scratch on the skin is exposed to dirt. It will heal only without its crust, at which point the condition is highly contagious. The entire bodies of some children are covered with this infection. Poorly treated, it leaves permanent scars. The other condition that is common at Grassy Narrows is a fungus infection that needs antibiotic treatment. Children have running sores from this condition on their hands, arms, feet, legs, and bellies.

19. On September 23, 1983, Toronto's *Globe and Mail* carried a feature story on the problem of gang rape at Grassy Narrows. The article reported a meeting between the chief and a visiting group of members of the Ontario parliament. In response to a question about sexual abuse, the chief admitted that gang rapes had been happening with increasing frequency in the context of drinking parties and that young teenage girls had been the prime victims.

20. The concept of promiscuity involves sexual behavior that is indiscriminate, random, and contrary to prevailing cultural norms. As long as people are drinking, however, it does not apply. It applies only to illicit sexual behavior when a person is sober.

21. On the old reserve, it was customary for courtships to be prolonged. The boy would normally live with the family of the girl and be judged on his skills as a provider. He could sleep with the girl, but not have intercourse, until the family approved the relationship. At that point, the couple would be considered to have formed a family unit and could openly and freely act as a married couple. As little as ten years ago, this was still the custom among "good families" of Grassy Narrows.

22. The custom of the new reserve with respect to family formation is a marked deviation from the traditional way. Now, if a girl conceives a child, the father, if his identity is known, may move in with her after the baby is born. Generally, however, there are no sanctions against the boy if he does not wish to live with the girl. In man–woman relationships, as one old woman put it, "nothing, nothing at all is left of the Indian way."

23. Grassy Narrows is a very small community in which everybody is related to everybody else at the second-cousin level through blood or marriage. It is impossible to know whether the incidence of children born with symptoms of mental slowness is related to chaos in bloodlines, alcohol, methyl mercury, or a combination of all three.

24. These statistics were contained in a letter dated February 20, 1978, from Dr. Connop, director of the Thunder Bay Zone of Medical Services, to Chief Simon Fobister.

## Chapter 2

1. By the nineteenth century, four main divisions of Ojibwa had emerged; the southeastern Ojibwa, the southwestern Ojibwa (Chippewa), the plains Ojibwa, and the northern Ojibwa. The four divisions were the result of a historic process that began in the mid-seventeenth century and involved trade, conquest, and migration. The plains Ojibwa moved into the province of Manitoba and adopted many features of plains tribes; the southeastern Ojibwa occupied the lower Michigan peninsula and parts of southern Ontario; and the southwestern Ojibwa gradually pushed into Wisconsin and Minnesota. The general agreement on the boundaries of the Ojibwa in these three regions does not extend to the northern Ojibwa, northwest of Lake Superior.

2. The ancestors of the present northern Ojibwa are believed to have occupied a territory from the east end of Georgian Bay on Lake Huron to Michipicoten Bay on the northeast shore of Lake Superior at the time of contact. Missionaries encountered large groups of these Algonquian-speaking peoples around Sault Ste. Marie, and it became the custom of the French to refer to them as the People of the Sault, or the Saulteaux. Even today, the Ojibwa Indians of northern Ontario are called Saulteaux to distinguish them from the Ojibwa of southwestern and eastern Ontario.

3. The movement of the Ojibwa westward and northward of Lake Superior was stimulated by the expanding fur trade. At first, the Ojibwa acted as middlemen in the fur trade to the Cree and Assiniboin, but later in the seventeenth century they became trappers themselves. As the Cree and Assiniboin moved eastward, the Ojibwa moved northward to Lac Seul and the region of the Lake of the Woods. Charles A. Bishop, *The Northern Ojibwa and the Fur Trade* (Toronto: Holt, Rinehart, and Winston of Canada Limited, 1974), pp. 3–7, 305–35.

4. Apparently the eight or ten groups of Ojibwa that had originally pushed north and west of Lake Superior in the 1720s and 1730s had increased to about thirty groups by 1780. The population of Ojibwa is believed to have doubled in the period 1730–80. Bishop, p. 331.

5. Martin H. Greenwood, *Big Trout Lake: A Pilot Study of a Northern Indian Settlement in Relation to its Resource Base* (Ottawa: Department of Citizenship and Immigration, Economic and Social Research Division, 1964), p. 5. On the Ojibwa and the fur trade, see also Harold Hickerson, *The Chippewa and Their Neighbours: A Study in Ethnohistory* (New York: Holt, Rinehart, and Winston, 1970); Arthur J. Ray, *Indians in the Fur Trade: Their Role as Trappers, Hunters, and Middlemen in the Lands Southwest of Hudson Bay, 1660–1870* (Toronto: University of Toronto Press, 1974); and Edward S. Rogers, "Changing Settlement Patterns of the Cree-Ojibwa of Northern Ontario," *Southwestern Journal of Anthropology* 19 (1963): 64–88.

6. An account of the treaty negotiations can be found in Alexander Morris, *The Treaties of Canada with the Indians of Manitoba and the Northwest Territories* (Toronto: Belfords, Clarke, 1880).

7. Although at the time of signing the treaty, Chief Sah-katch-eway represented the "single Mattawan and English River Band," in 1887, for administrative reasons, the government recognized these groups as separate bands with separate reserves. To this day, however, the Grassy Narrows people say they have always been one band although they had two reserves.

8. Both the date of the epidemic and the number of casualties are matters of dispute. Some people say that the epidemic took place in 1915, others in 1919. We have no records of the total population for Wabauskang prior to the epidemic, but the entire reserve was wiped out apparently, and "five or six bodies were buried every day." As legend has it, those who got sick at Grassy Narrows were given half a glass of rum by Donald Merchison, the Bay manager, "to sweat the fever from the body." Mr. Merchison is well remembered at Grassy Narrows for this aid, because he had to go to Kenora by dog team to get the rum. He lived around Grassy Narrows for a long time.

9. Kai T. Erikson, *Everything in Its Path* (New York: Simon and Schuster, 1976), p. 81.

10. The McIntosh residential school was built in 1923–24. Until 1949, when a road was built through McIntosh, access to the school was by water or rail. At its peak, this school could house about two hundred Indian children from northern reserves. The school residence burnt to the ground on March 19, 1965, but the classrooms are still standing. Many Grassy Narrows people attended the residential school at McIntosh.

## Chapter 3

1. Several books by Edward T. Hall illustrate variations among cultures with respect to time and space: *The Silent Language* (New York: Doubleday, 1959); *The Hidden Dimension* (New York: Anchor Books, 1969); and *Beyond Culture* (New York: Anchor Books, 1977).

2. The aspects of the traditional spatial orientation of the Ojibwa that do not relate directly to our discussion are the Ojibwa reliance on close observation of natural phenomena to maintain directional orientation, knowledge of terrain through direct experience of

topography and the spatial relation of one locality to another, "mental maps" that relate purposely to the active quest for food and the pursuit of livelihood, and "cosmic space" in the sense of a place for the major spiritual entities that exist on different planes in the universe.

For an exposition of these aspects of Ojibwa spatial perception, see A. Irving Hallowell, *Culture and Experience* (Philadelphia: University of Pennsylvania Press, 1955), pp. 184–202.

3. Carl C. Jung, *Memories, Dreams, Reflections* (New York: Vintage Books, 1965), pp. 300, 304–05.

4. Hallowell, p. 188.

5. As the life of plants, for example, becomes the subject of increased research, more of a scientific basis to the Indian belief of "a light coming off the land," or an "aura," may be discovered. The concept of aura has become familiar to us through Kirilian photography. Certain people with special sensitivities can also see auras around the human body. The aura is a light-wave phenomenon related to an energy field that cannot normally be seen by the naked eye.

6. This follows from the appraisal of the new reserve as "spiritually bad land." Obviously "good" land for human settlement would, by definition, have places of power in the general vicinity. There is, however, one place of power about four miles from the new reserve that was pointed out to me, although it is customary among Indian people to keep places of power secret. I know from personal experience that this "amplification point" does seem to be a place of high energy, uplifting to the spirit in a rather mysterious way. While communal spiritual rituals are no longer practiced on the new reserve, a few individuals still seek solitude and practice meditation in certain "personal places" that have special meaning for them.

7. Since in any solar year there are more than twelve and fewer than thirteen lunations, the Indians used to add an unnamed moon to the series. The other moons were named. For example, the people of the Berens River named the spring moons according to the birds that made their appearance in the area at that time. Thus, eagle, goose, and loon moons correspond to our months of March, April, and May. A similar naming system may have been used by the Grassy Narrows people in representing their moons by the animals characteristic of a particular season. Hallowell, pp. 226–27.

8. The sense of time that prompts people to begin activities "when the time is ripe and no sooner" seems to be characteristic of many Indian tribes. Hall elaborates on the sense of time among the Pueblo Indians and the Navajo in *The Silent Language,* pp. 31–41.

9. Hallowell, p. 99.

10. There is a rich literature on the importance of dreams and the puberty vision quest in the Ojibwa culture. Among the best sources are Diamond Jenness, *The Ojibwa Indians of Parry Island, Their Social and Religious Life* (Ottawa: National Museum of Canada, Bulletin no. 78, 1935); Edward S. Rogers, *The Round Lake Ojibwa* (Toronto: Royal Ontario Museum, Occasional Paper 5, 1962); and Rev. S. A. Sieber, S.V.D., *The Saulteaux Indians* (St. Boniface, Manitoba: The Provincial House, 1948).

11. Normally, it is forbidden to speak of the knowledge gained from the vision quest, particularly if the person is granted some special power or skill by his guardian spirit. In this example, the information is limited to time perception.

## Chapter 4

1. The Ojibwa sharply delineate two categories in their kinship terminology: (1) kinsmen who are patrilateral relatives (father's brother's family, brother's family, and brother's son's family) and matrilateral relatives (mother's sister's nuclear family); (2) non-

kinsmen who are all others in the society and who are literally not related. This dichotomy of kin and nonkin is absolute and has important implications for marriage. For extensive treatment of the subject, see R. W. Dunning, *Social and Economic Change among the Northern Ojibwa* (Toronto; University of Toronto Press, 1959), pp. 71–108; and Edward S. Rogers, *The Round Lake Ojibwa* (Toronto: Department of Lands and Forests for the Royal Ontario Museum, 1962), pp. B10–81.

2. Rogers states that the term literally means "those whom I lead"; therefore, if the context is hunting, a man might use the term to refer to all members of his hunting group. The most common context, however, is that of kinship, referring to a group of kinsmen for whom a man is responsible. These are determined according to a number of principles. The first is that of patrilineal descent. The second involves the solidarity of brothers— that is, an older brother is responsible for his younger full brothers and their descendants. The third relates to the dependency of women: unmarried and widowed women are under the care of the father first, then brothers, and sometimes sons. These principles provide the means of determining, in theory, the composition of the Ojibwa family. Rogers, p. B82.

3. Dunning makes a distinction between this family group, or extended family, and the household, or nuclear family, by calling the first group a co-residential group and the second group a commensural unit. Dunning, p. 55.

4. An important aspect of the difficulty in transplanting the linkages and support systems of the extended family to the new reserve has already been alluded to in the previous chapter. The physical (or spatial) layout of houses on the new reserve itself, dictated by government bureaucrats, made it impossible for the family group to live together. Indian people were given numbers, houses were allocated to individual households, and households were scattered randomly around the new site. To make matters worse, houses were arranged in a straight line and pressed closely together. Had government planners bothered to visit the old reserve and learn something about customary settlement patterns, they would have seen that each family group assumed a separate physical identity in space. At Grassy Narrows, one used to be able to see a cluster of houses or tents, like a family compound, with the various clusters at least a quarter mile apart on the shores of the English-Wabigoon River. Of course, for most of the winter, the old reserve was deserted as families scattered to their traplines.

5. One family at Grassy Narrows tries to keep [the memory of] the naming ceremony alive. The ceremony is no longer performed by a medicine man, of course, since all the recognized medicine men have died. But the custom of asking old people to name a child remains, although it is difficult to assess to what extent the spiritual context of the ritual has been preserved.

6. The *manitos* were entities who ruled the universe. They were the sources of the Ojibwa Indians' existence. Without their aid, without their blessings and protection, man was helpless; he could not achieve success in life. Success, symbolized by hunting achievement, good health, ability to divine and to cure, and, above all, long life, could come only as a gift from the manitos.

7. Ruth Landes, *The Ojibwa Woman* (New York: AMS Press, 1971), p. 124.

8. In the Western kinship system, it is customary to classify all the children of one's aunts and uncles on both sides of the family as cousins. The Ojibwa, however, make a distinction among cousins that we do not make. They consider that a man can marry his "cross-cousin" (the daughter of his mother's brother or his father's sister), because these women are not related to him. He cannot marry his "parallel cousin" (the daughter of his mother's sister or his father's brother) because such women are considered to be as closely related to him as his own sisters. Although all Ojibwa make the same identifications in their kinship terminology, not all Ojibwa bands favor cross-cousin marriage. In

her work in southwestern Ontario, Ruth Landes found that the Emo band forbade marriage between relatives, whereas the Kenora Ojibwa strongly preferred cross-cousin marriage. Landes, pp. 52–62.

9. In 1948, Sieber published his study of the Saulteaux of northwestern Ontario, which included Grassy Narrows. He recorded thirteen totems, or totemic clans, on the Grassy Narrows reserve: caribou, lynx, loon, sturgeon, bear, eagle, moose, kingfish, bullhead, pelican, mallard duck, rattlesnake, and common snake. (Only the first seven totems have survived in the contemporary setting.) The totem was passed by the father to his descendants; the woman did not lose her clan affiliation at marriage, but she did not pass it on to any of her children. Although the clan system as a formal means of social organization is believed to have disappeared sometime in the nineteenth century, what did remain until recently was the strong feeling of close kinship and solidarity among members of the same totemic clan. One could always turn to one's clanmates in times of need, but marriage between members of the same totem was forbidden. In the 1940s, Sieber had already observed that with regard to marriage customs, "the most outstanding decline took place in the matter of clan exogamy . . . the disregard of totemic clan affiliations." S. A. Sieber, S.V.D, *The Saulteaux Indians* (St. Boniface, Manitoba: The Provincial House, 1948), pp. 51–53.

## Chapter 5

1. Robert Redfield, *The Little Community* (Chicago: University of Chicago Press, 1960). See the chapter on social structure, which describes the importance of lineage family groups in primitive society.

2. A detailed and comprehensive study of the genealogies of Grassy Narrows families, from the signing of the treaty in 1873 to the present, revealed that practically every member of the Grassy Narrows band is related to everyone else at the second-cousin level. The information for this study was compiled from pay lists of annual treaty money (available from the archives of the Department of Indian Affairs) and from the private records of births, marriages, and deaths kept by the Mennonite missionaries since 1958. Melva Zook, one of the Mennonites resident at Grassy Narrows, undertook the laborious task of collating the information. Her work was part of the community research project that I directed in 1977–78. A copy of the report, entitled "Grassy Narrows: Family Histories," was distributed to the heads of all the major family groups, as well as to the chief and the band council.

3. Robert Redfield suggests that a "little community" is characterized by four qualities: distinctiveness (where the community begins and ends is apparent), smallness (its size enables it to be a unit of observation), homogeneity (the activities and states of mind of people of the same age and sex are similar), and self-sufficiency (the community provides for all or most of the activities and needs of the people in it). According to this definition, Grassy Narrows can certainly be called a little community.

4. The Medewiwin movement apparently had its origins in the late eighteenth century. This movement involved the formation of associations of specialized spiritual leaders. In its fullest form, in the late nineteenth century, it included elaborate initiations, a hierarchical priesthood, training and fees for members, and regular ceremonies and meetings. The Medewiwin ceremonies were performed on the old reserve and are remembered by many people at Grassy Narrows. However, these ceremonies were of an extracommunity character, attended by people from other reserves in northwestern Ontario.

A detailed discussion of the Medewiwin Society can be found in C. Vecsey, "Traditional Ojibwa Religion and Its Historical Changes" (Ph.D. diss., Northwestern University, 1977), pp. 202–26.

5. A study of the Round Lake people confirmed that the settlement pattern of the Ojibwa before the advent of year-round residence in one village or reserve was typified by small neighborhood subcommunities based entirely on the origin of the families and their kinship ties. Only in the summer did people gather more closely together "to form a type of village life, and for the most part . . . the summer settlements for each subcommunity were separate . . . . It cannot be overemphasized that concentrated village life is new to the Round Lake people, and much evidence is on hand that they still feel more comfortable when the nearest neighbors who are not close kin are located some miles distant." Ontario, Department of Lands and Forests, "The Round Lake Ojibwa: The People, The Land, The Resources 1968–70" (Paper prepared for A.R.D.A., Project 25075, December 1971), pp. 242, 244.

6. The Christmas feast was sometimes organized by the Hudson's Bay Company manager. Missionary priests tried to be on the old reserve at Christmastime in order to say Mass. Of all the Christian traditions, Christmas seems to have been the most important for the Grassy Narrows people. The Christmas feast is a community tradition to this day.

7. Jenness describes nine ways in which sorcerers used to kill or injure their enemies, including sketching the victim's image on the ground and placing poison on the spot to be harmed and tying a carved wooden image of the victim to a tree with a thread and waiting for the thread to break as a sign of the victim's death. Many of these methods seem to have been based on visualization techniques and the effecting of death through the magical separation of the soul from the body. Jenness, *Ojibwa Indians of Parry Island*, pp. 85–86.

8. Rogers, *Round Lake Ojibwa*, pp. D3–D31.

9. Maggie Land comments on the shaking tent ceremony, which she witnessed several times. She describes the ability of a medicine man to call the soul of a person to the tent. But I have never heard anyone at Grassy Narrows speak of the use of this ritual to cause harm or misfortune to others. The people say it was used for curing, for communication, or for other problem-solving situations. This does not invalidate the opportunity inherent in this ceremony to cause permanent separation of the soul from the body, resulting in death.

10. In general, the old people of Grassy Narrows have great difficulty in explaining the sharp deterioration in community life on the new reserve. Traditionally, a misfortune such as sickness or an epidemic that befell an entire band was never interpreted as having been caused by impersonal forces; rather, it was a punishment for offending the Great Spirit "by not living in the proper way." Although to some extent bad medicine was part of the norm of social relations in traditional Indian communities, perhaps the elder quoted here is implying that on the old reserve, the practice went beyond the norm and might therefore have been a factor in bringing about the present troubles.

11. See A. Irving Hallowell, *Culture and Experience*, chapters 13–15. Hallowell writes that the absence of overt aggression in face-to-face situations was an outstanding feature of interpersonal relations in Saulteaux society. "The culturally sanctioned channels for hostility are of two kinds. The first is typified by . . . unformalized ways and means [like gossip] . . . . The second channel is sorcery and magic. [By the latter means, the Indian could] vent anger with greater effectiveness than would be possible by verbal insult or even physical assault short of murder. [One could] make a person suffer a lingering illness, interfere with his economically productive activities and thus menace his living . . . make his children sick, lure the wife away by love magic . . . or kill" (pp. 280–81). In this context, it is clear that the ways of knowing about the nature of "power," its acquisition, and its deployment were basic to social relations and constituted a necessity for the spiritual elder of each major family group.

12. Hallowell, p. 147.

13. Stu Martin has worked with the Department of Indian Affairs for over twenty-five years. He described the situation in an interview: "Not so long ago, at Pekangikum, the Chief and Council functioned quite differently. They were organized in their own way, and this had nothing to do with us [the department]. Every person on that council had a different responsibility. For example, the band had its own policing system. They had a policeman. During the year, they used to pay him with groceries. He would get money only on Treaty Day. The people would simply take care of him, and he, in turn, would do the policing job. There was no need for lots of government people on the reserves. I would visit the reserves only four times a year. The Chief and Council took care of their own community and made sure that people made a decent living. Now, of course, the government has taken over many of the functions of the old Chief and Council."

14. In 1962, the Department of Indian Affairs was particularly anxious that the Grassy Narrows people elect a chief the government could deal with. The people had been resisting the move to the new reserve, and government-built houses had been lying vacant on the new site for over a year. Finally, a new chief was elected, and he presided over the implementation of the relocation in 1963–64. It is interesting to note that this chief subsequently became the only Grassy Narrows band member ever to be granted a permanent civil service job with the Department of Indian Affairs.

15. H. B. Hawthorn et al., *The Indians of British Columbia* (Toronto: University of Toronto Press, 1958), p. 39.

16. R. W. Dunning, "Some Problems of Reserve Indian Communities: A Case Study," *Anthropologica* 6 (1964):35–36.

## Chapter 6

1. These developments on the frontier included the building of a second transcontinental railway (the CNR line) in 1909, midway between the Grassy Narrows reserve and the CPR railway line, which passed through Kenora. In the 1920s, the lumbering industry was given a boost by the construction of a pulp mill in Kenora. Later in the same decade, a gold rush started around Red Lake, a town about 125 miles north of Grassy Narrows. Minaki Lodge, catering to wealthy tourists and sports fishermen, opened in 1916 near the rail crossing of the Winnipeg River. In the early 1930s, the Trans-Canada Highway was built through the town of Kenora, thus facilitating access to the region from points both east and west.

   For a more extensive discussion of the Indians' participation in the economy of northwestern Ontario before World War II, see an unpublished report prepared for the Anti-Mercury Ojibwa Group, the Islington Band, and the Grassy Narrows Band by Peter Usher, Patricia Anderson, Hugh Brody, Jennifer Keck, and Jill Torrie, "The Economic and Social Impact of Mercury Pollution on the Whitedog and Grassy Narrows Indian Reserves, Ontario," Ottawa, July 1979, pp. 87–89.

2. Department of Indian Affairs and Northern Development, *Annual Reports*. Report of John McIntyre to the Superintendent-General of Indian Affairs in Ottawa, 1885, pp. 166–67.

3. Report of E. McColl to the Superintendent-General of Indian Affairs in Ottawa, *Annual Reports*, 1885, p. 127.

3a. The description of provincial government policy regarding Indian land use presented in pp. 115 and 116 draws substantially on the more detailed analysis of this subject in Usher et al., pp. 90–91, 96–98, 106.

4. For a detailed examination of the evolution of the Indian Act, see "The Historical Development of the Indian Act" (Paper prepared by the Treaties and Historical Research Centre, Department of Indian Affairs and Northern Development, Ottawa,

August 1978).

5. Joint Committee of the Senate and the House of Commons, *Proceedings and Evidence* 16 (1961):605–18.

6. This amendment to the Indian Act made it possible to sell beer and other liquor to the Grassy Narrows guides in the tourist camps, to the men on railway section gangs around McIntosh, and to those who worked in the mines around Red Lake. On-reserve alcohol consumption, however, remained prohibited until the mid-1970s.

7. The difference in hospitality between the Cree and the Ojibwa Indians, for example, was noted by early explorers as well as by contemporary scholars. The Cree were known for their hospitality, and yet both Cree and Ojibwa communities are geographically isolated, and both cultures are based on clan groups. Thus, isolation by itself does not explain hostility to strangers.

8. Tuberculosis was a cause of many deaths on the old reserve, especially among children. There was initial resistance to the sanitariums, because "some people never came back, and the Indians thought the white people were killing them there."

9. Ira M. Robinson, *New Industrial Towns on Canada's Resource Frontier* (Chicago: University of Chicago Department of Geography Research Paper, no. 73, 1962). Indeed, Kenora in its early days must have borne a striking resemblance to Sioux Lookout (Crow Lake) in its ethnic composition, association with the railroad, and social structure. An excellent exposition of the development of Crow Lake is given by David H. Stymeist, *Ethnics and Indians, Social Relations in a Northwestern Ontario Town* (Toronto: Peter Martin Associates Limited, 1975), pp. 24–39.

10. Eleanor M. Jacobson, *Bended Elbow* (Kenora: Central Publications, 1976), p. 37. This book is a highly partisan and harshly negative account of Indians in Kenora, but it expresses feelings and perceptions that are widely shared among white residents of the town.

11. The federal government agencies include Indian Affairs, the Department of Manpower, and the Department of National Health and Welfare; the provincial government agencies are the Ministry of Natural Resources, Ontario Provincial Police, and Community and Social Services. Other government offices (Justice, Liquor Control Board, Mines, Highways, Transport, Post Office, and so on) serve both the Indian and the white populations.

12. Long-time Kenora residents confirmed the activities of bootleggers on the new reserve and the impact of road access on drinking patterns. Stu Martin said in an interview: "The drinking at Grassy Narrows really started when they were moved to the road, when the liquor began coming in. The taxi people, they exploited the Indians; they could bring in the booze very easily. The trouble at Grassy was related to alcohol, to the road, and to the relocation and the disruption of their way of life."

13. Jacobson, pp. 7–8, 5, 12.

14. See Stymeist, pp. 84–85, for a good discussion of the dimensions and implications of the existing exchange system between Indian people and the white organizations that serve them.

15. Ibid., p. 93.

16. An extensive and insightful discussion of strategies used by Indians to cope with the image whites have of them can be found in Niels Winther Braroe, *Indian and White* (Stanford: Stanford University Press, 1975), chapters 6–8.

17. Louis Cameron, Anishinabe interview, quoted in "Quicksilver and Slow Death" (Paper prepared for the Ontario Public Interest Research Group, October, 1976, p. 25.

18. Ibid., p. 26.

19. Jacobson, p. 33.

## Chapter 7

1. Father Lacelle had this observation about the berry-picking period at Grassy Narrows: "Because midsummer was kind of a slow period for the people, they used to socialize a lot before blueberry picking started. They would get into the picking areas about ten days before the berries were ready, and they would have all kinds of games and dances. This also happened around rice-picking time. There were two or three occasions in the course of the year where socializing would be combined, in a natural way, with economic activity. During these occasions, I would say that it was like clockwork—most of the children would be born nine months later."

2. This is Yngve Lithman's characterization of the ideology that permeated what he calls a new era in the history of Indian administration starting in the middle 1960s. Lithman's work, oriented toward the interaction between Indians and whites, is based on his field work at Fort Alexander, an Ojibwa Indian community in northern Manitoba. This band was not physically relocated but did get a new town-site in the mid-1960s, which, in Lithman's opinion, "caused a massive shift of community interests and sentiments." Yngve Georg Lithman, *The Community Apart* (Stockholm: University of Stockholm, Department of Social Anthropology, 1978), p. 175.

3. A more detailed examination of the decline of trapping at Grassy Narrows over the period 1948–78, as documented by MNR data on annual fur harvests, is contained in Peter Usher et al., "The Economic and Social Impact of Mercury Pollution on Whitedog and Grassy Narrows Indian Reserves, Ontario" (1979), pp. 149–53. The description of trends in the trapping of mink and muskrat contained on p. 137 draws on the information presented in this report, particularly pp. 185–187.

4. In the late 1970s, several attempts were made using government grants to cultivate vegetables on a two-acre site on the old reserve. This community garden quickly became just another government project with band members working for hourly wages. The project was unsuccessful and was abandoned after three years.

5. Usher describes the relationship between lodge owners and Indian guides as follows: "The owners of Ball Lake, for example, provided shelter for their Indian guides. But the Indians lived with their families in small shacks near the main lodge, out of sight of the guests. They were not allowed access to the main lodge and were not permitted to mingle with the guests. There was also a hierarchy among the workers of the camp based on race: white guides and staff came before Indian guides and staff." See Usher et al., pp. 111–112, 115.

6. Usher et al., pp. 113, 114.

7. Production data from the commercial fishery at Grassy Narrows for the period 1957–69 are available from the records of the Ontario Ministry of Natural Resources. These data probably underestimate the actual fish catch, but no one knows by how much. The band's fishing license called for collective reporting to MNR's district office in Kenora; yet each fisherman reported his catch on an individual basis. The aggregate record for the band as a whole, therefore, is only as accurate as the sum of the individual reports. The data do not include fish retained for domestic consumption. See Usher et al., pp. 154–156.

8. The situation in the province of Ontario prior to 1965 was as follows: Indian bands could participate under the Ontario General Welfare Assistance Act if they were willing/able to pay 20 percent of the total costs. Only one band (Six Nations) was able to do so. The other bands received welfare in the form of rations/vouchers from DIAND. In December 1965, the General Welfare Agreement between the federal government and the province of Ontario was signed. This provided for the extension of provincial welfare services to all bands in Ontario. These services included not only general assistance but also a foster child care allowance, special assistance for travel and funerals, supplementary aid for shelter, special allowances for advanced age, and so on. Under

provincial regulations, criteria, and rates of pay, the total amounts that DIAND had to reimburse the province for delivery of these services must have been considerably higher than the token amounts spent on Indian welfare services prior to 1965.

9. According to the responses to the survey concerning employment expectations and job preferences, the young generation (age 20–25) believe that the best work is, for example, working at the band office, managing a small business, or going to school. Persons in this age-group, with rare exceptions, have no desire to work in the bush and no trapping or hunting skills. In contrast, the older generation (age 45 and above) think that work in the bush is superior by far to any other kind of work. The middle generation straddles both worlds but prefers government-sponsored jobs that are steady and offer a decent wage.

10. Government of Canada, *Statement of the Government of Canada on Indian Policy*, 1969. This White Paper had as its ideological framework the notion that true equality for Indian people could be achieved only through removing the constitutional and legislative bases of discrimination. Toward this end, it proposed that the services to Indians should come through the same channels and from the same government agencies that service all Canadians. This line of reasoning led to some fairly radical proposals for policy change. First, the white paper suggested that the Indian Act be repealed, so that Indians could control lands and hold title to them. Second, it argued that the provinces should take over the same responsibilities for Indians as they had for all other citizens in the province. Third, it advised the "withering away" of DIAND. And fourth, it promoted substantial funds for Indian economic development.

    Indian leaders across Canada objected to the White Paper in the strongest possible terms because of what they saw as an ill-concealed attempt to take away their special status. They also saw in the transfer of responsibilities to the provinces an abrogation of treaty obligations by the federal government. In the elimination of DIAND, they believed that they would be overwhelmed by the maze of federal bureaucracy, with no agency especially responsible for their problems. Finally, they objected to the White Paper on the grounds that it had been written and released without any prior consultation with the Indian people.

    Although the White Paper was withdrawn as a result of Indian protest, the government of Canada still made three important changes in Indian policy. First, a commissioner was appointed to settle land claims; second, new funds were made available for Indian economic development; and third, instructions were issued to a number of government departments to provide their services to Indian people for the first time.

11. At Fort Alexander in northern Manitoba, for example, 51 percent of all income earned on the reserve is accounted for by band salaries and wages from DIAND-funded economic development programs. At Fort Hope in northern Ontario, economic development programs alone account for 43 percent of the band's total disposable income. The government's presence in the Fort Hope economy has been steadily increasing during the 1970s. Whereas total government investment accounted for 64 percent of the band's disposable income in 1969, in 1975 it accounted for almost 90 percent. Lithman, p. 157. Paul Driben and Robert S. Trudeau, *When Freedom is Lost: The Dark Side of the Relationship Between Government and the Fort Hope Band* (Toronto: University of Toronto Press, 1983), p. 36.

12. Driben and Trudeau, pp. 36–37.

13. Samuel Z. Klausner, Edward F. Foulks, and Mark H. Moore, *The Inupiat, Economics and Alcohol on the Alaskan North Slope* (Philadelphia: Center for Research on the Acts of Man, 1979), pp. 28–29, 40.

14. Michael Asch, excerpt from an interview for a four-hour radio series I prepared for the Canadian Broadcasting Corporation (CBC), entitled "Under Attack: Indian Life in Grassy Narrows," *Ideas* (Toronto: CBC Transcripts, 1982), p. 14.

15. Ibid., pp. 14–15.
16. Carol Farkas, "Components of the Northern Canadian Indian Diet and Mercury Toxicity" (Paper prepared for the Mercury Project, National Indian Brotherhood, Ottawa, 1976), p. 18.
17. Otto Schaefer, "Health in our time?" *The Canadian Nurse* 74 (October 1978):32–36.
18. Schaefer has suggested that there may be other related physiological effects of the change in nutritional patterns: a decreased ability to deal with stress; an increased susceptibility to other diseases such as atherosclerosis; an emergent hypertension, and so on. He has documented differences in growth and development in native populations related to nutritional changes. Schaefer, "Changing Dietary Patterns in the Canadian North: Health, Social and Economic Consequences," *Journal of the Canadian Dietetic Association,* 38 (January 1977):17–25.
19. Interview with Andrew Mikita, former senior policy adviser in the Corporate Policy Branch, Department of Indian Affairs and Northern Development, Ottawa, June 16, 1980.
20. The increase in income due to work opportunity projects, for example, should be balanced against the reduction in income arising from the displacement of land-based activities like trapping. Further, one of the consequences of wage labor and transfer payments has been the shift to store-bought food and a substantial reduction in the production of "country food" such as moose meat, wild rice, fish, rabbit and so on. These foods represent another form of income and have an annual income equivalent. The point here is that an analysis of the impact of economic development programs needs to take into account the loss of income as well as the gain in income.

## Chapter 8

1. Statement by J. W. Churchman, Director of Development, Indian Affairs Branch, to the Indian-Eskimo Association of Canada, Toronto, October 22, 1965. Churchman was a senior official in the Branch, responsible directly to the deputy minister of the Department of Citizenship and Immigration.
2. Ibid.
3. Over a period of two years, I conducted an exhaustive search of all DIAND files on Grassy Narrows (also called English River #21) pertaining to surveys, community planning, housing and school construction, lands and estates, and resettlement. It is remarkable and inexplicable that none of the files for the period of the early 1960s contained information concerning the relocation. In fact, aside from scattered fragments of financial data on construction costs for the new school and houses, the words *relocation* and *resettlement* do not appear in any of the files I examined. There were also no references to "community planning" or to "a new community." The unique piece of correspondence on the relocation was unearthed in the archives of the Kenora district office of DIAND.
4. Interview with David Nicholson, former assistant deputy minister of the Department of Indian Affairs and Northern Development, Ottawa, July 4, 1980.
5. A former assistant deputy minister of Indian Affairs, Cam Mackie, raised the subject of the Grassy Narrows relocation with John McGilp, director-general of the Ontario Region, in the early 1960s. McGilp did not have any specific memory of this event, but on the question of a possible "deal" with the Hudson's Bay Company, he admitted that "such an accommodation was entirely possible given the environment at that time."
6. Nicholson describes the policy context during the period within which many Indian reserves were relocated as follows:

   It seems to me that shortly after the Second World War, the plight of Indian people and their conditions was raised in the House of Commons in a special parliamentary committee. It was decided that something had to be done. So the delivery of support services by the department picked up in the 1950s and grew substantially since then. I would say that the problem of isolated Indian communities and our ability to provide housing and other services to them in a consistent way was identified in the late 1950s and 1960s. This brought in resettlement programs.

I can give a particular instance of resettlement from my own experience. Some years ago, I researched the records for a particular band that was relocated in the early 1960s in northern Manitoba. This was a band located on the banks of the Seal River, on the border between the Northwest Territories and Manitoba. At that time, the department was extending services to Indian bands in pretty well all areas— education, housing, community infrastructure, and social services. My research of the correspondence that led up to the decision to relocate the Seal River band indi- cated that the decision had a lot to do with the difficulty of extending such services to remote locations that did not have access by road. The situation of Grassy Narrows seems to be similar. The Seal River reserve was a fly-in situation. During spring breakup and fall freeze-up, there was a period of about six weeks at either end where you couldn't get into the community. You couldn't evacuate people for medical reasons, you couldn't bring in commodities, and so on. In the records I did find a BCR [Band Council Resolution] requesting relocation. In the context of the policy of Indian Affairs at the time relating to our responsibility to deliver services to Indian people, I take it that the department considered the relocation request as reasonable and viable in terms of dealing with the problem of how to extend services to a community in a remote and isolated location.

This is how the Seal River band was relocated to Churchill. It became the Dene Village in the city of Churchill. After the relocation, there was tremendous social upheaval and massive deterioration, but that's another story.

7. Letter from Eric Law to the Honorable W. Benedickson, July 8, 1964.
8. This letter was found in file number 29-2-13 at the DIAND Kenora district office. An almost identical letter was written by Richard Ashopenace to A. G. Leslie, Chief, Agen- cies Division, DIAND, Headquarters. This letter was dated July 23, 1964. At that time, it was unusual for an Indian person to write directly to headquarters for redress. This indicates the depth of the feeling of protest against what local officials were doing. It also reflects the perceived need to appeal to a higher level for intervention on the issue of locational choice.
9. This correspondence began when Norman Schantz and Pierre Taypaywaykejick wrote to David Rempel, the regional representative of the National Parole Board in Winnipeg, on January 16, 1964. Because Pierre was a parolee, and a condition of his parole was that he abstain from the use of alcohol, he, and many others in the community, wanted to live far away from the concentration of houses where there was drinking. Letters on Pierre's case were then exchanged between Rempel and Cook, the executive director of the National Parole Board. Cook wrote to Walter Rudnicki, Chief of the Welfare Division of DIAND, Ottawa. Rudnicki wrote to A. G. Leslie, Chief of the Agencies Division in Ot- tawa. Leslie wrote to Lapp, the regional supervisor of Northern Ontario, and Lapp finally wrote to Eric Law in Kenora.
10. Letter from A. G. Leslie to Ward Cook, National Parole Board, June 29, 1964.
11. Kai Erikson, "Memorandum to the People of Grassy Narrows." This excerpt is from the first draft of a report that Erikson and Christopher Vecsey prepared for the band council following their visit to the reserve in January 1979.

## Chapter 9

1. Bernardino Ramazzini, 1731 A.D., as quoted in Warner Troyer, *No Safe Place* (Toronto: Clarke, Irwin and Company Limited, 1977), p. ix.

2. Quoted in "Mercury and Its Compounds," *Occupational Health Bulletin* 25, no. 7–8 (1970).

3. Data on the volume of mercury emissions in Canada show that in 1970 the chlor-alkali industry accounted for about 32.1 percent of the total volume of mercury losses from all industrial plants. Inadvertent emissions of mercury from petroleum combustion constituted about 24.3 percent of the total. Paints, dental amalgams, instrumentation and electrical equipment, print manufacture, battery cathodes, pharmaceuticals, fungicides, and the recovery of gold, zinc, copper, and lead accounted for the remainder. Total emissions of mercury into the atmosphere in 1970 have been documented as 74.6 metric tons. Environment Canada, "National Inventory of Sources and Emissions of Mercury: 1970," Internal report APCD 73-6, 1973. See also L. M. Azzaria and F. Habashi, "Mercury Pollution—An Examination of Some Basic Issues," *CIM Bulletin* (August 1976), pp. 101–07.

4. Between 1955 and 1975, in the province of Ontario, for example, the Workmen's Compensation Board paid compensation to twenty-two workers who developed mercury poisoning. These workers held jobs in the following industries: hat manufacturing, gold refining, fungicides, battery manufacturing, and the electrical industry. Other cases of poisoning stemmed from working with mercury in a dental laboratory and from inhaling mercury vapor while firefighting. Two other cases of poisoning involved workers exposed to mercury in a chlor-alkali plant. It is inorganic mercury that is most often responsible for mercury poisoning among industrial workers. Troyer, p. 10.

5. In 1969, attorneys representing disease victims came to see Hosokawa, who had retired as the director of the Chisso Factory Hospital. He was very ill and dying, but he made a sworn statement that in 1959 he had informed Chisso executives that his research had demonstrated a direct link between Chisso effluent discharges and Minamata disease. In response to this information, management had stopped him from doing any further research and had clamped down on scientists trying to take samples of the effluent water. In public and during the court case, the company continued to deny that it had any previous knowledge of the link between its chemical operations and Minamata disease.

6. In 1956, 1960, and 1971–72, there were outbreaks of mercury poisoning in Iraq, where seed grain treated with mercury to prevent spoilage was diverted and milled for flour. Smaller outbreaks caused by eating mercury-treated seed grain occurred in Guatemala (1963–65), Ghana (1967), and Pakistan (1969). In 1964, in Niigata, Japan, 120 persons died from eating poisoned fish and shellfish in an outbreak similar to that at Minamata.

7. The process of biomethylation was first described in 1965 by two Swedish scientists, Alf Johnels and M. Olsson, who suggested that inorganic mercury of the kind used in chlor-alkali plants could be converted to methyl mercury in muddy lake bottoms. Within a few years, two more researchers documented more precisely how biomethylation works. See Soren Jensen and Arne Jernelov, "Biological Methylation of Mercury in Aquatic Organisms," Institute of Analytical Chemistry, University of Stockholm, 1969. In Canada, there is a continuing controversy as to when Canadian scientists were made aware of biomethylation and the dangers of polluting waterways with inorganic mercury.

8. A complete description of the type and distribution of lesions in the human brain caused by methyl mercury can be found in D. Hunter and D. Russell, "Focal Cerebral and Cerebellar Atrophy in a Human Subject due to Organic Mercury Compounds," *Journal of Neurology, Neurosurgery, and Psychiatry* 17 (1954):235–41; and T. Takeuchi, "Biological Reactions and Pathological Changes in Human Beings and Animals Caused by Organic Mercury Contamination," in *Environmental Mercury Contamination*, ed. R. Hartung and B. D. Dinman (Ann Arbor: Ann Arbor Science Publishers, 1972), pp. 247–89.

9. In 1953, in Niigata, Japan, a boy who had eaten large amounts of contaminated fish and shellfish over a period of only ten days was, seven years later, so severely affected by the poison that he could not attend school. Department of National Health and

Welfare Canada, "Task Force on Organic Mercury in the Environment: Final Report (1973)," p. 6.

10. The level of mercury in hair is given in units of parts per million (ppm). The criteria for "safe" levels of mercury vary for hair as they do for blood, but generally, for persons having minimal environmental exposure to mercury, levels in hair are about 6 ppm. In Japan, people who had hair values of 200 ppm or more in 1965 are now seriously ill with Minamata disease; some of those who had hair levels between 100 and 200 ppm are now certified patients; and a few with hair levels between 50 and 100 ppm have the initial symptoms of mercury poisoning. Memorandum from the Mercury Team, National Indian Brotherhood, to the Standing Committee on Mercury in the Environment, October 9, 1975.

11. Iraq has had three outbreaks of organic mercury poisoning, two of which were major. In 1960, approximately 1,000 persons were affected; in 1971 and 1972, 6,430 cases were recorded, of which 459 were fatal. The 1971–72 outbreak followed the ingestion of bread made from grain treated with a methyl mercurial fungicide. The symptoms of poisoning were similar, but not identical, to those found at Minamata. Whereas blood concentrations of Japanese victims were not fully documented at the time of exposure, in Iraq, blood samples were taken an average of sixty-five days after people stopped eating contaminated food.

An important question is whether the Iraqi data are relevant as a baseline for other populations. What the data show is that there is a risk of neurological damage for persons whose blood levels of methyl mercury are in the range of 100–500 ppb. The difference between the Iraqi situation and that in northwestern Ontario lies in the temporal nature of the exposure to mercury. In Iraq, the exposure was a brief one, with relatively large doses of mercury ingested over a period of one to three months. In Canada, the exposure of the Indian people is seasonal, with the highest blood levels of mercury falling at the end of the summer guiding period.

12. World Health Organization, *Environmental Health Criteria: Mercury* (Geneva: World Health Organization, 1976), pp. 23–24.

13. B. D. Dinman and L. H. Hecker, "The Dose–Response Relationship Resulting from Exposure to Alkyl Mercury Compounds," in *Environmental Mercury Contamination*, p. 290.

14. In 1966 and 1967, the Department of Health and Welfare was apparently warned by several sources that mercury contamination could be a serious health hazard. Scientists from the National Research Council approached federal health authorities but were told that there was no problem. That same year, direct communication from the World Health Organization in Geneva failed to move the federal bureaucrats in Ottawa to action. Yet a full account of Minamata disease had been published in English as early as September 1961. Troyer, pp. 22–23.

15. A comprehensive survey of mercury accumulation by all organisms in the system was carried out by the staff of the Freshwater Institute of the Fisheries Marine Service in Winnipeg. See A. L. Hamilton, "A Survey of Mercury Levels in the Biota of a Mercury-Contaminated River System in Northwestern Ontario," The Freshwater Institute, report No. 1167, 1972.

In 1971, Norvald Fimreite studied fish-eating birds and waterfowl on the English-Wabigoon river system. He found very high levels of mercury in the tissues of the birds. Similar mercury values were found in another study of birds around Clay Lake (K. Vermeer, F. A. J. Armstrong, and D. Hatch, "Mercury in Aquatic Birds at Clay Lake, Western Ontario," *Journal of Wildlife Management* 37 [1973]:58–61).

16. J. N. Bishop and B. P. Neary, *Mercury Levels in Fish from Northwestern Ontario 1970–1975*, Inorganic Trace Contaminants Section, Laboratory Services Branch, Ontario Ministry of the Environment, April 1976, p. 78.

17. After mercury discharges into a river system cease, natural restorative processes help to reduce the concentration of mercury in the sediment. These include the trapping and isolation of mercury by further sedimentation, the "flushing" of the system by the natural seasonal flow of water, and the transport of mercury further downstream. Between 1970 and 1975, for example, the level of mercury in the sediment twenty miles from the source of pollution in Dryden had decreased by half; further downstream, however, the level had increased. Recent indications are that the mercury burden continues to travel westward, downstream, away from the original source of the pollution.

18. J. A. Spence, "Inorganic Mercury Discharges and Emissions by the Dryden Chemical Co. Ltd., March 1962 to October 1975" (Unpublished paper, April 1977), p. 9. Estimates of mercury losses to the English-Wabigoon river system were based on known empirical relationships between chlorine production, mercury consumption, and mercury losses per ton of chlorine produced. Mercury was lost to the environment in wastewater from the plant, in sludge resulting from the precipitation of impurities in brine, and in atmospheric emissions from the mercury cell room. No direct estimate of aerial emissions of mercury has been made, although studies at similar plants have shown that such discharges form a substantial proportion of total losses; furthermore, they occur in the immediate vicinity and are then washed into the adjacent river system. The total inorganic mercury available to the English-Wabigoon river system (from both aerial and direct aquatic emissions) was estimated to be between 30,000 and 46,000 lbs (1962–75); the remainder (from estimated total losses of 50,000 lbs) was trapped in special disposal pits and buried.

19. Bishop and Neary, p. 78.

20. In describing the attempts to whitewash "the crimson history of mercury," Troyer includes the following excerpt from a press release prepared by Dryden Chemicals Limited "To dispell [sic] the notion that we have wantonly dumped mercury into the river, we should point out that the effluent from our plant even before the installation of the treatment system had a mercury concentration in the order of 1/30 the concentration of mercury in normal human urine." Troyer quips back: "The logic is not much better than the spelling—few of us manage to excrete 33 million gallons of urine daily" (Troyer, p. 98).

## Chapter 10

1. In Canada as a whole as of 1978, there were 546 individuals with mercury levels above 100 ppb, 402 (74 percent) from Quebec and 105 (19 percent) from Ontario. Indian people from Grassy Narrows and Whitedog made up most of the Ontario population considered to be at risk. About two-thirds of the Indians were males of working age (16–65) who were exposed to methyl mercury while working as guides in the fishing camps on the English-Wabigoon river system.

2. Masazumi Harada, "Epidemiological and Clinical Study of Mercury Pollution on Indian Reservations in Northwestern Ontario, Canada" (Unpublished manuscript, 1976), pp. 8–10, 13–14.

3. T. W. Clarkson, "Exposure to Methyl Mercury in Grassy Narrows and White Dog Reserves," a report prepared for the Medical Services Branch, Health and Welfare Canada, 1976, p. 43.

4. J. S. Prichard, excerpt from an interview for the CBC radio series on Grassy Narrows, *Ideas*, p. 21.

5. Of the ten individuals in the group found to have neurological abnormalities possibly

attributable to methyl mercury, seven had peak recorded mercury levels in their blood between 100 and 199, and three had peak levels of 227, 337, and 417 ppb, respectively. *Methylmercury in Canada* (Ottawa: Health and Welfare Canada, 1979), p. 192.

6. Shepard, David A. E., "Methyl Mercury Poisoning in Canada," *Canadian Medical Association Journal* 114(1976):471.

7. In Iraq, no symptoms were observed in patients who had blood mercury levels of less than 200 ppb, and no deaths were reported at exposure levels below 3,000 ppb. There was a striking variability in the severity of symptoms, even within families having similar blood levels. In contrast to Japan, mild to moderate cases, with the exception of fetal cases, showed a tendency toward improvement of clinical disabilities over time. Furthermore, the late appearance of symptoms did not occur in Iraq, as it did in Japan. *Methylmercury in Canada*, pp. 41–42.

8. Ibid., p. 79.

9. T. W. Clarkson, excerpt from an interview for *Ideas*, p. 21.

10. J. S. Prichard, excerpt from an interview for *Ideas*, p. 21.

11. Commercial fishing was much more restricted at Grassy Narrows than at Whitedog. The Grassy Narrows license was not valid (except for the waters within reserve boundaries), from April 1 to September 30, for example, exactly the months when most commercial fishing took place at Whitedog. Furthermore, the license limited the total catch of fish to no more than ten tons of pickerel (walleye) and pike combined, a total commercial value of about $5,250 (1969 prices), assuming a pike/pickerel ratio consistent with the overall catch in northwestern Ontario.

12. Fisheries biologists, through a combination of knowledge and intuition about the productivity of fish by species, use the concept of maximum sustainable yield to determine the amount of fish that can be harvested from any body of water without damage to stocks. They use their findings in setting constraints on fishing activity in certain lakes. These constraints take the form of regulations on the length of the season, the total catch by weight, and sometimes restrictions on gear (net size and type).

13. Prices for whitefish, walleye, and pike vary not only from year to year but from season to season. For whitefish, prices vary according to the size, condition, and grade of the fish; for walleye, according to whether the fish is dressed, round, or headless and dressed. The point is that average prices for each species in any given year are only approximations to the economic return for a year's fishing effort.

   In calculating the dollar value of economic losses to the Grassy Narrows band as a result of the closing of the fishery, the average prices per pound of fish in the late 1960s and early 1970s were used. They were as follows: walleye, $0.50; whitefish, $0.33; and pike, $0.17. In the early 1970s, these prices increased slightly from the levels prevailing in the late 1960s. This small increase is the reason why an inflation factor of only 6 percent has been chosen for the analysis. Given that price escalation has been much more rapid in the late 1970s and early 1980s, a sensitivity analysis using higher rates of price increase should be conducted, particularly if an estimate of economic losses is to be prepared for a legal claim against the polluter.

   The other point to be noted is that the estimate of economic losses is based only on the three species noted above. Over a thirteen-year period, however, coarse fish (suckers, mooneyes, ling, tullibees, and others) accounted for 9 percent of the total harvest of fish by weight. Since most such species have low commercial value, they have been left out of the calculation given above.

14. On the basis of production figures of an annual average level of 15,869 pounds of whitefish, 8,829 pounds of walleye, and 7,704 pounds of pike, Brian Felske estimates the total economic loss to the Grassy Narrows band to be $441,618.16 for the years 1970–90. To arrive at this figure, he used 1977 fish prices and an inflation rate of 7 percent per year for the period 1978–90. Brian Felske, "Certain Aspects of the Com-

mercial Fishery at White Dog and Grassy Narrows" (Unpublished paper, January 25, 1978).

In another study, the minimum estimate for the average annual catch and value of the commercial fishery during the late 1960s is given as 70,000 pounds of fish valued at $24,500. Peter Usher et al., "The Economic and Social Impact of Mercury Poisoning on Whitedog and Grassy Narrows Indian Reserves, Ontario" (Unpublished paper, 1979), p. 175. Even if one takes into account the likelihood that MNR records of the total fish harvest underestimate the true production levels, this estimate seems high. For one thing, the band's annual production of whitefish averaged only about 15,400 pounds; moreover, its catch of pike and pickerel combined was limited by license to 20,000 pounds.

15. "Payments Made to Fishermen—Grassy Narrows Band, 1970–1973" (Memorandum prepared for the Ontario Ministry of Natural Resources). The relatively greater importance of the commercial fishery at Whitedog is indicated by the fact that the Ontario government paid out a total of $55,141 to Whitedog commercial fishermen over the same period.

16. Ignatius E. La Rusic, "A Report on Mercury in the Environment in the Communities of Whitedog and Grassy Narrows: The Dietary Aspects and Problems of Communicating with the Local Populations" (Paper prepared for the Medical Services Branch of the Health and Welfare Canada, July 31, 1973), pp. 9–10.

17. Troyer, for example, quantifies the economic loss to Grassy Narrows resulting from the closing of Ball Lake Lodge as follows: "The men of Grassy Narrows and Whitedog worked, happily and faithfully, as guides at the tourist lodges and fishing camps. They cooked and shared those ambrosial shore lunches with their guests, fishermen from Toronto and New York, from Chicago, Detroit, Dallas, Los Angeles and St. Louis . . . . The largest lodge, Barney Lamm's Ball Lake Lodge, put a $300,000 *annual* payroll into Grassy Narrows reserve and alone employed virtually every employable Grassy Narrows adult . . . . Its closure means, over forty years . . . lost wages totaling $12 million" (Troyer, *No Safe Place*, p. 49).

In his book *Grassy Narrows,* George Hutchison devotes a chapter to Ball Lake Lodge and describes the romance, adventure, and splendor ("the stuff of memories") of summers at Ball Lake. Aside from portraying the lodge as a paradise for the Grassy Narrows guides who worked there, Hutchison also portrays the closing of the lodge as a catastrophe for the community economy. He asserts that seventy-five persons from Grassy Narrows were employed at Ball Lake and that the people "benefited by tying their fortunes to Barney's Ball Lake Lodge" (Hutchison, *Grassy Narrows* [Toronto: Van Nostrand Reinhold Ltd., 1977], p. 50).

18. It is difficult to estimate total income from guiding (sports fishing and hunting) because we do not have data on how many people were employed in guiding hunters in the fall. In the late 1960s, at the rate of $12 per day for guiding sports fishermen, a man could easily earn about $1,600 in wages, with about $500 in tips, if he guided every day for the full season, from mid-May to the end of September. If he also guided hunters in October, at a daily rate of $15, he could add, with tips, another $800–900 to his earnings. It is therefore possible that gross income from guiding brought $90,000–110,000 into the community economy.

19. Press release of February 4, 1971, by Leo Bernier, then member of the provincial parliament for Kenora, on the intention of the government to assist tourist camp operators affected by the mercury contamination.

20. Grassy Narrows band, "Brief to the Provincial Interdepartmental Task Force on Mercury," March 8, 1973.

21. Letter from G. James Stopps to Colin Myles, November 16, 1972; letter to the Grassy Narrows band council, February 27, 1973. Emphases added.

22. *Winnipeg Free Press,* March 10, 1973.
23. Health and Welfare Canada, "Task Force on Organic Mercury in the Environment: Final Report" (Unpublished paper, Ottawa, 1973), p. 18.
24. Government of Ontario, "Fourth Report of the Mercury Task Force (1973)," p. 13.
25. Federal officials recognized the Ontario government's reluctance to undertake any measures that might be interpreted as compensation. In their task force report, they stated: "Indications are that the government of Ontario is hesitant to discuss the question of compensation for lost economic opportunities, though it is understood that favourable considerations may be given to requests from the Indian people for extensions to pulpwood cutting areas and to the provision of alternative mercury-free commercial fishing grounds." Health and Welfare Canada, "Task Force on Organic Mercury," p. 9.
26. Ibid., p. 15. The final report of the task force recommended that the residents of Whitedog and Grassy Narrows be recognized as at risk and that surveillance measures (hair and blood tests) continue, especially for the subgroup previously omitted from testing. "As a matter of priority," it also advised the federal government "to institute a program of social and economic development" in both communities. The task force report made no reference at all to the disruptive impact of the relocation.
27. Letter from the chairman of the standing committee, E. Somers, to Clive Linklater of NIB, May 2, 1975.
28. The state of interdepartmental communications as late as November 28, 1974 (four years after mercury was discovered), is well illustrated by a single line from an internal DIAND memorandum. The director-general of the Ontario region, H. Rodine, telexed John McGilp in Ottawa to say that "Actions taken [with respect to mercury] by Department of National Health and Welfare unknown." Within DIAND, the representative to the standing committee, H. Rogers, admitted frankly that the department had no policy on mercury and that there was a breakdown in communications between headquarters, the region, the district, and the Indian people.
29. These concerns were voiced emphatically in a letter from Alan Roy to John Reid, member of Parliament for Kenora, May 14, 1975.
30. Leo Bernier apparently called the Japanese doctors "a bunch of troubadours." The Health Minister, Frank Miller, told a reporter that Harada was "a psychiatrist, not a neurologist," and that he should be viewed with suspicion because of his left-wing political views. It is fair to say that some Ontario cabinet ministers felt that the Japanese doctors were predisposed to find cases of mercury poisoning in Ontario. By this time, however, the mercury issue had become politicized, and government people felt that the Japanese were adding fuel to the fire of political confrontation.
31. On the day before DIAND was to make a presentation to the standing committee, John McGilp, director of operations in Ottawa, wrote to Howard Rodine, regional director-general in Ontario as follows: "I am sure you will agree that we need to be able to indicate that some positive action as well as some appropriate planning is taking place in Indian Affairs." DIAND policy was to be shaped by two concerns: the need to find and make accessible alternative sources of protein, and the need to find employment opportunities to replace lost jobs. (Letter from J. McGilp to H. Rodine, May 15, 1975).

In a report dated the next day, the department was "able to indicate" to the standing committee that it had, astonishingly: (a) initiated a program of economic support which would enable the Indians of Grassy Narrows and Whitedog to fish in uncontaminated lakes close to their reserves; (b) designed and implemented a community education program; (c) initiated discussions with the two bands on long-term economic development; and (d) gathered a "cadre of specialists" to deal with the mercury issue. "Report of the Department of Indian Affairs and Northern Development to the Interdepartmental Committee on Mercury in the Environment," May 16, 1975. None of these "programs," however, had yet been discussed at the community level, let alone initiated.

32. In file no. 487/17-10 of DIAND for 1975, one can find copies of the letters written by the minister's special assistant to concerned citizens about the mercury issue. The letters state that DIAND was running a community education and information program (see below), that it had "located a few noncontaminated lakes and is assisting the Indians who are harvesting those lakes and catching 'clean' fish" (a statement of good intentions only); and that it was "considering schemes for making wild game and cattle products more accessible" (these schemes never went beyond internal bureaucratic memoranda).

33. They were accompanied by Aileen Smith, coauthor with Eugene Smith of *Minamata;* Quaker physician Peter Newberry; Jill Torrie, a researcher for NIB; and Barney Lamm. The federal government paid the air fares of Aileen Smith and the Indians as part of the "community education program." The funds were justified on the grounds that the trip to Japan would "sensitize a group of Indian leaders to the seriousness of mercury poisoning in order that they could return to their reserves and communicate directly with people to avoid eating contaminated fish." Telex from P. B. Lesaux, assistant deputy minister, DIAND, to the Canadian Embassy in Tokyo, July 22, 1975. This trip to Japan, however, was the only tangible evidence of a DIAND-sponsored community education program on the two mercury-affected reserves in 1975.

34. As has been noted, the symptoms of mercury poisoning can easily be attributed to other maladies. The objective of an epidemiological study is to determine whether the occurrence of particular symptoms associated with mercury poisoning is significantly higher among an exposed population than among a control group that has not been exposed. A much higher incidence of neurological symptoms of damage in the exposed population would indicate that mercury is the causal factor.

35. Text of an AMOG statement prepared for the chiefs of Whitedog and Grassy Narrows entitled "Reasons Why the Wabigoon-English River System Should Be Closed."

36. According to one of the old-timers at Ball Lake, prior to 1970 Lamm had started to fly his guests off the river system in any case. As soon as the English-Wabigoon area became accessible by road, the wealthy clients who came for "the wilderness experience" did not wish to be followed around by "the pork 'n beaners," the people who "drove in with their trailers and campers and noisy children." Ball Lake lost its exclusivity, and the lodge ceased to attract "the same quality of customers . . . . The clientele began to change . . . and the rich people wanted to go up north to the arctic." To what extent these factors, in addition to mercury, put intolerable strains on the operations of the lodge cannot be known for certain.

37. As recently as 1983, Lamm again proposed to the band council of Grassy Narrows that the band buy Ball Lake Lodge, this time for the sum of $1.2 million out of the "compensation money" forthcoming from the federal government. Given that he had already decided that the lodge was no longer a reasonable business proposition, one has to wonder what benefits would accrue to the Indian people as a result of such a transaction.

38. During 1975, Indian Affairs officials were giving serious consideration to the relocation of Whitedog and Grassy Narrows. A "strictly confidential memorandum" of October 27, 1975, from P. Jacobs (Kenora district office) to H. Rodine (Ontario regional director-general) noted that the Indian people would probably reject the offer of relocation. Jacobs admitted that because the promises of the first relocation had been broken, the Indians had little faith in the ability of DIAND to safeguard their interests. In a rare acknowledgment of the adverse effects of past government actions, the memo contained the following paragraph: "To date, the consequences of the previous relocation have not been solved. The violence and apathy evident on these reserves [Whitedog and Grassy Narrows] are at least as much a result of the relocations as of loss of traditional

livelihood . . . . While this [social] disintegration has been aggravated by lost income after closing of the fisheries, it was present following the first relocation." This statement is the only one on record indicating an awareness within DIAND of the disastrous consequences of the earlier relocation. As predicted, the chiefs of both bands rejected the relocation offer made by the DIAND minister in November 1975.

39. Internal DIAND memorandum to the minister, Judd Buchanan, July 1976, file no. 487/17-10.

40. Memorandum from P. Jacobs, Kenora District Office, to Cam Mackie, assistant deputy minister of DIAND, December 10, 1976.

41. "Briefing Notes: Grassy Narrows and Whitedog" (prepared for the Minister of Indian Affairs, December 1976).

42. On March 3, 1977, the Grassy Narrows band submitted another lengthy and detailed brief to both governments outlining precisely the steps that each government could and should take to help the band plan its long-term development. By then, I had already been recruited as the band's adviser and community planner, so I had ample opportunity to observe the governments' reactions to band proposals. The adviser for the Whitedog band was Bruce Crofts, a Toronto insurance executive who had become genuinely committed to finding a solution to the social disintegration at Whitedog. Like me, he was appalled by the inability (or unwillingness) of the governments to commit the level of resources required. In a letter to DIAND minister Judd Buchanan, dated December 1, 1975, he put it very well: "No white community would be permitted to destroy itself, as many [Indian] communities are doing, without massive government assistance and aid."

43. Based on Chief Simon Fobister's "Submission to the Royal Commission on the Northern Environment," January 18, 1978.

44. The Royal Commission on the Northern Environment, *Interim Report & Recommendations*, April 4, 1978, p. 5.

45. Ibid., p. 24. It is revealing that Justice Hartt did not deal with the issue of the closing of the river in his *Interim Report*, since neither the Whitedog nor the Grassy Narrows bands referred to it in their submissions to the Royal Commission.

46. "Memorandum of Understanding," December 15, 1978, signed by the governments of Canada and Ontario and the Grassy Narrows and Islington (Whitedog) bands. The issue of flooding was particularly relevant to Whitedog, the latter having been relocated as a consequence of flooding by Ontario Hydro. The issue of raising and lowering of water levels was included because of the adverse effects on muskrat trapping and the harvest of wild rice caused by the actions of the Lake of the Woods Control Board.

47. Grassy Narrows Band, "Presentation to the Governments of Canada and Ontario" (Paper given at the opening session of the mediation process, May 29, 1979), p. 24.

48. This passage is a composite of excerpts from tape-recorded interviews with the heads of families pertaining to the mediation, January–February 1979.

49. Lorne Henderson, Minister of Resources Development, 1982.

50. Dennis Timbrell, Minister of Health, 1977.

51. Leo Bernier, Minister of Northern Affairs, 1977.

52. Russell Ramsey, Minister of Labor, 1981.

53. Since the signing of the mediation agreement, there have been three ministers of DIAND (Hugh Faulkner, Jake Epp, and John Munro); three deputy ministers (Arthur Kroeger, Paul Tellier, and M. Lafontaine); and four assistant deputy ministers in the Indian Program (Cam Mackie, Huguette Labelle, David Nicholson, and Don Goodwin). The need to reeducate each new senior civil servant on the mediation process is evident. Over time, the responsibility for the mediation process within DIAND has shifted downward to lower and lower levels of authority.

## Postscript

1. The Indians' use of alcohol has been the subject of an extensive scholarly debate. Very briefly, some observers believe that Indians cannot handle liquor for genetic or physiological reasons and are predisposed to react to it in a particularly disinhibited and violent manner. Others argue that the pathological or self-destructive use of alcohol has nothing to do with "Indianness" but rather is correlated with the circumstances under which Indians began to lose their independence and bargaining power in their relationship with Europeans. They point to a historical relationship between pathological drinking, powerlessness, and the deprivation of the means of validating Indian identity; as Indians' frustration with their conditions mounted and it became harder to express aggression against whites, their anger turned inward and began to be manifested in essentially self-destructive behavior.

   For a discussion of differing perspectives on Indian drinking, see Nancy Oestreich Lurie, "The World's Oldest On-Going Protest Demonstration: North American Indian Drinking Patterns," *Pacific Historical Review* 40, no.3 (August 1971). See also Craig MacAndrew and Robert B. Edgerton, *Drunken Comportment, A Social Explanation* (London: Thomas Nelson and Sons, 1970); and Joseph Westermeyer, "Options Regarding Alcohol Use Among the Chippewa," *American Journal of Orthopsychiatry* 42 (1972):398–403.

2. Kai Erikson, *Everything in Its Path* (New York: Simon and Schuster, 1976).

3. Department of Indian Affairs and Northern Development, *Indian Conditions, A Survey* (Ottawa, 1980), p. 109.

4. It is significant that with respect to resource development in the Canadian north, government officials continue to think of progress for the Inuit people as a linear movement from nature to culture. See Hugh Brody, "An Overview," a paper submitted to the Berger Inquiry in the hearings on the MacKenzie Valley Pipeline, April 1976, pp. 18–19.

# INDEX

Alcohol abuse: effects, 3, 11, 21; factors frustrating information about, 18–19; diagnosis as alcoholic, 20; expenditures for alcohol, 20–21; by age and sex, 22–23; hospital admissions for, 23–25; social inequality and, 25; guilt and punishment for rejected, 25, 34, 47, 241; school dropout problem, 35–36; debate over Indian abuse, 265*n*1. *See also* Drinking behavior

American Indian Movement, 132, 216

AMOG: formation of, 217; closing the river campaign, 218–20; focus of, 220

Anti-Mercury Ojibway Group. *See* AMOG

Asch, Michael, 155

Ashopenace, Richard, 171

Assimilation: public policy's main thrust, 107, 118

Ball Lake Lodge: described, 139–40; "closed system" of earning, 141; closing of, 142, 199, 203–04, 261*n*17. *See also* Guiding; Lamm, Barney

Band government: Chief and Council described, 99–101; federal government's impact on, 101; administrators' behavior, 104, 106–07; bureaucracy, creation of, 151. *See also* Federal government; Provincial government

Banks, Dennis, 132

Barrow study: Inupiat people, 152

Beaver. *See* Fur trade

Beliefs: land as abode of spirits, 71–73; Great Spirit, 72; dream experiences, 76–77; death, 90–92; sorcery, 95–99

Benedickson, Honorable W., 167

Bernier, Leo, 206–07, 208, 212–13, 218, 221

Berry picking, 61, 94; socializing during, 252*n*1. *See also* Economy

Billingsley, Robert, 190–91

Binges. *See* Drinking behavior

Blind Persons Act, 117

Breast-feeding: decline of, 157–58

Brunelle, René, 207, 218, 226

Buchanan, Judd, 221–22

Burnt, 44. *See also* Gas sniffing

Cameron, Louis, 131

Canada–Ontario Mercury Committee, 219, 223; creation of, 221

Canadian National Railway, 57

Canadian Pacific Railway, 56

Canadian Shield, 1; mercury in environment of, 190. *See also* Mercury pollution

Caron, C. E., 219

Cat dancing disease. *See* Minamata disease

Ceremonies: Treaty Day, 60–61, 94, 118–19; shaking tent, 62, 250*n*9; naming, 85–86; burial, 91; Christmas, 95, 250*n*6; wild rice, 116

Chief and Council: obligations and responsibilities, 99–100; structure of authority, 101–02; relationship with DIAND, 102, 251*n*14

—after relocation: political role of, 102–03; instability of leadership, 103–04. *See also* Band government

Children: suicide, 16–18; gangs, 32; rites of passage, 32, 85–88; crime as escape from reserve life, 33; roots of problems with, 33–34; treatment on old and new reserves contrasted, 40–41; puberty vision quest, 77, 85–88; naming ceremony, 85–86; sugar intake, 157–58; impetigo, 245*n*18

—neglect of: social pathology indicated by, 10, 38; statistics on, 38; treatment on new reserve, 39–41; effect of spree drinking, 41–43, 102; desertion, 43; coping mechanisms, 43–45; infant deaths, 48. *See also* Education; Gas sniffing; Suicide